# Learning PostScript

## A Visual Approach

### Ross Smith

Peachpit Press
Berkeley, California

Learning PostScript: A Visual Approach
© 1990 Ross Smith

Peachpit Press, 1085 Keith Avenue, Berkeley, California 94708 (415) 527-8555

The illustration facing the opening page of the Introduction is *Square-recursion,* a PostScript rendering by John M. Pratt based on *Square-limit* by M.C. Escher.

The illustration on the Introduction table of contents page is a labyrinth rendered in PostScript as a logo for Bedford Microcomputer consultants, San Francisco.

**Notice of Liability**
The information in this book is distributed on an "As Is" basis, without warranty. While every precaution has been taken in the preparation of this book, neither the author nor Peachpit Press, Inc. shall have any liability to any person or entity with respect to any liability, loss, or damage caused or alleged to be caused directly or indirectly by the instructions contained in this book or by the computer software and hardware products described herein.

**The Name PostScript**
The name PostScript® is a registered trademark of Adobe Systems Incorporated. All instances of the name PostScript in the text are references to the PostScript Language as defined by Adobe Systems Incorporated, unless otherwise stated. The name PostScript is also used as a product trademark for Adobe Systems' implementation of the PostScript language interpreter.

**Trademarks**
Throughout this book trademarked names are used. Rather than put a trademark symbol in every occurrence of a trademarked name, we state that we are using the names only in an editorial fashion and to the benefit of the trademark owner with no intention of infringement of the trademark.

**Library of Congress Cataloging-in-Publication Data**
Smith, Ross.
       Learning PostScript: a visual approach / Ross Smith.
       Includes index.
       1. PostScript (Computer program language) I. Title.
QA76.73.P67S55 1990
005.13'3—dc20        89-49111
ISBN 0-938-151-12-6

0 9 8 7 6 5 4 3 2 1
Printed and bound in the United States of America

# Author

**Ross A. Smith**, consultant, author, and columnist, is a former IBM systems engineer and Ernst & Young consultant, and the founder of Smith Consulting Group, a Santa Rosa, California, firm specializing in desktop publishing and presentation graphics. He is a regular contributor to various personal computer magazines, and is presently an editor of *PC Publishing*, for which he writes the monthly PostScript column.

Mr. Smith's earlier book, *EUREKA! The Six Stages of Creativity*, is the culmination of fifteen years experiential research into the subject of logical/visual communication between our left and right brain hemispheres. Many of the principles learned from that research are utilized here, including the design of the visual page grids.

# Co-author and Technical Editor

**Ross R. Smith**, son of Ross Smith, is an independent microcomputer consultant and a software engineer for Smith Consulting Group. He is a beta tester for PostScript hardware and software developers, and has consulted in the development of PostScript interpreters and software applications.

Mr. Smith is responsible for the sample programs shown on these pages. He has made a substantial contribution to this book by developing original design ideas created with novel PostScript page descriptions.

# Editor and Producer

**Steve Roth** is a writer, editor, and book packager specializing in desktop publishing. He is the editor of *Real World PostScript* (Addison-Wesley), co-author of *ScanJet Unlimited*, (Peachpit Press) and *Real World PageMaker* (Bantam Books), and he's a regular contributor to *Macworld, PC World*, and *Personal Publishing*.

The programs in this book are available on disks for IBM-compatible and Macintosh computers. See the back of the book for details.

# Foreword

It's somewhat ironic to find myself writing the foreword for a book whose purpose is to teach the PostScript language to nonprogrammers, using a visual approach.

Why? Because in developing PostScript, our aim was to create something that is mostly invisible—an unseen layer of software between the computer and the output device.

For the typical computer user, that aim has been achieved. Using virtually any personal computer application in conjunction with one of the scores of different output devices equipped with PostScript interpreters, you can press the Print button and take the rest for granted. The nitty-gritty details—such as whether the output device happens to be a 300-dot-per-inch laser printer or a 2400-dot-per-inch imagesetter—are handled by that invisible layer.

Still, there are many reasons for someone to be curious about how to write PostScript programs or modify existing ones. The best graphic artists and publishers have always had a desire to master their tools to the utmost extent, and what better way to do so in the electronic age than to learn PostScript? Also, powerful graphics tools have always been an invitation to play. For those who want to experiment with type, graphics, and images, the PostScript language is a stimulating intellectual experience.

By its very nature, PostScript begs to be taught by means of a visual, interactive method. I am impressed by the extent to which Ross Smith has drawn on PostScript's own strengths as he leads the reader through a process of discovery and understanding. This book is a fresh, effective approach to learning PostScript, and I recommend it as an introductory resource to all students and teachers of the language.

*John Warnock, Adobe Systems*

# How This Book Was Made

Most of this book was produced on plain-paper desktop laser printers at a resolution of 600 dots per inch (dpi). The text pages and the character sets in appendix A were produced on a Varityper VT-600 laser imager with an Adobe Systems interpreter. The example drawings were produced on a Hewlett-Packard LaserJet Series II printer using a 600-dpi DP-Tek PS600 controller with a QMS Ultra-Script interpreter.

The finished mandalas and cover backgrounds in chapter 6 and at the beginning of each chapter were prepared on a Canon 400-dpi laser engine using an EiconLaser 840 controller with an EiconScript interpreter. The separations for the color drawings in chapter 8 were produced at 2540 dpi on a Linotronic L-300 imagesetter with an Adobe Systems interpreter.

# Acknowledgements

We gratefully acknowledge the following vendors who have made available Post-Script hardware, software, and other resources used in the preparation of this book.

**Hardware**

CalComp (5913 Colorview 300-dpi thermal color printer/plotter/CAI interpreter), Anaheim, CA

Canon USA (various printers and laser engines used with various interpreters and controllers), Lake Placid, NY

DP-Tek (Laserport PS600 controller/UltraScript interpreter), Wichita, KS

Eicon Technology (EiconLaser 840 400-dpi laser engine/EiconScript 800-by-400/400-dpi controller), Montreal, Quebec

Hewlett-Packard (various printers used with various interpreters and controllers), various locations

NewGen Systems (NewGen TurboPS/480 Canon 400-dpi laser engine/RIPS 800-by-400-dpi interpreter), Fountain Valley, CA

Pacific Data Products (PacificPage laser printer cartridge/PhoenixPage interpreter), San Diego, CA

Laser Connection (QMS JetScript controller/Adobe Systems interpreter), Mobile, AL

Qume Corporation (Qume ScripTen 300-dpi printer/Adobe Systems interpreter), Milpitas, CA

Raster Image Processing Systems (RIPS Image 4000 controller/400-dpi Canon engine/RIPS Interpreter), Boulder, CO

**Software**

Adobe Systems (typeface outlines), Mountain View, CA

Applications Techniques (Pizazz Plus screen capture utility), Pepperell, MA

Bitstream (Fontware typeface outlines), Cambridge, MA

Computer Support Corporation (Decipher EPS conversion utility) Dallas, TX

Custom Applications, Inc. (Freedom of Press interpreter), Billerica, MA

Eicon Technology (EiconView programming environment), Montreal, Quebec

Emerald City Software (LaserTalk programming environment), Menlo Park, CA

The Font Company (URW typeface outlines), Phoenix, AZ

GammaLink (GammaScript interpreter/fax conversion utility), Palo Alto, CA

ImageSoft (PS View interpreter), Port Washington, NY

LaserGo (GoScript interpreter), San Diego, CA

Laser Tools (PrintCache print spooler, Trading Post printing utility), Emery-ville, CA

Legend Communications (PSPlot text editor/typeface downloader), Brampton, Ontario

Pan Overseas Company (PreScript interpreter), Pine Brook, NJ

QMS (UltraScript interpreter), Mobile, AL

Systems of Merritt, Inc. (Advanced PostScript Error Handler programming/debugging aid), Mobile, AL

## Other Resources

Adobe Systems Incorporated (technical specifications, programs, and other information and support), Mountain View, CA

*Micro Cornucopia* ("PostScriptals" [PostScript Fractals], Larry Fogg, Issues 49 & 50), Bend, OR

The Other Woman (BBS), Sonoma, CA, 707-938-3508

Pipeline Associates (*PostScript Language Journal*), Parsippany, NJ

We would like to thank Frank Braswell, Ron LaFon, Steve Sharpe, David Blatner, and Susie Hammond for reading the manuscript, and for their helpful comments and suggestions. We also acknowledge the technical support of other individuals too numerous to mention by name.

# Contents

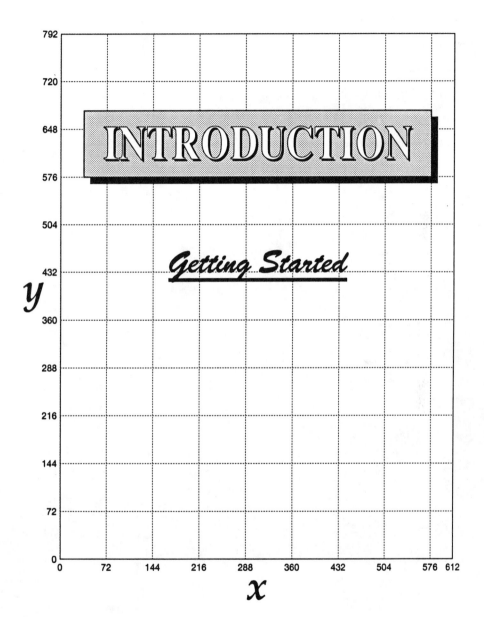

# INTRODUCTION

## Getting Started

# Introduction

# Learning PostScript Visually

PostScript is about visualizing information, and this book is about visualizing PostScript.

Our purpose here is to demonstrate how to create PostScript page descriptions quickly and easily, using a "visual page grid" that we developed especially to *show* you how the language works—using PostScript to demonstrate itself, rather than trying to just explain it abstractly.

This is the first book about learning PostScript that is intended primarily for nonprogrammers—desktop publishers, graphic artists, typographers, printers— and others who are currently using or who will be using this powerful page description language to communicate information. And it is the first book to present PostScript visually.

Because PostScript is a page description language as well as a programming language, it is ideally suited to being learned visually. Instead of explaining conceptually how PostScript works, this book shows you what each PostScript operation does, so you can see how this unique language performs its magic.

Each sample program is accompanied by a brief explanation and a visual representation that shows you what the program does, precisely as it would appear on a full-sized page. The accompanying visual page grid lets you see exactly how PostScript instructions manipulate text and graphics to place them on the printed page or visual display.

The integration of verbal explanation with visual demonstration is ideally suited to the presentation of information, because it involves both our verbal and visual brain hemispheres in the process of assimilating the ideas. Indeed, pictures can replace many thousands of words.

This integration of words and pictures is what a page description language like PostScript is designed to do. And this book utilizes these inherent capabilities of the language in presenting PostScript to you.

# What Is PostScript?

If you're reading this book, it's probably because you are currently using PostScript or are thinking about using PostScript. Or maybe it's because you've heard so much about PostScript and want to know "why all the fuss?"

In a nutshell, PostScript is a programming language, just like BASIC, Pascal, or any of the dozens of other programming languages that have come into being over the past few decades. PostScript is different from other programming languages, though, because it is specially designed for creating text and graphics on a printed page.

As you might expect, the PostScript language contains a rich vocabulary of graphics commands—for drawing lines and curves, filling graphic shapes, etc. In fact, one of the particular strengths of the language is that it is based on a coherent, unified model in which text characters are merely a special kind of graphic. The letter Q, for example, is handled by PostScript as a set of curves that constitute the outline, filled with solid black.

Because the Q is essentially a graphic, it can be manipulated like any other graphic: scaled to any size, stretched or squeezed, filled with a pattern or solid black, and so forth. The flexibility that results from PostScript's unified approach to text and graphics is one reason for the language's wide popularity.

# How Does PostScript Work?

While PostScript is a computer programming language, it is also a page description language. This means that writing a typical PostScript program amounts to nothing more than writing a description of what you want the printed page to look like, using simple, English-like commands.

Just as the graphics you're interested in printing may vary from a simple graphic to a complex and intricate illustration, a page description written in the PostScript language might range from a few simple commands to a lengthy program with thousands of lines of code.

In either case, the next step after creating the page description is to send that description to a "PostScript interpreter." The job of the interpreter is to convert the various PostScript commands for lines, curves, and so forth into actual dots on paper or film.

When PostScript was first introduced, it was embodied in the Apple LaserWriter. Since then, a variety of different interpreters have emerged. Some interpreters are PostScript cartridges that plug into a slot on a laser printer. Others are controller boards that plug into a slot inside a personal computer. Still others are dedicated computers called RIPS (raster image processors) that talk only to a high-resolution PostScript imagesetter. Finally, there are software-based PostScript interpreters. These come on floppy disks and run in computer memory like any other software.

Perhaps the most important hallmark of PostScript is that it is device-independent. Any page description written in the PostScript language can be run on any device equipped with a PostScript interpreter.

Since PostScript's first unveiling in 1985, this device independence, combined with the power resulting from PostScript's unified and flexible approach to graphics and text, have led to the language's rise to the status of an international standard both in the personal computer industry and the publishing industry. Indeed, it is primarily due to PostScript that the distinction between those two industries has become blurred, and a new industry known as desktop publishing has emerged.

# How to Use This Book

You don't have to have a PostScript printer to use this book. You can use one of the controllers or software-based interpreters on the market, which make it possible to print PostScript page descriptions on non-PostScript dot-matrix, ink-jet, and laser printers, or even display the output on screen.

The book is intended to be used interactively. Each new concept or command is illustrated with a short PostScript program, which you can try out on your own printer. Because of the variety of output devices that contain PostScript interpreters, there are a number of ways in which you can print your PostScript programs. Let's first consider the options.

# Printing from the IBM PC

There are two primary methods for working with PostScript programs on an IBM PC or compatible.

If you have a printer with a PostScript interpreter, the easiest way to send your PostScript programs to the printer is to type them into a text editor or a word processor that can create straight ASCII text files with no special formatting. Then send the file to the printer by typing the following at the DOS prompt.

copy filename.ext prn

In this command, you will want to replace "filename.ext" with the name of your PostScript text file, and replace "prn" with the name of your printer port—either parallel (LPT1:, LPT2:, etc.) or serial (COM1:, COM2:, etc.). For instance, to send a file named MANDALA.PS to a parallel port, type *copy mandala.ps lpt1:*.

If you are using a serial port, you must type the following command at the beginning of your session to establish communication between the computer and the printer.

mode comx:= 9600,n,8,1,p

If you don't have a PostScript printer, you can use one of the new software-based interpreters (discussed in appendix B of this book). These interpreters support most popular dot-matrix and ink-jet printers. Some even allow you to preview the output of your program on the computer display.

For more on working with various devices and PostScript interpreters, and other methods of sending PostScript from DOS, see appendix B.

# Printing from the Macintosh

On the Macintosh, there is nothing similar to the DOS *copy* command that lets you send files directly to the printer. Instead, you use an application or desk accessory that sends the file over AppleTalk. Or you can use communications software and a serial connection, just as you can with DOS machines. Just as with DOS, though, you will need to edit your PostScript with a word processor or text editor, and save it as straight text (many Mac programs refer to this as "text only.")

There are at least three utilities for sending PostScript files to a printer that's connected to your Macintosh via AppleTalk. SendPS from Adobe Systems is free from user groups or on-line bulletin boards. One such bulletin board is the Adobe Conference on CompuServe, which can be accessed by typing *go adobe* from the CompuServe! prompt. LaserStatus is a desk accessory from CE Software (515/224-1995) that lets you send PostScript while you're working in another program. LaserTalk from Emerald City Software (415/368-8303) is a PostScript programming environment (also discussed in appendix B).

# PostScript Books

This book is an introduction to the world of PostScript, but it is not the whole world. You'll notice that we often refer you to other books that provide good coverage of various topics. These are more advanced books; refer to them when you've worked through this book and feel comfortable with what you've learned here.

Throughout this book you'll find us referring to the Red, Blue, Green, Orange, and White books. The universe of PostScript books is still small enough that several of them are referred to by those monikers. The Red, Blue, and Green books (published by Addison-Wesley) are all from Adobe Systems, the creators of the PostScript language.

*PostScript Language Reference Manual.* The Red book is the official manual for the PostScript language. Refer to this book for complete information on all PostScript operators.

*PostScript Language Tutorial and Cookbook.* The Blue book contains many examples of PostScript programs. You may find it useful (especially the cookbook section) after you've completed this book.

*PostScript Language Program Design.* Written by Glenn Reid, the Green book provides more insight into programming techniques and the best ways to construct PostScript programs.

*Real World PostScript.* The Orange book, from Addison-Wesley, is a collection of essays on various PostScript topics by a variety of PostScript programmers, designers, and users. It was edited and partially written by Steve Roth, and provides especially good sections on halftoning and color.

*Inside PostScript.* Written by Frank Braswell, the White book (Peachpit Press) is the definitive look inside Adobe PostScript interpreters. It explains and documents all the internal procedures, dictionaries, and other arcane matters.

*Understanding PostScript Programming.* Written by David Holzgang and published by Sybex, this book is a good introduction to the language.

*PostScript Programmer's Reference Guide.* Published by Scott, Foresman, this book documents the PostScript language much as the Red book does, but also includes the newer color operators.

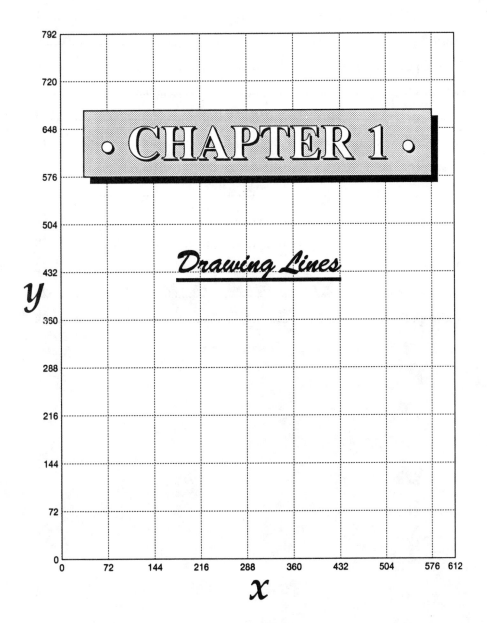

# · CHAPTER 1 ·

## *Drawing Lines*

# Chapter 1

# PostScript Coordinate System

The first step in learning PostScript is understanding the PostScript coordinate system. This is the secret to learning the language quickly and easily.

PostScript page descriptions are constructed with reference to "points" on a page. With most printers this is a standard 8.5-inch wide by 11-inch high letter-sized page, but some devices might use a different size page. We will use the standard letter-size page throughout this book, unless otherwise noted.

Points on the page are specified by means of an x/y coordinate system. Coordinates are expressed as pairs of numbers that can describe any point on the page. The first coordinate always represents the horizontal x axis, and the second the vertical y axis.

The x/y coordinates 0, 0 refer to the "origin" of the coordinate system, which is located at the lower-left corner of the page. Increasing the value of x moves toward the right side of the page, and increasing the value of y moves up toward the top of the page.

In PostScript there are normally 72 points per inch. This corresponds to the standard "point" system used in the printing industry to measure the size of text.

The total number of points along each axis is the product of 72 points per inch multiplied by the length of the page along the axis. Thus, the x/y coordinates 612, 792 describe the upper-right corner of the standard 8.5-by-11-inch page.

$$X = 8.5 \times 72 = 612$$
$$Y = 11.0 \times 72 = 792$$

# Visual Page Grid

The visual page grid on the right was designed to assist in the learning process by showing visually how each sample page description in the book would look if printed on a full-size page.

The grid is an exact half-scale replica of an 8.5-by-11-inch page superimposed on the underlying PostScript page coordinates. Grid lines are drawn at one-inch intervals, with corresponding X/Y coordinate values shown to the left and below respectively, for easy cross-reference.

We produced the grid with a PostScript program that resizes and repositions each example within the grid. The result appears exactly as it would on a full-size page, but reduced to a half-inch scale so it will fit on the pages of this book.

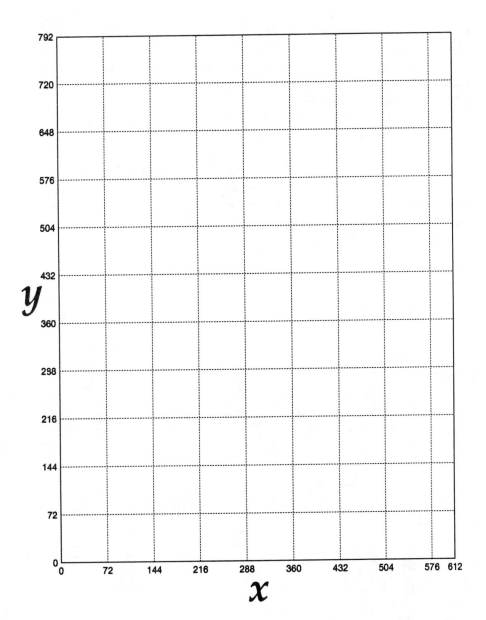

# Paths, Operators, and Operands

Now that you understand what PostScript coordinates are, there are only three additional concepts you need to understand to create a PostScript page description. These are "paths," "operators," and "operands."

PostScript page descriptions are made up of one or more paths. These paths can comprise graphical shapes, text, and images. An imaginary (and whimsical) path is shown on the facing page.

The PostScript language is comprised of special command words that you use to define paths, for drawing graphical shapes, text, and images. These command words are known as operators. An example of a PostScript operator is *moveto*.

PostScript operators are normally preceded by operands, usually numeric values, that provide specific information the operator needs to perform an operation. An example of two operands would be the x/y coordinates of a location on the page where a new path would begin, for instance *72 612 moveto*.

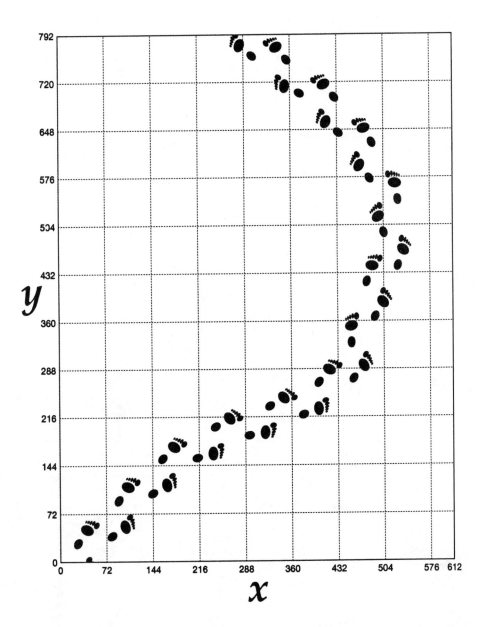

# moveto

PostScript page descriptions often start with the *moveto* operator. The *moveto* operator establishes a new path starting at a given point on the page. This point is known as the current point.

For example, to begin a new path at x/y coordinates 72, 612, you use the following instruction.

72 612 moveto

This instruction initiates a new path at the point designated by the small arrow on the facing page. (The arrow is not a part of the page description.) As yet, the page is still unmarked, and would be blank if sent to the printer.

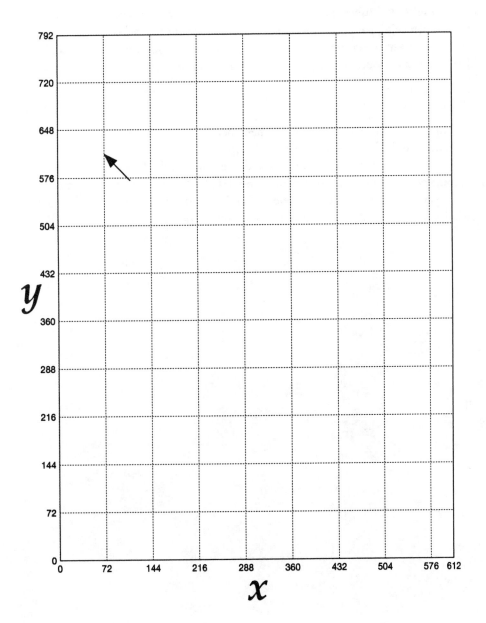

# lineto

Once you've established a current point, you then describe subsequent elements of the path using path construction operators. The simplest is *lineto.*

Beginning at the current point designated by *moveto,* you can draw a straight line to another point on the page using *lineto,* as follows.

```
72 612 moveto
360 612 lineto
```

This constructs a straight-line segment beginning at the current point and extending to the location specified by the operands 360, 612.

The resulting line is represented by a dashed line on the following page. The current point is now at the x/y coordinates 360, 612, as indicated by the arrow.

As yet, the page is still blank. The dashed line and arrow show where the line will be drawn, and the location of the new current point.

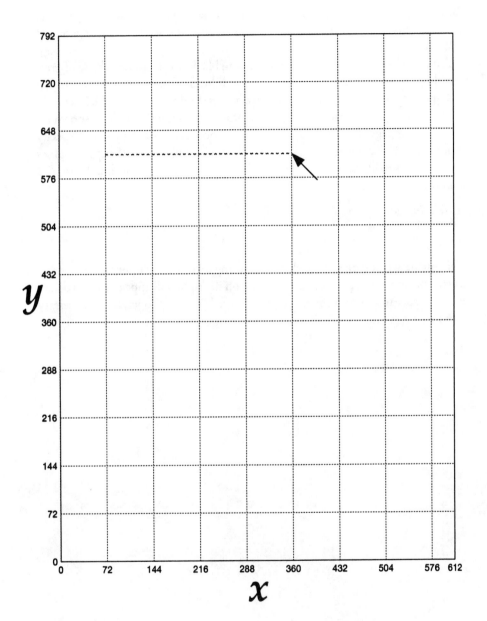

# *stroke*

The next step consists of applying "paint" to the path, using a PostScript painting operator. This might also be called rendering; it takes the as-yet invisible path and makes it visible.

You can apply paint in any color, including black, white, or any shade of gray, according to your requirements and the capabilities of the output device. If you don't specify a color, PostScript automatically uses the default color, which is black.

The *stroke* operator paints a line of any thickness along the path, as shown on the following page. Painting operators require no operands, but you can specify attributes such as color, line thickness, etc. by modifying the PostScript "graphics state" (discussed in chapter 3). The default value for the line width is 1, or 1/72 of an inch.

```
72 612 moveto
360 612 lineto
stroke
```

If you are writing directly to the screen using a PostScript interpreter that displays each path as it is painted, the drawing on the right will appear. But if you are sending a page to a printing device, one additional PostScript operation is necessary to produce a printed page.

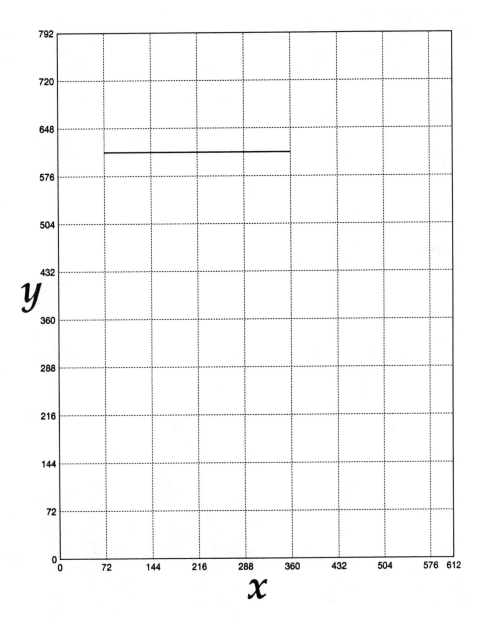

# showpage

PostScript page descriptions are not limited to single paths. Most pages consist of several paths, combining text and graphics at several locations on the page. A finished page description can be quite elaborate, as we'll see later in the book.

But the one thing that all PostScript page descriptions have in common is that they are all terminated by *showpage* or its equivalent.

The *showpage* operator sends the current page to the current output device (be it a laser printer, high-resolution imagesetter, fax machine, or any other printing device). This causes the objects that have been "painted" to actually appear on the page. The *showpage* operator then erases the current page and reinitializes the graphics state parameters in preparation for the next page description.

```
72 612 moveto
360 612 lineto
stroke

showpage
```

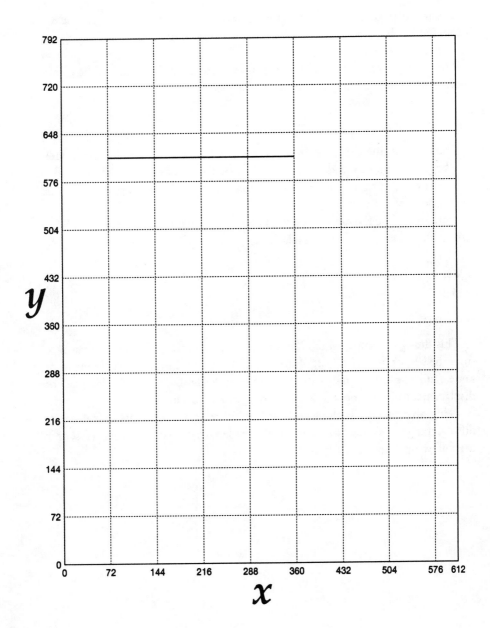

# rlineto

The previous page description resulted in a horizontal line being drawn at 8.5 inches (612 points divided by 72 points per inch) from the bottom of the page on the vertical or Y axis.

The length of this horizontal line, as measured along the X axis, is the difference between the first and second X coordinates.

360 - 72 = 288
288 / 72 = 4 inches

The X/Y coordinates used with the previous *lineto* operator are absolute values. The beginning point was defined absolutely by the two operands for the *moveto* operator; the ending point was defined absolutely by the two operands for the *lineto* operator.

You can achieve the same result with the *rlineto* (relative *lineto*) operator. With *rlineto*, the movement is always relative to the current point.

```
72 612 moveto
288 0 rlineto
stroke

showpage
```

This draws the same 4-inch horizontal line, extending 288 points measured from the beginning point (72) of the X axis. But in this instance the Y value is the same, and the line remains on the same vertical plane of 612. Hence, the displacement of the Y operand is 0 relative to the current location of Y.

Being able to express the length of lines in relative terms makes it easier to draw rectangular shapes, when you know the length of two adjoining sides, as in the following example.

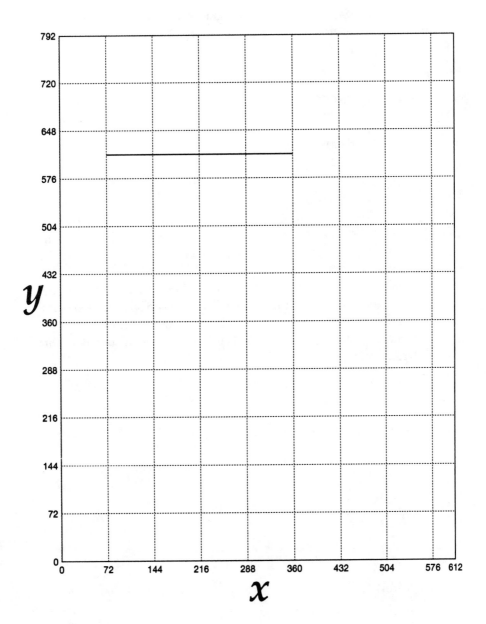

# closepath

Beginning with the 288-point (4-inch) line segment from the previous example, we can draw a rectangle with the short side measuring 1⁄4 inch, or 18 points, with the following instructions.

```
72 612 moveto

288 0 rlineto      % Side one
0 18 rlineto       % Side two
-288 0 rlineto     % Side three
closepath          % Side four

stroke

showpage
```

Note that a negative value is used to draw the third side of the rectangle. Otherwise, it's the same as the instruction for the first (opposite) side. The negative value for x constructs a line segment from right to left, moving in the opposite direction.

Because the interpreter can "remember" the origin of the current path, the fourth side can be constructed with *closepath*. The *closepath* operator appends a straight-line segment to the current path, connecting the current point to the origin of the current path, which was specified by the initial *moveto*. Some operators such as *closepath* require no operands.

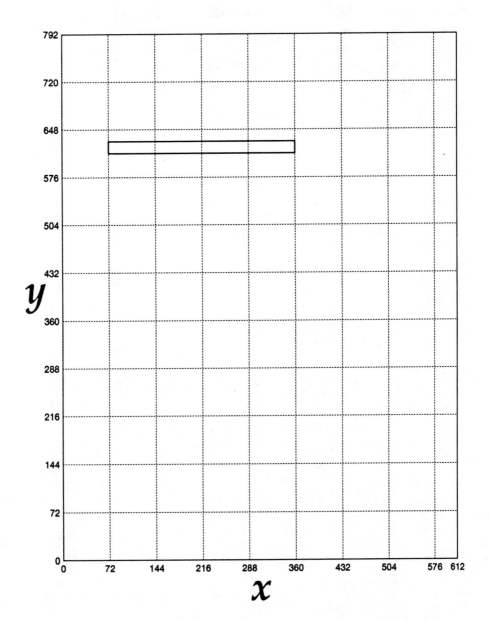

# fill

In the previous example, we painted the four sides of a rectangle with *stroke*.

Here, we use the same instructions to construct an identical rectangular path. But instead of stroking the four sides of the rectangle, we substitute the *fill* operator to paint the entire rectangle with the current color.

```
72 612 moveto
288 0 rlineto
0 18 rlineto
-288 0 rlineto
closepath

fill

showpage
```

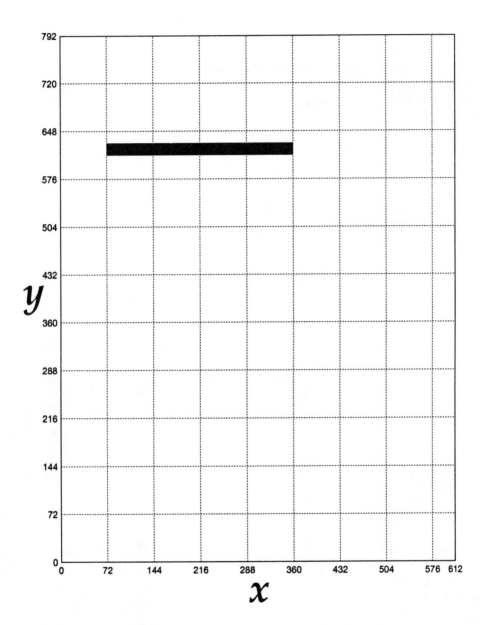

# Diamond Exercise

For simplicity, the lines drawn in this chapter have been perpendicular to either the horizontal or vertical axes. However, PostScript can connect any points on the page moving in any direction.

Starting with the instructions below, on a separate piece of paper complete the instructions necessary to draw a symmetrical diamond in the center of the following page. Then turn the page and look at a solution to this problem, before going on to chapter 2.

```
486 396 moveto
-180 180 rlineto      % Side one...
```

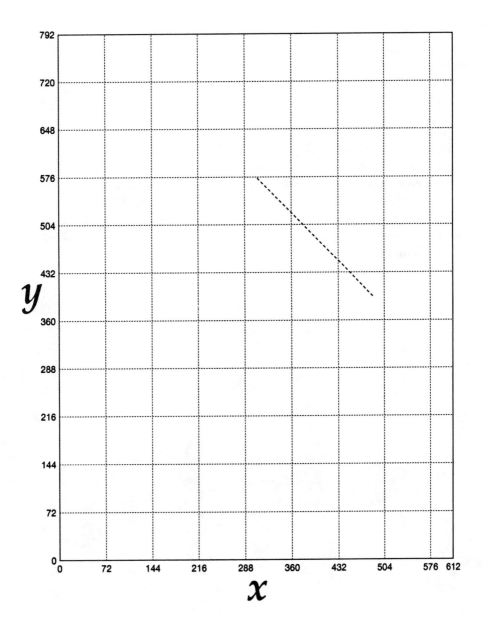

# Finished Diamond

```
486 396 moveto
-180 180 rlineto      % Side one

-180 -180 rlineto     % Side two
180 -180 rlineto      % Side three
closepath             % Side four
stroke

showpage
```

We drew side two by moving left and down 180 points each, relative to the current point. Hence, both operands are negative numbers.

Side three moves right and down the same number of points relative to the current point, requiring a positive and negative number, respectively.

Side four is constructed with *closepath,* which completes the diamond.

Finally, we paint the diamond with *stroke,* and use *showpage* to send the finished diamond to the printer.

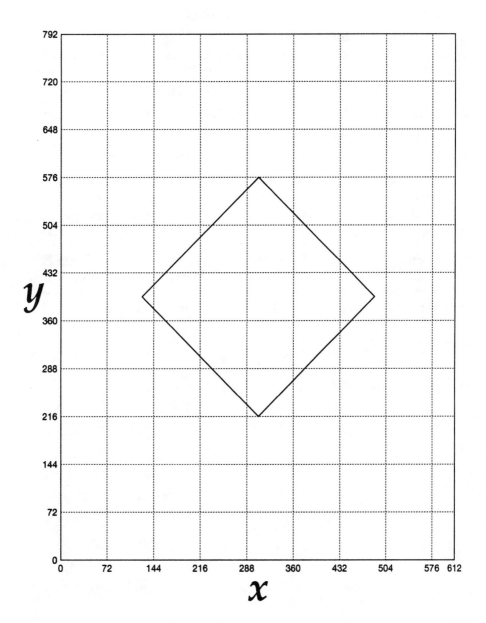

# PostScript Syntax

Observe the following rules of syntax when creating PostScript page descriptions.

A PostScript page description is an ASCII file—a straight text file made up of upper- and lowercase letters, numbers, and special characters (see the Red book, pages 21–22). You can create or modify an ASCII file using a text editor, or word processor capable of producing straight text files with no special formatting.

PostScript is case sensitive. Except for certain literal names that will be discussed later, all instructions must be in lowercase characters.

PostScript uses postfix notation, a system in which operands precede operators.

PostScript treats space, tab, and new line (carriage return or line feed) characters—even several in a row—as a single space character. You can use these characters to make your code more readable and understandable without changing the way it operates.

In PostScript, the percent sign (%) is a special character denoting "comment following." The PostScript interpreter ignores all text following a percent sign, until it encounters the end of the line (carriage return or line feed). As you'll see throughout this book, comments make it easier to understand programs.

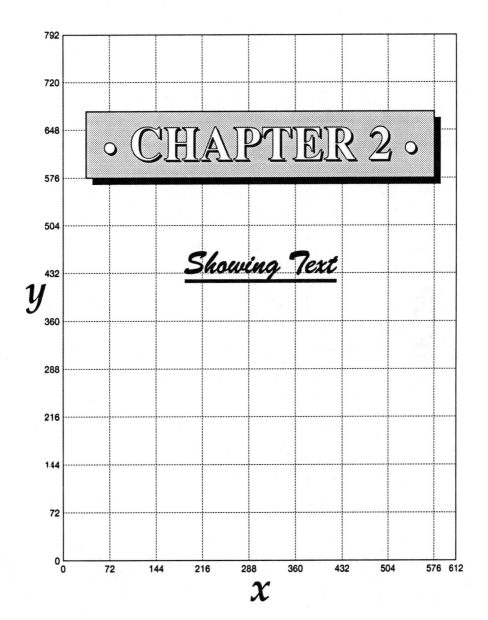

· CHAPTER 2 ·

*Showing Text*

# Chapter 2

# Text as Graphics

Although PostScript is best known for graphics drawing, one of the main reasons for choosing PostScript is for its superb font-handling capabilities. Using Post-Script for text processing provides two primary benefits.

First, the characters in any PostScript typeface are stored as individual Bézier outlines that can be scaled to form a font of any desired point size on demand. This makes PostScript very versatile and storage-efficient, compared to other typographical methods that require pre-formed font bitmaps for each point size.

Secondly, the outlines from which the PostScript interpreter generates individual characters are based on the same model used for rendering graphics. Fonts are therefore subject to all types of graphic manipulation, including rotation, scaling, reflection, skewing, and clipping. Thus, in PostScript, text is said to be "fully integrated" with graphics. Elaborate textual designs can be created as easily as other graphics.

Bézier curves are one of several ways of representing curved surfaces in computer graphics. Because they define the curves' endpoints and use two other control points to define the shape of the curve, they are ideally suited for use in interactive computer graphics, where a pointing device such as a mouse can be used to mold the curve to the desired shape.

# Bézier Outlines

The Bézier model that PostScript uses for forming text characters is the model on which the entire page description language is based.

Bézier outlines are specialized pre-formed graphics that have all the elements of a PostScript page description: an underlying X/Y coordinate system with a point of origin in the lower-left corner, an initial *moveto* instruction to begin a path, a series of *lineto* and *curveto* instructions necessary to construct the straight and curved line segments that comprise the character shape, and a final *closepath* instruction that completes the character.

The accompanying uppercase "T" from the Times-Roman typeface is a representation of an actual Bézier outline, with the resulting character that is formed from the outline shown in gray. The dashed lines connect control points and end points that are used to form the straight and curved line segments that comprise the character, using PostScript *lineto* and *curveto* operators. (Curved lines are discussed in chapter 5.)

The dots on the character outline represent the succession of current points where the initial *moveto* and successive *lineto* and *curveto* instructions begin and end. These are connected to represent the "character path," the perimeter of the lightly-filled area in the sample drawing.

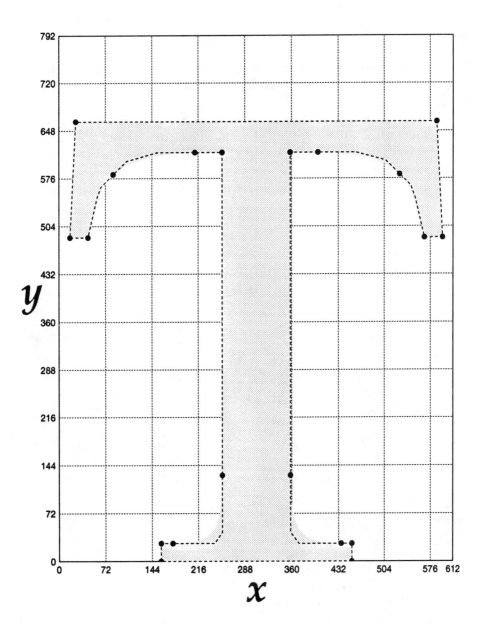

# Font Selection

To select a font in PostScript it is first necessary to identify the desired typeface.

/Times-BoldItalic

The slash character (/) at the beginning of this instruction is a special Post-Script character that always identifies a "literal" name—in this instance, "Times-BoldItalic."

"Times" identifies the typeface family, of which this particular typeface is a part. Many typeface families used in desktop publishing contain four typefaces: a normal, a bold, an italic or oblique, and a bold-italic version—although these precise names may not be used.

The four typefaces available in the Times typeface family are shown on the right.

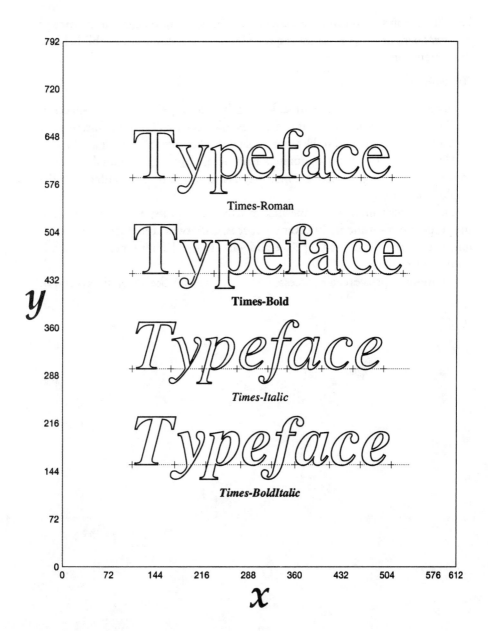

# findfont

PostScript stores the outlines for available typefaces internally. The PostScript *findfont* operator searches for the requested font, and if it finds it, establishes it as the current font.

/Times-BoldItalic findfont

PostScript interpreters contain at least 13 internal typefaces: four typefaces in the Times, Helvetica, and Courier families, plus the Symbol font. Interpreters with 13 typefaces are said to be compatible with the original Apple LaserWriter.

Most recent PostScript interpreters have access to the 35 internal typefaces shown on the facing page. These interpreters are said to be compatible with the Apple LaserWriter Plus.

The typeface name must be specified exactly as it appears, with any hyphens in the proper position and no intervening spaces. Otherwise, the interpreter will be unable to locate the desired typeface and will use the default typeface, which is normally Courier.

Additional typefaces can be accessed by the interpreter. See appendices A and B.

35 Standard Typefaces:

AvantGarde-Book
*AvantGarde-BookOblique*
**AvantGarde-Demi**
***AvantGarde-DemiOblique***
**Bookman-Demi**
***Bookman-DemiItalic***
Bookman-Light
*Bookman-LightItalic*
Courier
**Courier-Bold**
***Courier-BoldOblique***
*Courier-Oblique*
Helvetica
**Helvetica-Bold**
***Helvetica-BoldOblique***
Helvetica-Narrow
**Helvetica-Narrow-Bold**
***Helvetica-Narrow-BoldOblique***
*Helvetica-Narrow-Oblique*
*Helvetica-Oblique*
**NewCenturySchlbk-Bold**
***NewCenturySchlbk-BoldItalic***
*NewCenturySchlbk-Italic*
NewCenturySchlbk-Roman
**Palatino-Bold**
***Palatino-BoldItalic***
*Palatino-Italic*
Palatino-Roman
Σψμβολ (Symbol)
**Times-Bold**
***Times-BoldItalic***
*Times-Italic*
Times-Roman
*ZapfChancery-MediumItalic*
✳❂□❖✦❊■❋❂❀▼▲ (ZapfDingbats)

# scalefont

Once you've selected a typeface with *findfont,* you can set the size of the type with the *scalefont* operator.

Because characters are scaled uniformly in both the x and y directions, the *scalefont* operator requires only one operand. (Nonuniform scaling of characters is discussed in chapter 4).

/Times-BoldItalic findfont
72 scalefont

Bézier outlines are stored internally as 1000-point outlines that *findfont* factors by .001 to return a 1-point font. This is then scaled to the point size specified for *scalefont.*

The drawing at the right depicts the letter "T" from the Times-BoldItalic typeface, scaled to 72 points.

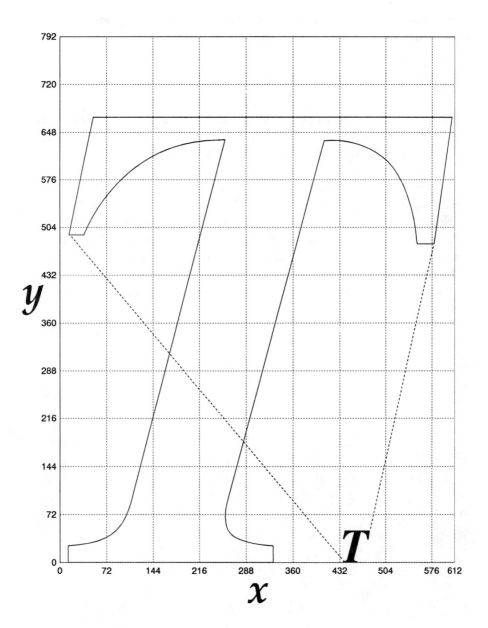

# *setfont*

The *setfont* operator establishes the specified typeface and font point size as the current font, to be used for subsequent character operations.

```
/Times-BoldItalic findfont
72 scalefont
setfont
```

The accompanying example shows the alphabetic and numeric characters from the Times-BoldItalic typeface, printed in a 108-point (1.5-inch) size for clarity. The sample was produced by a separate program (not shown).

Each character is shown in relation to its path bounding box, represented by the dashed line around the character, and to the baseline, also a dashed line. Beginning and ending points of origin are shown as small crosses on the baseline.

Notice how many characters have negative "left side bearings," indicated by overlapping path bounding boxes. This is common with italic or oblique character sets, and particularly true of characters with descenders on the left side, such as J, f, g, j, p, and y.

For further discussion of character paths, path bounding boxes, and complete character sets, see appendix A.

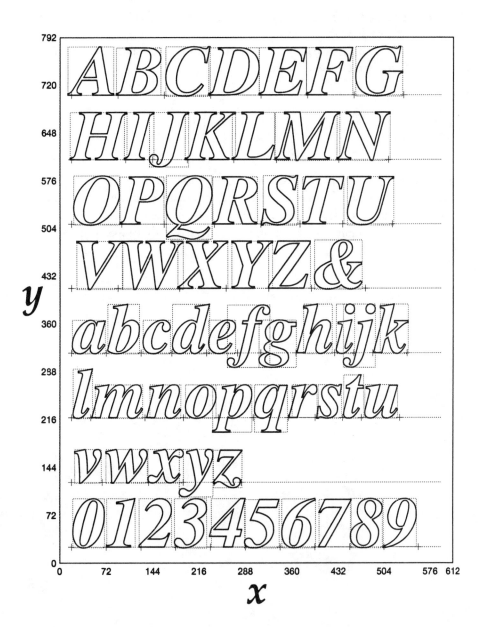

# Character Strings

Once you've defined a current font, you're ready to tell the PostScript interpreter what characters to draw in that font.

First you establish a new path with an initial *moveto* instruction. Then specify the string of characters to be printed.

```
/Times-BoldItalic findfont
72 scalefont
setfont
72 648 moveto
(Typeface)
```

You use left and right parentheses in PostScript to identify a string of characters (a string may be made up of a single character, many characters, or even no characters). In this sample, the string "Typeface" is enclosed in parentheses.

The page description you see at right was created with a separate program (not shown).

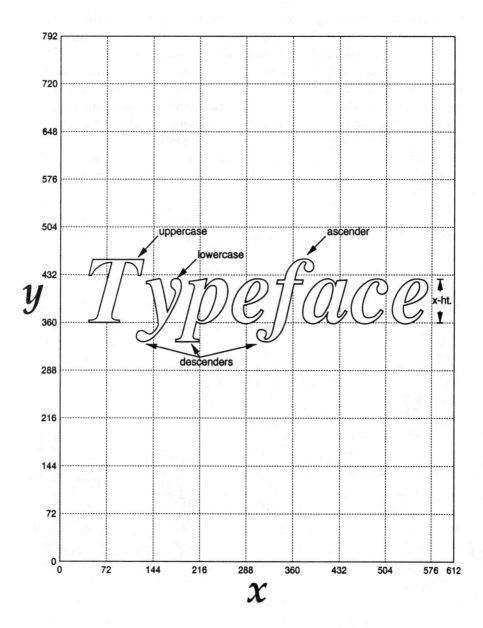

# String Width

The accompanying drawing depicts the character string specified on the previous page, created by a separate PostScript program. It identifies the elements of the character string, and shows the relationships between the characters.

Note that there is only one point of origin between each character in the string. This is because the ending point of origin for each character coincides with the beginning point of origin for the next character. The horizontal distance between the beginning point of origin of the first character and the ending point of origin of the last character is known as the "string width."

The light gray box surrounding the character string identifies the actual horizontal and vertical space occupied by this particular character string, which is shown in an arbitrary 120-point (1 2/3-inch) size.

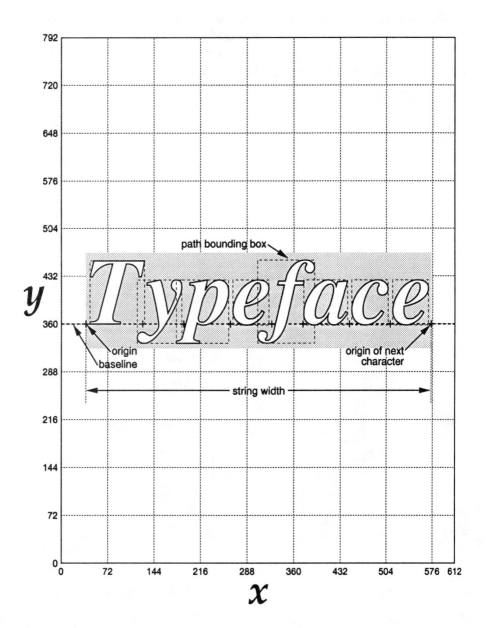

# *show*

Finally, the character string is ready to be painted. This is accomplished with *show*—a special PostScript operator that is used only with text.

The *show* operator fills the specified character string with the current color, and moves the current point to the end of the string.

```
/Times-BoldItalic findfont
72 scalefont
setfont
72 648 moveto
(Typeface) show

showpage
```

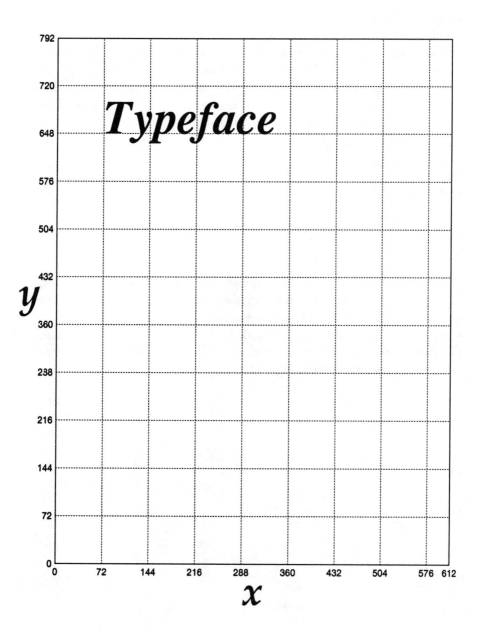

# ashow

There are other PostScript operators besides *show* that you can use for painting text characters. One of these is *ashow.*

The *ashow* operator provides the means to modify the distance between the characters in any string, either along the horizontal or vertical axis.

The following page description is identical to our first sample of the *show* operator. But here, the *ashow* operator is used to alter first the horizontal, and then both the horizontal and vertical spacing between each character.

```
/Times-BoldItalic findfont
72 scalefont setfont
72 648 moveto
12 0 (Typeface) ashow

72 648 moveto
12 -72 (Typeface) ashow

showpage
```

The *ashow* operator requires three operands—the X and Y values of additional spacing that will be inserted between each character, in either or both the horizontal and vertical directions, and the string of characters to be drawn.

As with other X/Y values, the operands for *ashow* specify distances in points. The first instance of *ashow* moves each character 12 points right. The second moves each character 12 points right and 72 points down.

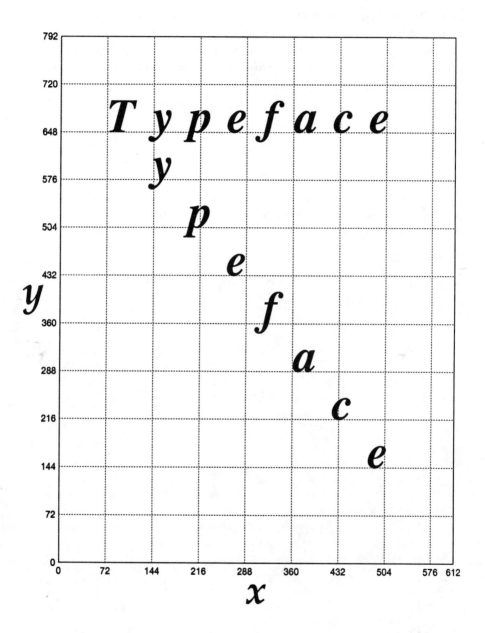

# charpath

Where the PostScript *show* operator fills text characters with the current color, the *stroke* operator produces character outlines by painting along the character path (*true charpath*) of each character. The *charpath* operator, combined with the operand *true*, defines the *cha*racters' *path*—the outline of the characters. You can then act on that path as you can any other path.

```
/Times-BoldItalic findfont
72 scalefont setfont
72 648 moveto
(Typeface) true charpath
stroke
```

Note that the following instructions accomplish the same thing as the *show* operator. Using *true charpath fill* is slower than *show*, but it's sometimes useful when you're writing procedures.

```
/Times-BoldItalic findfont
72 scalefont setfont
72 504 moveto
(Typeface) true charpath
fill

showpage
```

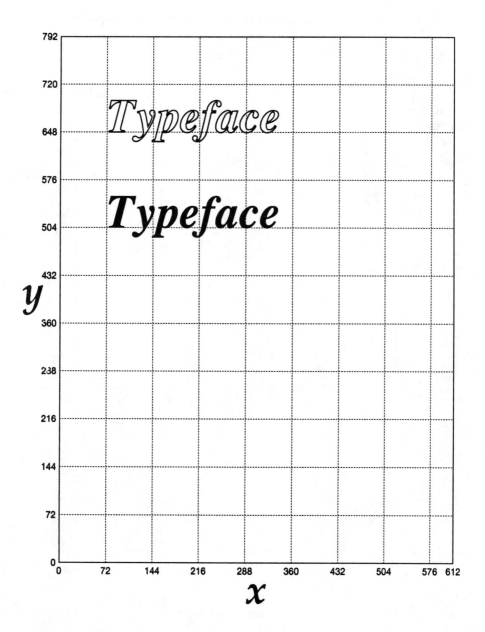

# Underlined Text

The following page description combines the sample code used to produce the word "Typeface" on page 2-16 with the sample of the rectangle shown in chapter 1, to create a heavy underline below a character string.

```
/Times-BoldItalic findfont
72 scalefont setfont
72 648 moveto
(Typeface)
show

72 612 moveto
288 0 rlineto
0 18 rlineto
-288 0 rlineto
closepath
fill

showpage
```

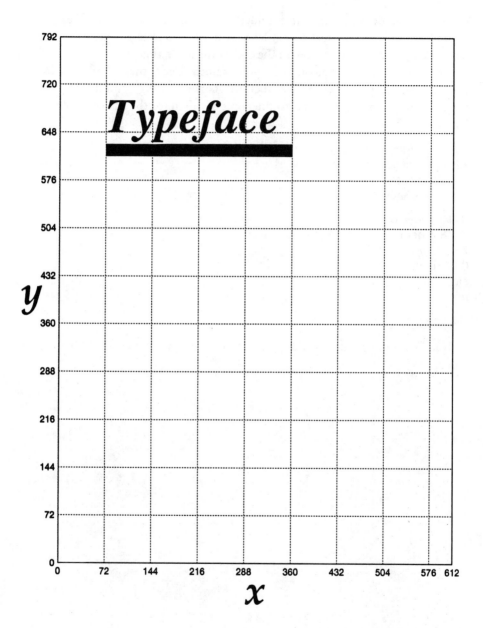

# rmoveto

In the previous example, the 4-inch underline used in chapter 1 extends too far beyond the width of the text string. So we use *rmoveto* to align the end of the rectangle used as an underline with the end of the text string.

We accomplish this by moving to a point directly under the end of the string (the new current point that results when we show the string), and drawing the rectangle from right to left, back to the point of origin for the string, which we know is at 72 x.

```
/Times-BoldItalic findfont
72 scalefont setfont
72 648 moveto
(Typeface) show

0 -18 rmoveto
0 -18 rlineto
72 612 lineto
0 18 rlineto
closepath
fill

showpage
```

Note how both *rlineto* and *lineto* instructions are used to create the underline.

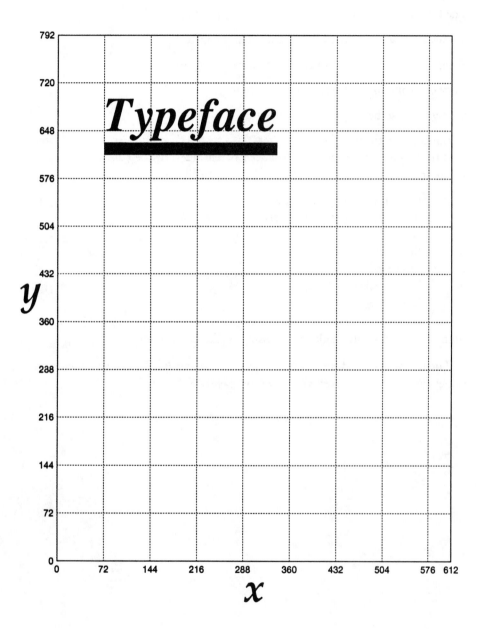

# PostScript String Syntax

The following special rules apply to PostScript strings.

Strings are always enclosed in left and right parentheses.

Strings can contain special PostScript characters such as "%."

They can contain ((balanced)) left and right parentheses.

Strings can also be empty, or nul, as with ().

Within a string, the backslash character (\) is a special PostScript "escape" character used to define things such as unbalanced parentheses, or the continuation of a string on a new line.

| | |
|---|---|
| \( | unbalanced left parenthesis |
| \) | unbalanced right parenthesis |
| \r | carriage return |
| \n | line feed |
| \f | form feed |
| \t | horizontal tab |
| \b | backspace |
| \\ | backslash |
| \nnn | octal character code for accessing ASCII characters |

The use of octal codes is shown on pages 5-10 and A-12, and octal character values for various characters are shown on pages A-15 to A-24.

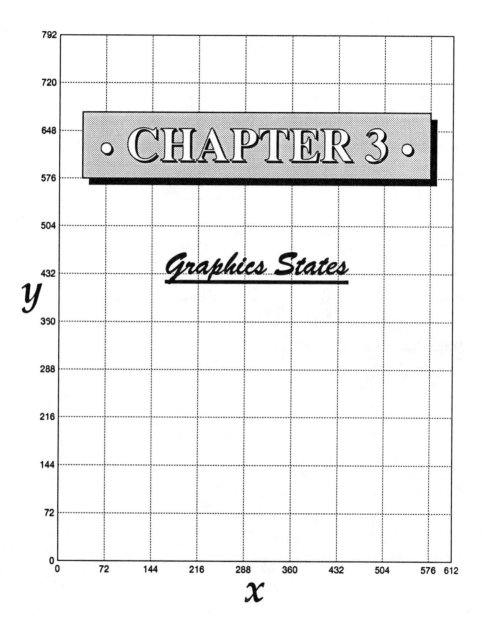

CHAPTER 3

*Graphics States*

# Chapter 3

# Graphics States

As we have seen, a PostScript page description is built up by applying paint to graphics and text with the *stroke, fill,* and *show* operators. The paint can be applied in black, white, or any shade of gray, or, for devices that have the capability, any color.

You can modify elements of the current graphics state in much the same way that a graphic artist changes a brush or color of paint before rendering text and graphic elements on a page.

The PostScript interpreter "remembers" the current graphics state parameters. Any of these parameters can be modified either temporarily or permanently at any point in a page description to affect a specific area or an entire page.

In chapter 1 we discussed how to initialize and modify two of the most fundamental graphics state parameters: the current point and the current path. And in chapter 2, we showed how to select the set of graphics shapes or characters that define the current font.

In this chapter we will examine two graphics state parameters that are used to change the appearance of graphics or text: the width of the line produced by the PostScript *stroke* operator, and the color of the graphic produced by the painting operators—*stroke, fill,* and *show.*

Of the remaining graphics state parameters, several—line cap, line join, miter limit, dash pattern, and flatness—affect only the *stroke* operator, and are described in the Red book, pages 214–222. We discuss the *setflat* operator briefly in chapter 6.

Other parameters—the CTM (current transformation matrix), halftone screen, and clipping path—are of major importance, and will be discussed in chapter 8.

# Color

Because black and white are the colors used by the vast majority of PostScript users in laser printing and imagesetting, the other colors will be discussed separately in chapter 8. We will concentrate here on black, white, and various shades of gray.

To begin, examine the effects achieved by the following instructions, as shown on the facing page.

```
0 0 moveto
612 0 rlineto 0 792 rlineto -612 0 rlineto
closepath fill
```

```
/Times-BoldItalic findfont 24 scalefont setfont
306 100 moveto
1 setgray
(graphics states . . .) show
```

```
showpage
```

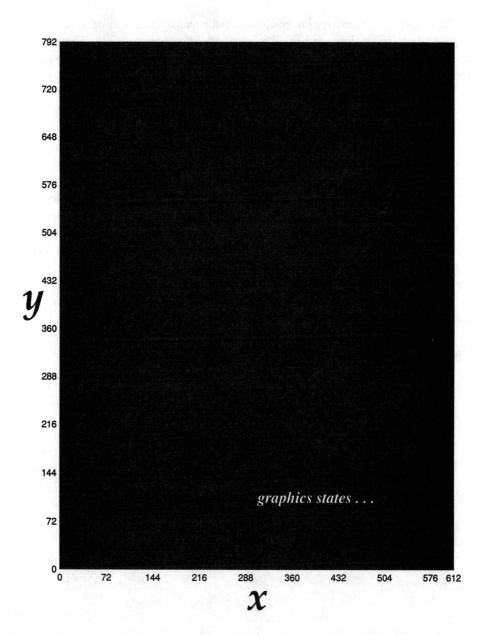

graphics states . . .

# setgray

In the previous page description we constructed a rectangle the size of the entire page, 612 by 792 points, and filled it with the default color, black. Then we selected a font and showed the string "graphics states" at a specified position on the page.

The *1 setgray* instruction caused the text to be painted in the color white. This technique is referred to as a "reverse," because it reverses the natural order of printing black characters on a white page.

The *setgray* operator is one of the simplest in the PostScript vocabulary. In addition to reversing the natural order of black on white, it can also be used to create the illusion of depth or three-dimensionality by altering background and foreground colors, and by shading some graphic elements in relationship to others.

The *setgray* operator requires only one operand, ranging from 0 for black (solid color), to 1 for white (no color), or any intermediate value representing a percentage of white to black. For example, .1 is 10 percent white, or dark gray; .5 is an equal amount of black and white, or medium gray; and .99 is nearly all white, or very light gray.

PostScript uses "halftoning" to represent shades of gray. For a complete discussion of PostScript's halftoning methods, see chapter 10 of the Orange book.

The example on the following page shows the results produced by a range of *setgray* operations from 0 to 1.

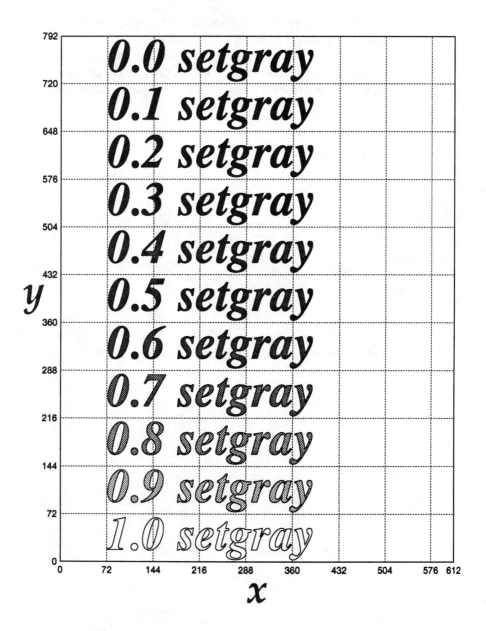

# Layering

The order in which the *setgray* operator applies text and graphics to the page, using black and white or various shades of gray, is important.

On the following page, the "shadowing effect" of the text produced by the *.9 setgray* instruction must be applied before the black text produced by the *0 setgray* instruction, or the shadow would be "on top" of the solid black text, instead of underneath it.

```
/Helvetica-Bold findfont 72 scalefont setfont

.9 setgray          % Gray first
200 400 moveto
(Stand) show
225 325 moveto
(Out) show

0 setgray           % Then black
220 425 moveto
(Stand) show
245 350 moveto
(Out) show

showpage
```

The technique of applying paint to text and graphics in a certain order is known as "layering."

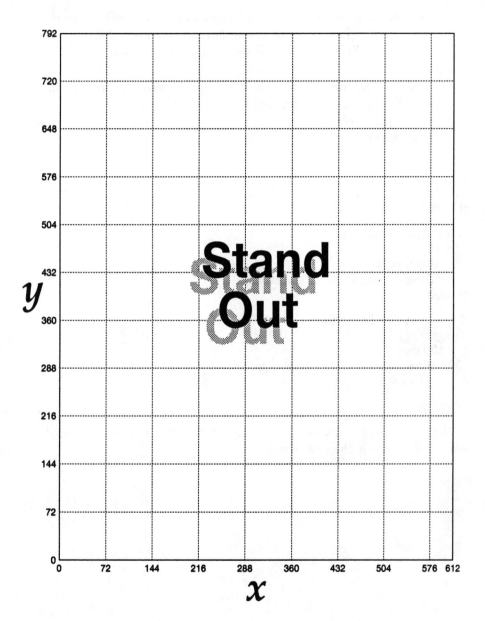

# Shadowing

To the eye, the rectangle on the following page appears to be a solid white box, outlined with a black line, and with a black shadow underneath that causes the box to "stand out" from the page. The shadow underneath creates the illusion of depth.

But as you can see from studying the PostScript instructions below, this illusion is actually constructed by drawing three separate boxes: a filled black box underneath, a second white-filled box slightly offset on top of it, and a third which is outlined with the *stroke* operator.

```
% Box 1—fill black box
115 385 moveto
200 0 rlineto 0 300 rlineto -200 0 rlineto
closepath fill

% Box 2—fill white box
1 setgray
100 400 moveto
200 0 rlineto 0 300 rlineto -200 0 rlineto
closepath fill

% Box 3—stroke box outline
0 setgray
100 400 moveto
200 0 rlineto 0 300 rlineto -200 0 rlineto
closepath stroke

showpage
```

Note that the *moveto* instruction for the first box is offset 15 points to the right and down, relative to the other boxes.

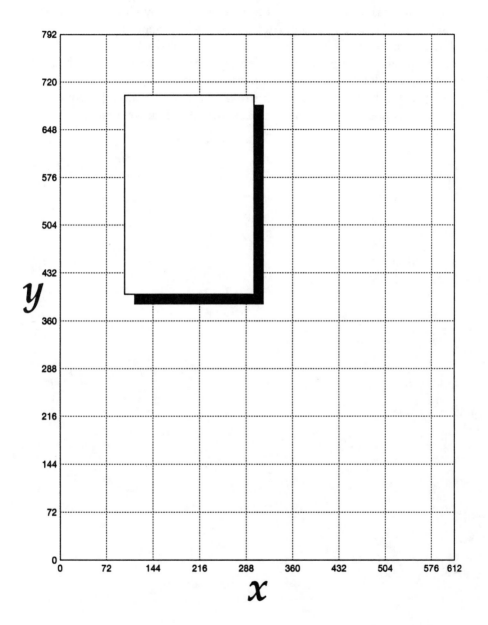

# Opaque Paint

PostScript paint is opaque, so any subsequent color entirely obscures any paint which is applied to text or graphics that are on any layer applied previously.

The drawing on the facing page shows the three layers that comprise the white box in the previous example, with the white layer showing the entire black box in the first layer underneath it, as though it were translucent.

The path of the third layer, which strokes the box with a black outline, is shown by a dashed white line where it passes over the black box underneath.

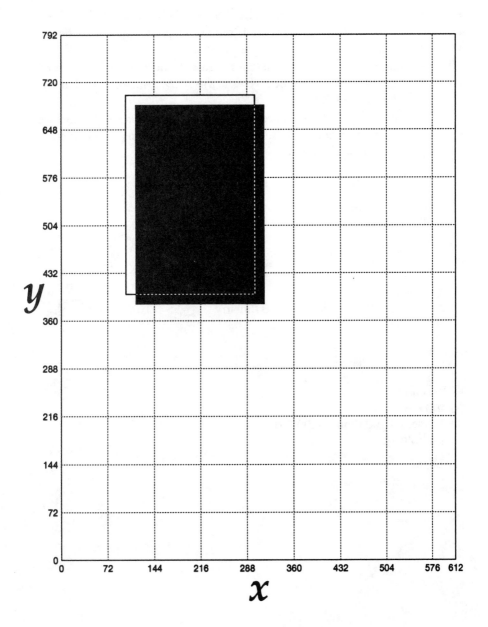

# gsave and grestore

This sample shows the same shaded white box, but the instructions have been altered slightly, to show how to "save" and "restore" graphics state parameters to temporarily change one or more of the parameters.

In this example, we use the *gsave* operator to save the default black color used to paint the first solid black box, then we issue the *1 setgray* instruction that sets the color for the second white box.

The *grestore* instruction then restores the black color that was saved before we issued the *1 setgray* instruction. Thus, there is no need for a *0 setgray* instruction prior to painting the black outline.

```
% Box 1—solid black
115 385 moveto
200 0 rlineto 0 300 rlineto -200 0 rlineto
closepath fill

% Box 2—white
gsave
    1 setgray
    100 400 moveto
    200 0 rlineto 0 300 rlineto -200 0 rlineto
    closepath fill
grestore

% box 3—black outline
% 0 setgray not needed
2 setlinewidth
100 400 moveto
200 0 rlineto 0 300 rlineto -200 0 rlineto
closepath stroke

showpage
```

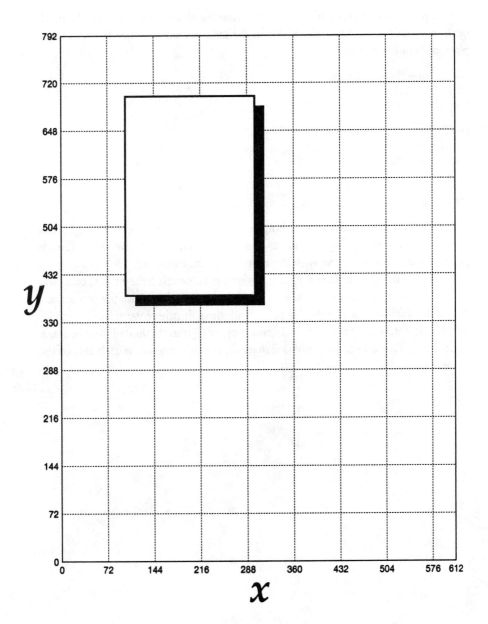

# setlinewidth

On the previous page, we added the instruction *2 setlinewidth* to thicken the black outline stroked around the white box. In the sample below, we use *setlinewidth* in place of filling a rectangle.

```
/Times-BoldItalic findfont 72 scalefont setfont
72 648 moveto
(Typeface) show

0 -27 rmoveto
72 621 lineto
18 setlinewidth
stroke

showpage
```

Instead of constructing and filling a rectangular box 18 points high, and underlining the string "Typeface," as was done in chapter 2, the same effect is produced by stroking a line with the same 18-point thickness.

Note that instead of beginning the underline 18 points below the text, as was done in chapter 2, and then drawing a box 18 points high, we use the instruction *18 setlinewidth* to produce the 18-point underline. But here we start the line 27 points below the end of the text (*0 -27 rmoveto*), or 18 plus 9 (one-half the thickness of the line). This is because *setlinewidth* strokes equal weights on each side of the current path.

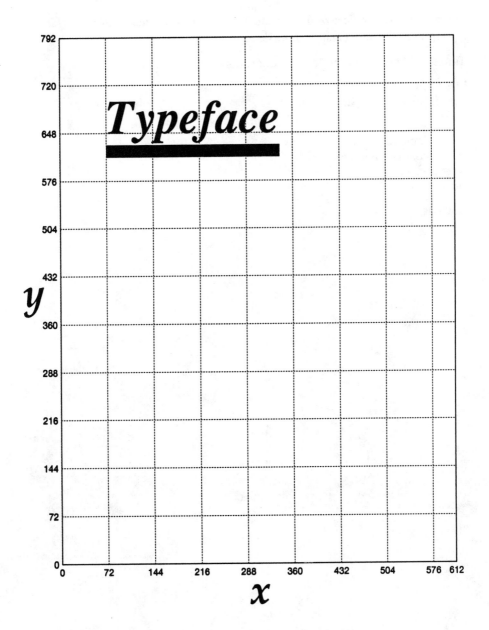

# Thin Text Outlines

You can also use *setlinewidth* to create a line that is thinner than the default 1-point line width, to create a more delicate appearance.

```
/Times-BoldItalic findfont 72 scalefont setfont

72 648 moveto
(Typeface) true charpath
stroke

72 504 moveto
(Typeface) true charpath
.5 setlinewidth
stroke

showpage
```

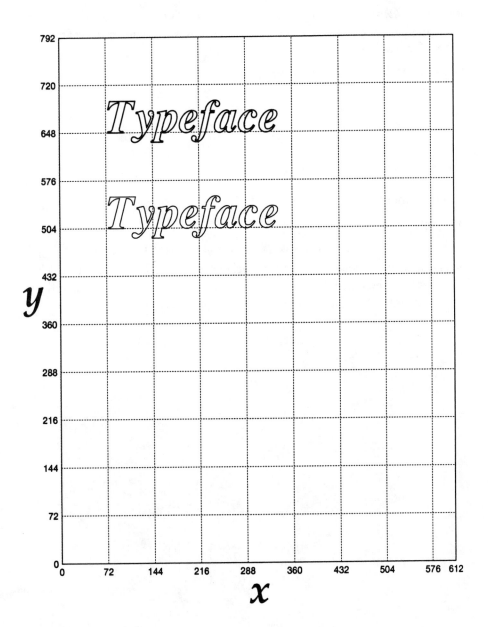

# Thick Text Outlines

Because the *show* operator simply fills a character's outline, the *setlinewidth* operator, in conjunction with the *stroke* operator, is the only way to enlarge the character outline, for creating thicker characters.

/Times-BoldItalic findfont 72 scalefont setfont

72 654 moveto
(Typeface) true charpath
12 setlinewidth
stroke

72 654 moveto
1 setgray
(Typeface) show

showpage

Note that this is really a two-step operation, with the thicker text created with the first series of instructions using the black default color. We painted the thick black text first, then used *1 setgray* to change the current color to white, and the *show* operator to paint the white text on top of the black.

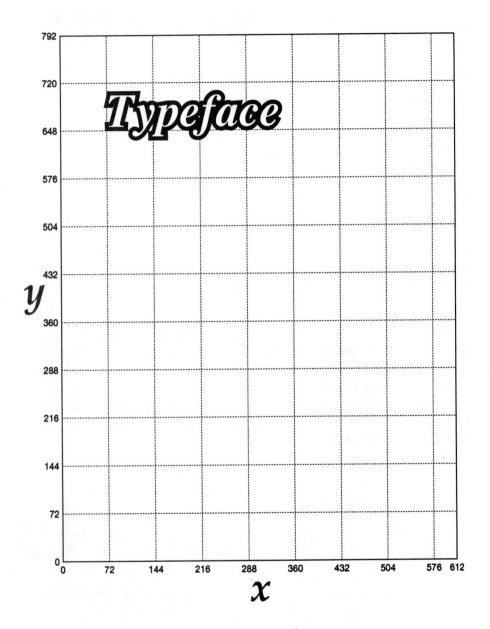

# Fancy Text Outlines

We can use this same principle to achieve more intricate textual effects, by using three layers. The three-layer composite resulting from the following sample is shown at Y 360 in the example.

```
/Times-BoldItalic findfont 72 scalefont setfont

72 360 moveto
(Typeface) true charpath
fill

72 360 moveto
(Typeface) true charpath
3 setlinewidth
stroke

72 360 moveto
(Typeface) true charpath
1 setlinewidth
1 setgray
stroke

showpage
```

The first layer (shown also on Y 648) fills the string of text—a string which could also have been painted with *show*. The second layer strokes a thicker (3-point) outline around the first layer as shown on Y 504, to create filled text that is slightly thicker than normal.

Finally, the third layer adds a 1-point white outline (using *1 setlinewidth* and *1 setgray*). It follows the normal shape of the character outlines, but is "inside" the thicker black outline painted in layer two.

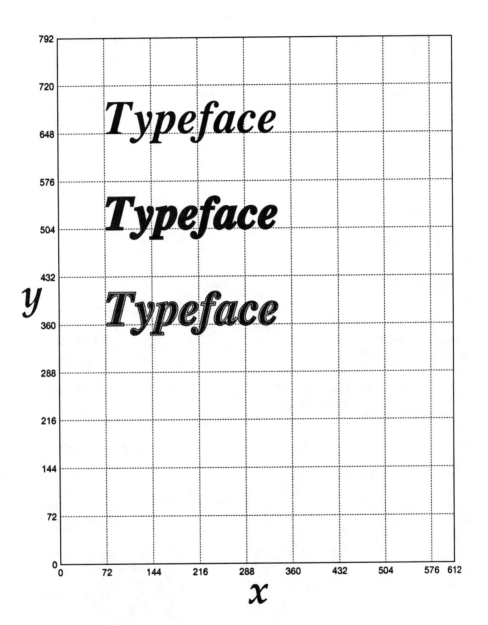

# Shaded Box

We can use the same technique to create multiple-layered objects combining text and graphics, starting with a three-layered box that is similar to the box shown on page 3-8. Note the use of *gsave* and *grestore* to save and then restore the black color for use in the third layer.

```
% Shadow box
46 566 moveto
540 0 rlineto 0 100 rlineto -540 0 rlineto
closepath fill

% Background box
gsave
     36 576 moveto
     1 setgray
     540 0 rlineto 0 100 rlineto -540 0 rlineto
     closepath fill
grestore

% Outline box
36 576 moveto
2 setlinewidth
540 0 rlineto 0 100 rlineto -540 0 rlineto
closepath stroke
% Continued on next page
```

You will need a *showpage* to produce the drawing at right, which is the first stage of the drawing produced by the next sample.

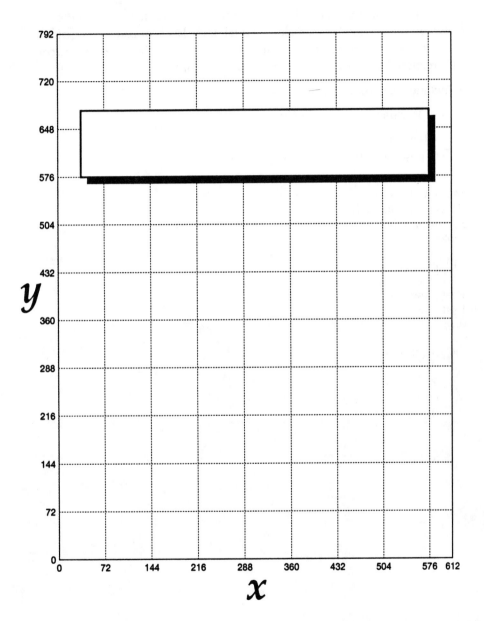

# Shaded Box with Fancy Text

We can now construct and paint three layers of text inside a box like the one shown on the previous page, making a total of six layers of combined graphics and text. These layers must be constructed in the order in which they are presented here, in order to paint each layer in the proper order.

```
% Include code from previous page

/Times-Bold findfont 108 scalefont setfont

140 590 moveto
(TITLE) true charpath
fill

140 590 moveto
(TITLE) true charpath
3 setlinewidth
stroke

140 590 moveto
(TITLE) true charpath
1 setlinewidth
1 setgray
stroke

showpage
```

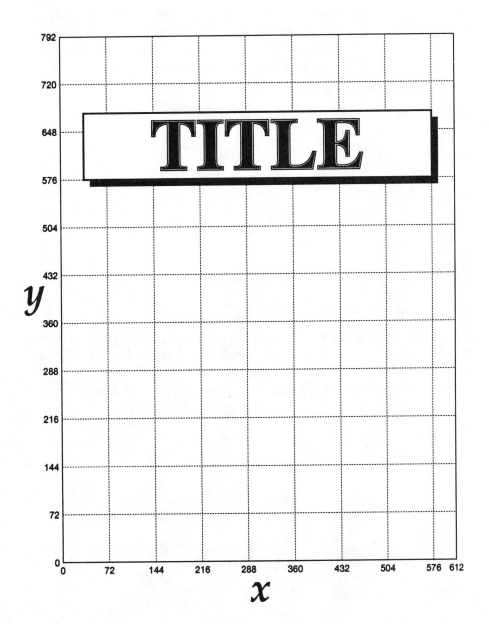

# Shaded Box and Shaded Text

We can achieve a very different effect by changing only one line in the routine for drawing the background box. We change *1 setgray* to *.95 setgray*, and offset a shadow under the text in the same manner as we used with the three boxes. This is the same box-drawing routine as before, but the text is changed slightly.

```
/Times-Bold findfont 108 scalefont setfont

90 587 moveto
(T I T L E) show

gsave
    1 setgray
    87 590 moveto
    (T I T L E) show
grestore

.5 setlinewidth
87 590 moveto
(T I T L E) true charpath
stroke

showpage
```

Note how we offset the first layer of text 3 points to the right and down from the white text in the second layer, and how the final black outline is needed to differentiate the white text from the light gray background.

Notice also that we inserted a single space between the characters in the string "T I T L E" to better fill the box along the horizontal axis.

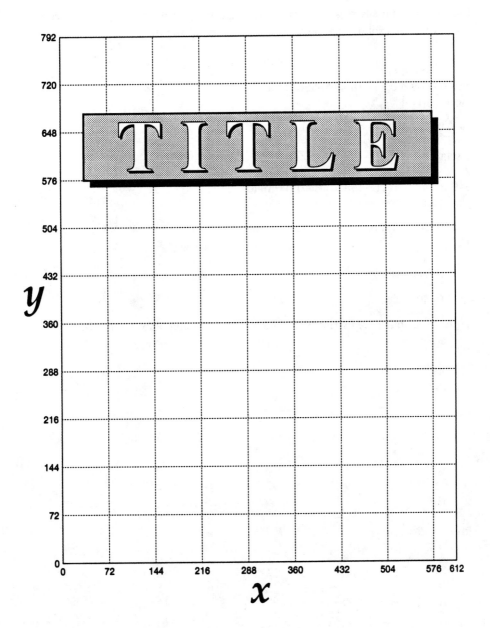

# Box in Box

Finally, we can easily create a formal-looking title by stroking a white box inside the borders of a solid black box, using white text for the title.

```
% Black box
31 571 moveto
550 0 rlineto 0 110 rlineto -550 0 rlineto
closepath fill

% White outline inside
36 576 moveto
1 setgray
2 setlinewidth
540 0 rlineto 0 100 rlineto -540 0 rlineto
closepath stroke

/Times-Bold findfont 108 scalefont setfont
1 setgray
92 590 moveto
24 0 (TITLE) ashow

showpage
```

In this instance we used *ashow* to increase the spacing between the characters.

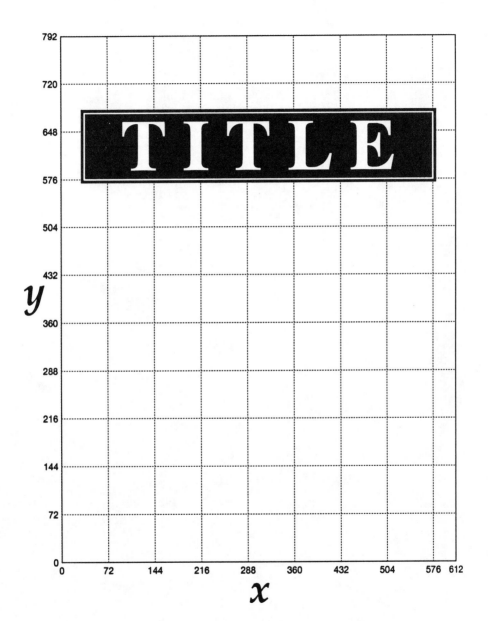

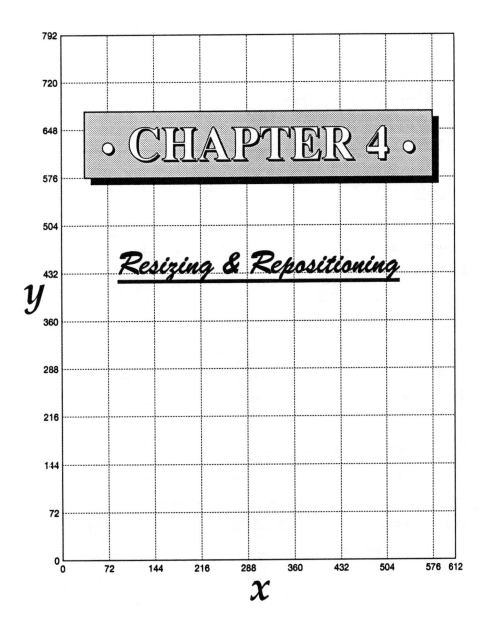

CHAPTER 4

Resizing & Repositioning

# Chapter 4

# Transformations

Perhaps the most powerful aspect of PostScript is its ability to support transformations of the underlying coordinate system. In PostScript, you can literally transform the underlying page into something very different from what we have been working with in the previous three chapters.

This is an important concept to understand. When you use transformation operators, you are changing the size, origin, and/or orientation of the underlying coordinate system. This, in turn, transforms the appearance of anything subsequently drawn on the page.

In this chapter we will examine the three most common kinds of transformations: scaling, translation, and rotation—each of which is supported by a PostScript operator.

The *scale* operator changes the unit size of either the X or Y axis or both, without affecting their origin or orientation.

The *translate* operator moves the origin of the coordinate system to a new location, while leaving unit size and orientation of the X/Y axes unchanged.

The *rotate* operator turns the axes of the coordinate system by any specified angle, without affecting unit size or origin of the axes.

Individually, these are powerful features. Collectively, the ability to scale, translate, and rotate any text and graphics means that, with PostScript, there is virtually nothing that can't be drawn on a page.

# *scale*

The ability to scale any object to any size is perhaps PostScript's single most important capability, for it is scaling that gives the language its unique ability to be used with any raster imaging device of any resolution.

We first encountered scaling in chapter 2, where we used the PostScript *scalefont* operator to scale typeface outlines to produce a font of any desired point size.

Unlike *scalefont,* which requires only one operand to scale typefaces uniformly along both the x and y axes, the *scale* operator requires two operands for scaling any object independently or uniformly along either or both axes.

Observe how the instructions below can produce our familiar 72-point "Typeface" from a 36-point font, by scaling by a factor of 2 uniformly along both the x and y axes.

```
/Times-BoldItalic findfont 36 scalefont setfont

gsave
    72 648 moveto
    2 2 scale
    (Typeface) show
grestore

showpage
```

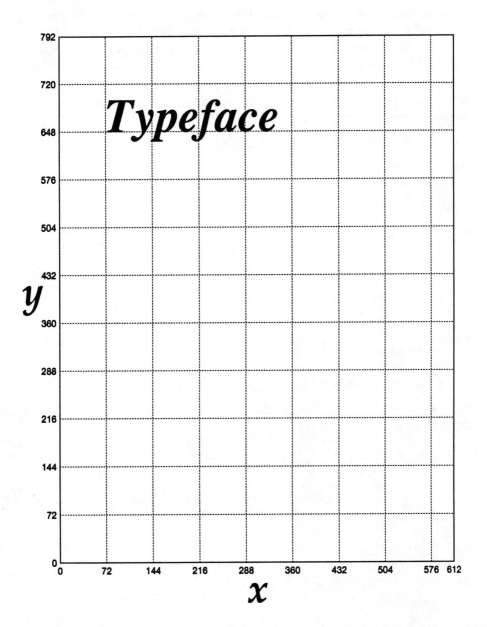

# Horizontal Scaling

In the accompanying example, we show three ways to stretch the same 72-point "Typeface" by scaling it only along the horizontal axis. As you can see (at Y 648), the *2 1 scale* instruction, which doubles the size for only the X axis, produces a string that appears too long for the page.

We can modify this by changing the scale factor for the X axis to 1.75 (see Y 504); or, better still, by leaving the scale factor at 2 and using *ashow* to draw the individual characters closer together (see Y 360).

```
/Times-BoldItalic findfont 72 scalefont setfont

gsave
    72 648 moveto
    2 1 scale
    (Typeface) show
grestore

gsave
    72 504 moveto
    1.75 1 scale
    (Typeface) show
grestore

gsave
    72 360 moveto
    2 1 scale
    -5 0 (Typeface) ashow
grestore

showpage
```

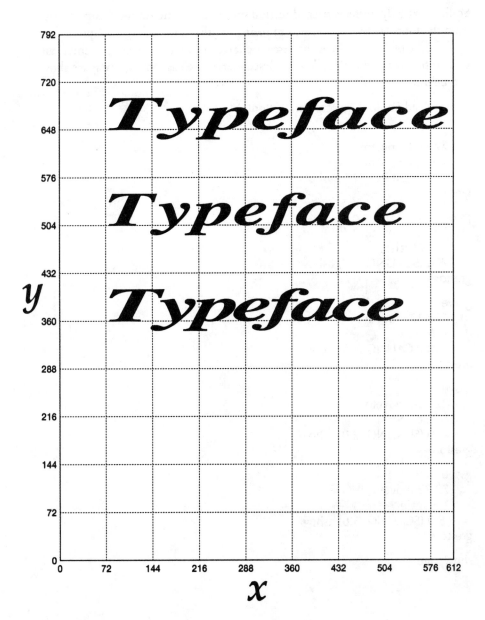

# Vertical Scaling

Scaling text only in the vertical direction produces an interesting change of pace from the fonts we are accustomed to seeing. Notice how scaling a 72-point font by a factor of 1.5 produces uppercase characters that are exactly 1 inch tall. Remember that point sizes allow for descenders as well as some white space above and below.

```
/Times-Bold findfont 72 scalefont setfont

gsave
    72 648 moveto
    1 1 scale
    -5 0 (SCALING  1.0) ashow
grestore

gsave
    72 504 moveto
    1 1.5 scale
    -5 0 (SCALING  1.5) ashow
grestore

gsave
    72 432 moveto
    1 .5 scale
    -5 0 (SCALING .5) ashow
grestore

gsave
    72 288 moveto
    1 2 scale
    -5 0 (SCALING  2.0) ashow
grestore

gsave
    72 72 moveto
    1 3 scale
    -5 0 (SCALING  3.0) ashow
grestore

showpage
```

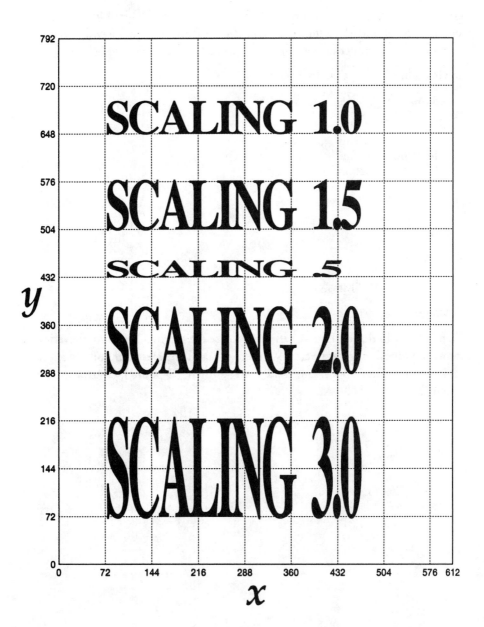

# Emphasizing and Fitting Text

Vertical scaling is useful for emphasizing certain aspects of a graphic (as in the word "SALE" on the following page), and also for fitting text into a width that is determined by the other elements of the graphic (as in the last line below).

```
/Helvetica findfont 72 scalefont setfont

72 648 moveto
(PRE-SEASON) show

gsave
    /Times-Bold findfont
    144 scalefont setfont
    72 191 moveto
    1.25 4 scale
    (SALE) show
grestore

72 72 moveto
.72 1 scale
(THURSDAY, MAY 5) show

showpage
```

Notice how in the last line we were able to use the original 72-point Helvetica font without specifying it explicitly. We used *gsave* and *grestore* to temporarily select the 144-point Times-Bold font, and then restored 72-point Helvetica as the current font.

# A Word of Caution

When using the *scale* operator, be careful to use *gsave* and *grestore* before and after if you don't want succeeding instructions to be affected. This is true not only for the size of the object, but also for its location on the page.

The instructions below show how text intended for coordinates 144, 288 is moved to 72, 144 due to the previous *scale* instruction. The accompanying example superimposes the new visual page grid that results from the *.5 .5 scale* instruction, to demonstrate what has occurred.

```
/Times-BoldItalic findfont 72 scalefont setfont
144 576 moveto
(Sample One) show

144 432 moveto
.5 .5 scale
(Sample Two) show

144 288 moveto
(Sample Three) show

showpage
```

As a general rule you should use *gsave* and *grestore* before and after issuing *scale* instructions, and move to the desired location before scaling.

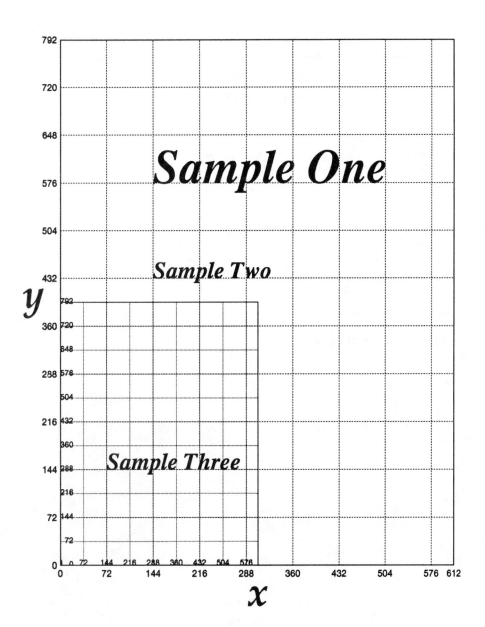

# Reflections

You can also use *scale* to invert any object by specifying negative values for either the X or Y operands. Negative X inverts the object on the horizontal axis (right to left), and negative Y inverts the object bottom to top. When both values are negative, the object is inverted in both directions.

```
/Helvetica-Bold findfont 36 scalefont setfont

gsave
    306 396 moveto
    1 3 scale
    (REFLECTIONS-1) show
grestore

gsave
    306 396 moveto
    -1 3 scale
    (REFLECTIONS-2) show
grestore

gsave
    306 396 moveto
    1 -3 scale
    (REFLECTIONS-3) show
grestore

gsave
    306 396 moveto
    -1 -3 scale
    (REFLECTIONS-4) show
grestore

showpage
```

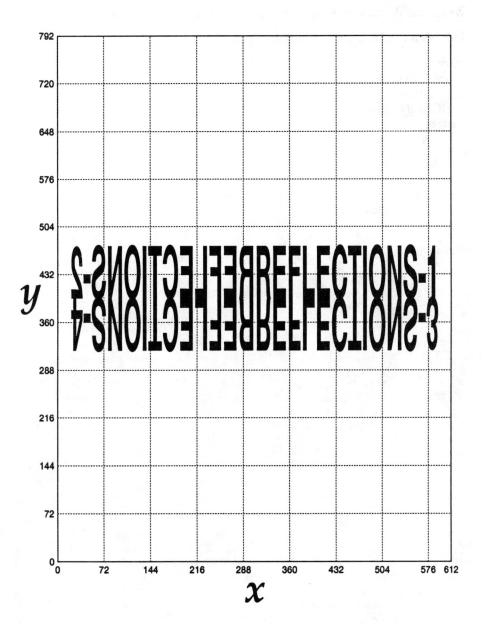

# Mirror

We can use the same technique to create interesting effects with *setgray.*

/Helvetica-Bold findfont 144 scalefont setfont

```
gsave
    54 396 moveto
    1 3 scale
    (GEMINI) show
grestore

gsave
    54 396 moveto
    .8 setgray
    1 -3 scale
    (GEMINI) show
grestore

showpage
```

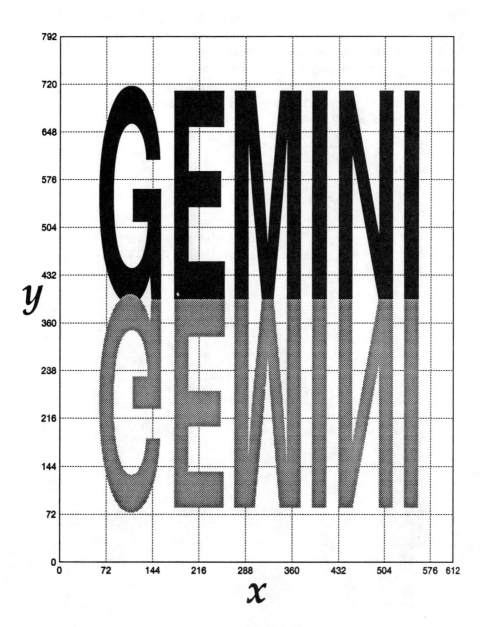

4-15

# *translate*

Where *scale* is used to resize elements of a page description, the *translate* operator is used for repositioning certain elements of a page description or an entire page description. It moves the origin of the entire page from the lower-left corner to the x/y coordinates you specify in the operands for *translate*.

To demonstrate the change, we'll compare two similarly produced examples. For the first, take the following instructions which produce our familiar "Typeface," this time at coordinates 72, 72.

/Times-BoldItalic findfont 72 scalefont setfont

72 72 moveto
(Typeface) show

showpage

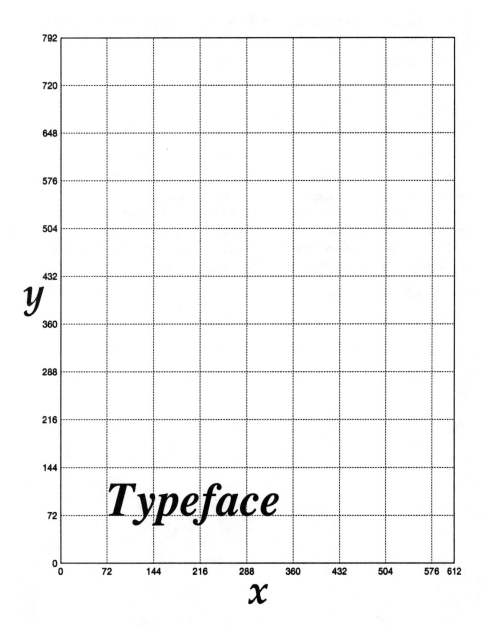

# Repositioning

You can achieve the same results as in the previous example with the following instructions.

/Times-BoldItalic findfont 72 scalefont setfont

72 72 translate

0 0 moveto
(Typeface) show

showpage

As you can see from this and the previous example, "Typeface" was printed at the same location—with respect to the *original* coordinate system.

But because the *72 72 translate* instruction displaces the origin of the underlying coordinate system, the *moveto* instruction is different.

Thus, *translate* provides the ability to locate any set of instructions anywhere on the page, making it easy to relocate PostScript routines.

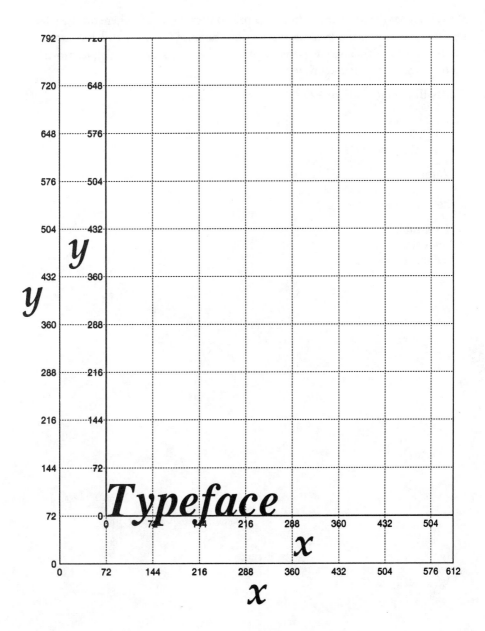

# Repetition

We can repeat the same result from the previous example anywhere on the page by simply repeating the *translate* instruction. Because the *scale* and *translate* instructions are not enclosed in *gsave* and *grestore,* the effects are cumulative, moving up the page 72 points each time.

/Times-BoldItalic findfont 72 scalefont setfont

72 72 translate
0 0 moveto
(Typeface) show

0 72 translate
0 0 moveto
(Typeface) show

0 72 translate
0 0 moveto
(Typeface) show

% Etc.

showpage

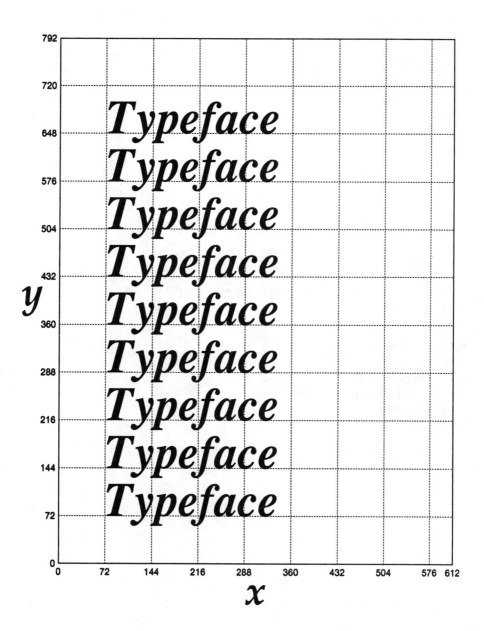

# *Similarity*

With *translate,* we can reuse the same drawing routines, positioning the results at different coordinates.

Compare the instructions below with those on page 3-22. Because of the *10 -10 translate* in the shadow box routine below, we can initiate all three boxes with the same *36 576 moveto* instruction.

```
% Shadow box
gsave
      10 -10 translate
      36 576 moveto          % Replaces 46 566 moveto
      540 0 rlineto 0 100 rlineto -540 0 rlineto
      closepath fill
grestore
```

```
% Background box
gsave
      36 576 moveto
      1 setgray
      540 0 rlineto 0 100 rlineto -540 0 rlineto
      closepath fill
grestore
```

```
% Outline box
36 576 moveto
2 setlinewidth
540 0 rlineto 0 100 rlineto -540 0 rlineto
closepath stroke
showpage
```

Being able to reuse routines as "procedures" is an important aspect of PostScript. We explore this capability in chapter 7.

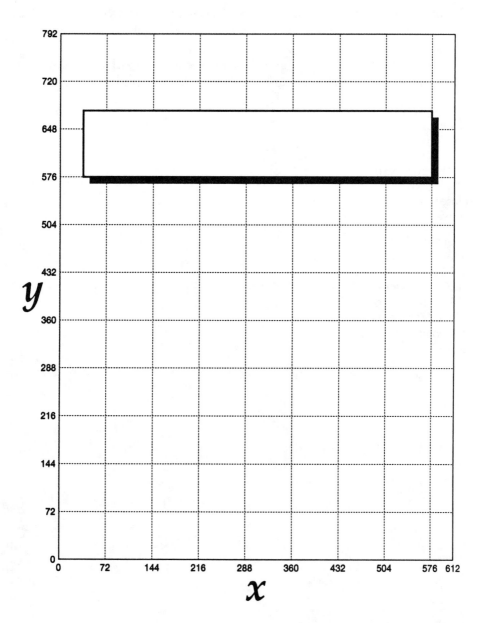

# Enlarged Diamond

We can also use the *translate* operator to permanently reposition an entire page, so that the effect of scaling will have no effect on the position of certain objects on the page.

For example, if we take the diamond-drawing routine from chapter 1 (page 1-22), and attempt to scale the diamond using *1.5 1.5 scale,* the larger diamond moves off the page.

```
% Original diamond
486 396 moveto
-180 180 rlineto
-180 -180 rlineto
180 -180 rlineto
closepath
stroke

% Scaled diamond
486 396 moveto
1.5 1.5 scale
-180 180 rlineto
-180 -180 rlineto
180 -180 rlineto
closepath
stroke

showpage
```

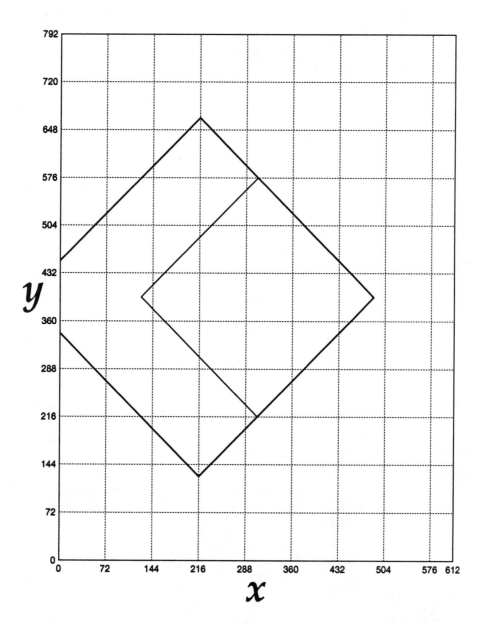

# Center Origin

Had we planned ahead when we drew the initial diamond, we could have drawn it in such a way that it could be easily resized.

One way to accomplish this is by repositioning the origin at the center of the page, using the following instruction.

306 396 translate

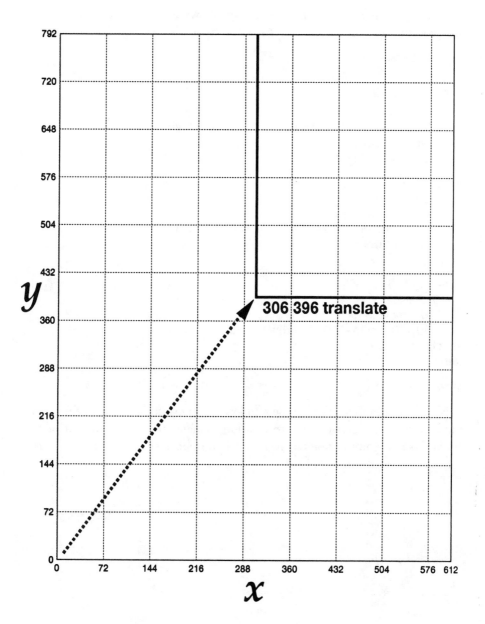

306 396 translate

# Center Page Grid

Relocating the origin at the center of the page allows us to draw diamonds of any size, repeating all instructions except for the one that scales each diamond.

306 396 translate

```
gsave
    1 1 scale
    180 0 moveto
    -180 180 rlineto -180 -180 rlineto 180 -180 rlineto
    closepath stroke
grestore

gsave
    1.5 1.5 scale
    180 0 moveto
    -180 180 rlineto -180 -180 rlineto 180 -180 rlineto
    closepath stroke
grestore

gsave
    .5 .5 scale
    180 0 moveto
    -180 180 rlineto -180 -180 rlineto 180 -180 rlineto
    closepath stroke
grestore

showpage
```

Note how the origin for both the x and y axes is now in the center of the page, and how we use negative values to position elements that are to the left of or below this new point of origin. The new origin is reflected in the x and y values that accompany the new grid.

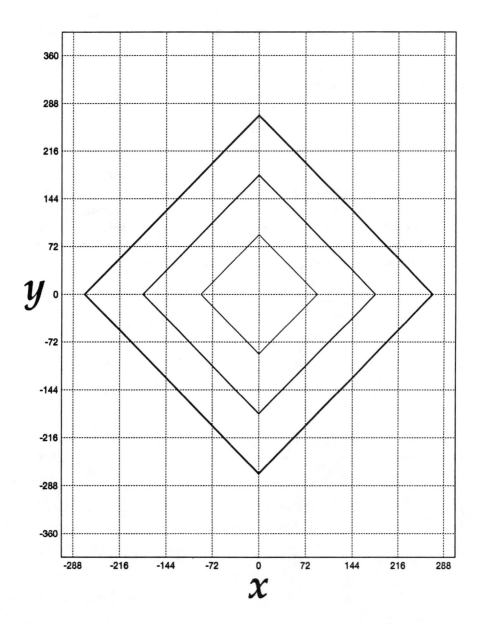

# scale and translate

You can combine the *translate* and *scale* operators to perform specific tasks such as reducing the size of a full-page description to one-half its normal size, as we did to show the examples in this book.

```
153 198 translate      % 612/4 and 792/4
.5 .5 scale            % Half-size page

0 0 moveto
612 0 rlineto 0 792 rlineto -612 0 rlineto
closepath stroke

showpage
```

We first translate the point of origin one quarter page right and up from the original point of origin, then scale both axes by one half. Note that the rectangle being drawn is for a full 612-by-792-point page, scaled by one-half.

If the box at right looks vaguely familiar, it should. This is the same technique we used to create the visual page grids throughout this book.

# *rotate*

You can use *rotate* to reorient the page, without affecting the page size or origin.

The *rotate* operator turns the grid counter-clockwise the number of degrees specified in the single operand.

For instance, to show a single line of text perpendicular to text on the rest of the page, we rotate the coordinate system 90 degrees (temporarily—using *gsave* and *grestore*) before stroking the text outlines in normal orientation.

```
/Times-BoldItalic findfont 72 scalefont setfont

gsave
    72 72 moveto
    90 rotate
    (Typeface) true charpath fill
grestore

72 72 moveto
(Typeface) true charpath stroke

showpage
```

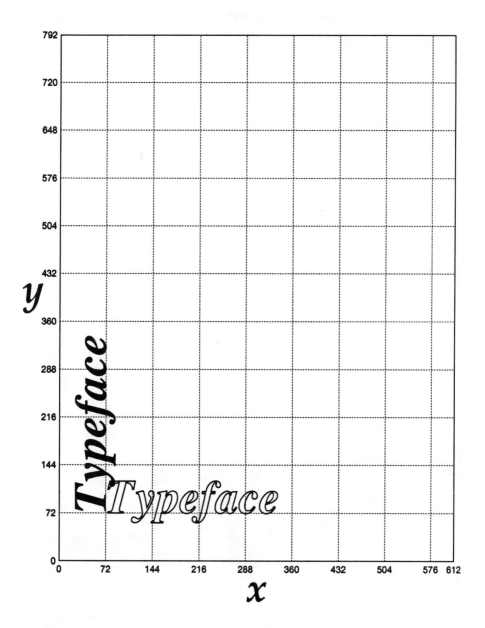

# Negative Rotation

A negative value for the *rotate* operand rotates the page in a clockwise direction.

/Times-Roman findfont 72 scalefont setfont

306 396 translate

0 0 moveto
-45 rotate
(-45 rotate) show

showpage

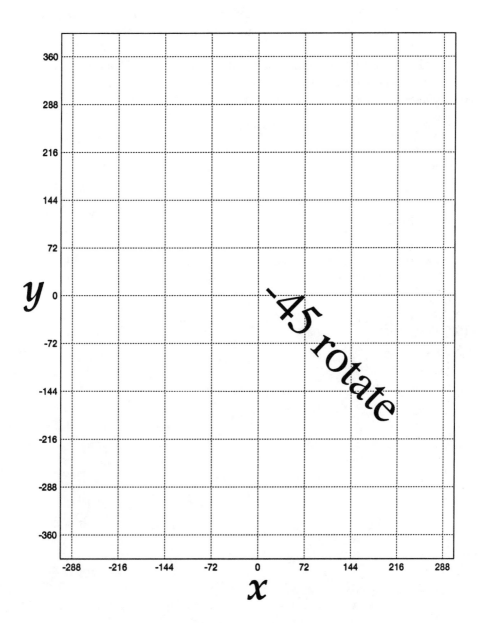

# Cumulative Rotation

Like *scale* and *translate,* the effects of successive *rotate* operations are cumulative. In this example, we permanently translate the origin to the center of the page, then rotate a fixed number of degrees.

This technique can be used effectively with "repeat loops," which we discuss in the next chapter. Notice how we use an initial negative rotation so that each successive rotate instruction is similar.

```
/Times-Roman findfont 60 scalefont setfont

306 396 translate
-90 rotate

90 rotate
0 0 moveto
(0 rotate) show

90 rotate
0 0 moveto
(90 rotate) show

90 rotate
0 0 moveto
(180 rotate) show

90 rotate
0 0 moveto
(270 rotate) show

showpage
```

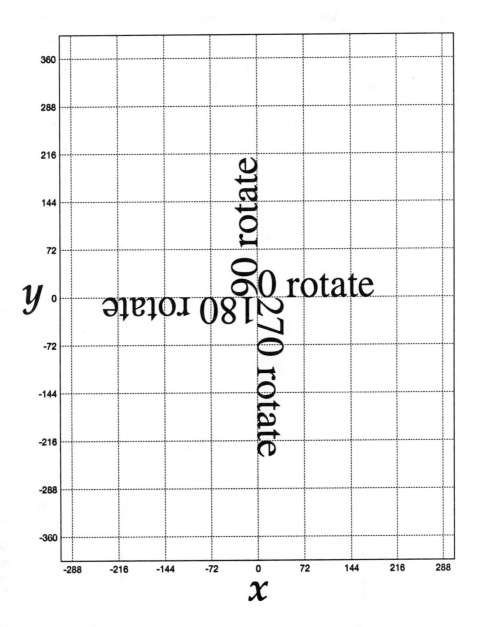

# translate and rotate

We can also combine *translate* and *rotate* to change the origin and orientation of the entire page for all subsequent operations—a useful technique for changing a page to "landscape" orientation.

The landscape orientation, which prints perpendicular to the normal vertical page orientation, is popular in desktop publishing for creating things like three-column brochures.

In this two-step procedure, the first step is to translate the origin from the lower-left corner to the lower-right corner.

612 0 translate

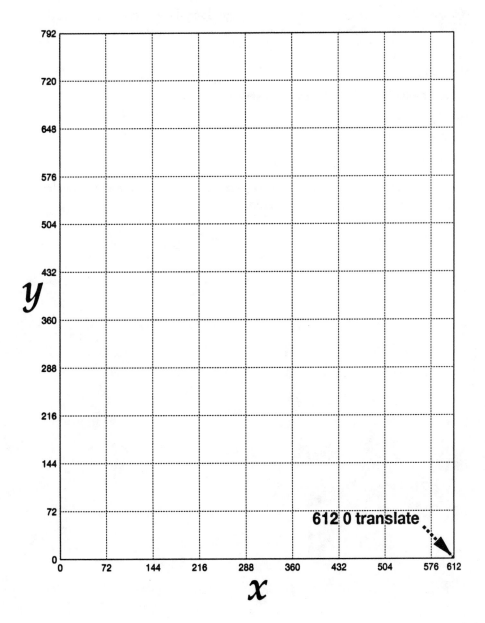

612 0 translate

# Landscape Orientation

Next, a *90 rotate* instruction reorients the page along the vertical axis, so that the former lower-right corner becomes the new lower-left corner.

```
612 0 translate
90 rotate
```

```
/TimesBoldItalic findfont 72 scalefont setfont
```

```
72 72 moveto
(Landscape) show
```

```
showpage
```

As you can see, we have created a new page grid that makes it easy to visualize the page in this new landscape orientation.

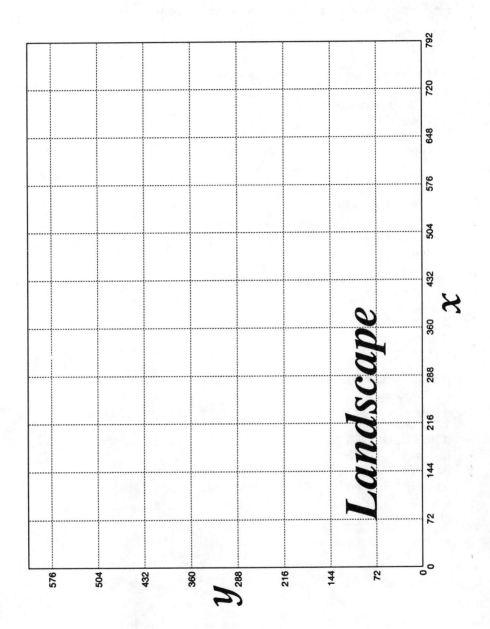

*Landscape*

# *translate, rotate, and scale*

Finally, we can combine all three transformation operators in one program.

```
612 0 translate
90 rotate

/Helvetica-Bold findfont 84 scalefont setfont
gsave
      396 190 moveto
      1 4 scale
      (DEBATE) show
grestore

gsave
      .8 setgray
      396 190 moveto
      -1 4 scale
      (DEBATE) show
grestore

/Times-Bold findfont 72 scalefont setfont
54 504 moveto
.8 setgray
(FORBES v) show
0 setgray
(s FULLER) show

/Helvetica-Bold findfont 32 scalefont setfont
36 72 moveto
.8 setgray
1 2 scale
(CIVIC AUDITORIUM, FRI) show
0 setgray
(DAY, MAY 24, 7:30 ) show
/Helvetica-Bold findfont 30 scalefont setfont
0 6 rmoveto
(p.m.) show

showpage
```

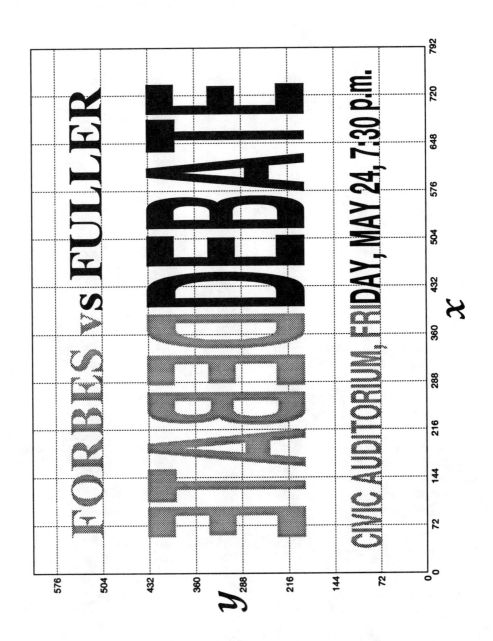

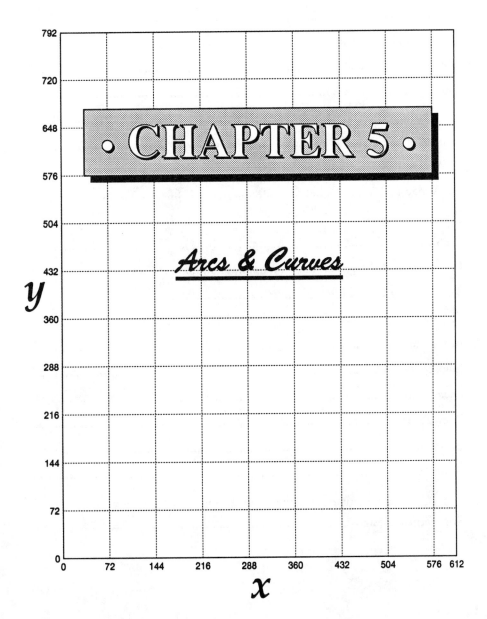

# CHAPTER 5

## Arcs & Curves

# Chapter 5

# Drawing Curves

This chapter discusses both the simplest and most difficult graphic shapes that can be constructed in PostScript: arcs and curves. They are also the most versatile.

The PostScript *arc* operator is perhaps the simplest of all the PostScript operators for drawing graphic shapes. It is much easier, for instance, to draw circles with the *arc* operator than it is to construct rectangles.

The same *arc* operator draws arcs of any length or radius at any position. You can use it in conjunction with *lineto* to draw semicircles or pie wedges of any radius and orientation. You can use *fill* and *stroke* to paint the resulting shape with any color. Used in conjunction with *scale*, the *arc* operator can also be used to draw ellipses.

A variation, *arcto*, can be used to connect intersecting lines with curved line segments. Although more difficult to use than *arc*, it is ideal for constructing rectangles with rounded corners.

Finally, there is the PostScript *curveto* operator, the most powerful of all the PostScript operators, and also the most difficult to use. We will briefly explain *curveto* at the end of this chapter, and in chapter 6 we'll show you how to use curves and arcs to create elaborate symmetrical designs.

# arc

As shown in chapter 1, it takes five PostScript operations to construct a simple rectangular shape: one *moveto,* three *lineto* or *rlineto* instructions, and a *closepath.* Compared to rectangles, circles are a breeze.

A circle can be of any size at any location, and can be easily drawn using a single *arc* operator together with its five operands. These five operands describe, in order, the x and y coordinates for the center of the circle, the radius of the circle, and the beginning and ending angles of the arc. For circles, the beginning and ending angles are 0 and 360.

The sample below produces a circle with a 2-inch radius, centered on the page.

306 396 translate

0 0 144 0 360 arc
stroke

showpage

Because we used *translate* to move the point of origin to the center of the page, the x/y coordinates for the center of the circle are 0, 0.

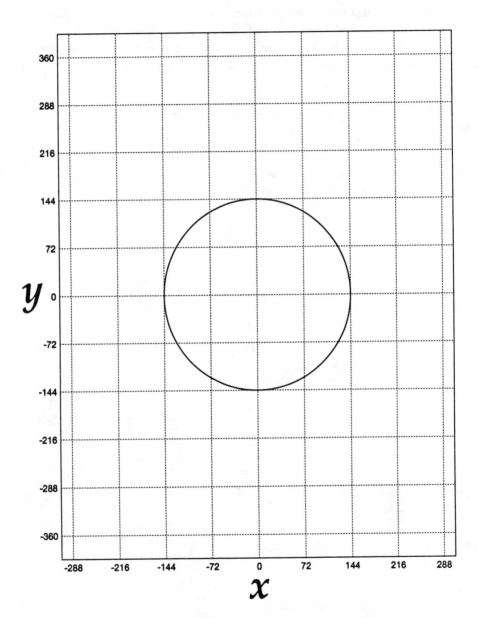

# Donut

This is the same 2-inch-radius circle, but this time the PostScript *fill* operator paints the circle with the default color, and then fills a 1-inch-radius circle with white. Because PostScript painting operators apply opaque paint, the inside circle obscures the portion of the black circle underneath, creating a "donut" effect.

```
306 396 translate

0 0 144 0 360 arc
fill

1 setgray
0 0 72 0 360 arc
fill

showpage
```

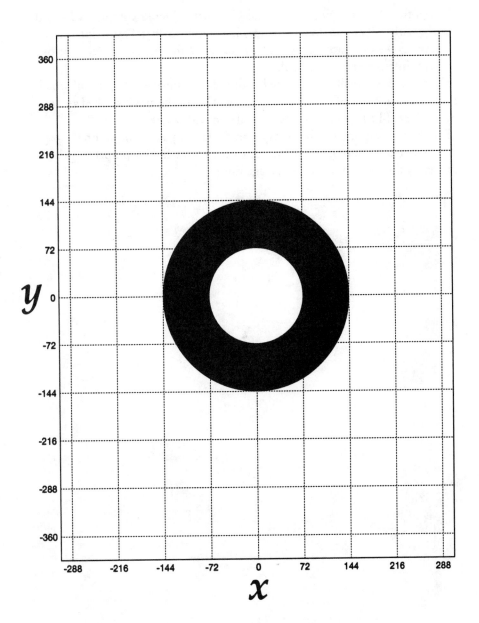

# Tao

Although the accompanying Tao (or Tai-Chi) symbol looks complicated—and would be fairly difficult to draw by hand—it is simple to do in PostScript. It is the first drawing we ever attempted, and we use it all the time to check that our PostScript interpreter is functional.

The symbol is actually constructed with only six *arc* operators, five of which are full circles and one of which is a semicircle. One of the arcs is stroked and five of the arcs are filled—three with black and two with white.

The page description for the example on the facing page is shown on the page following. It is important to paint each of the arcs in the proper sequence, particularly the two white circles in stage three.

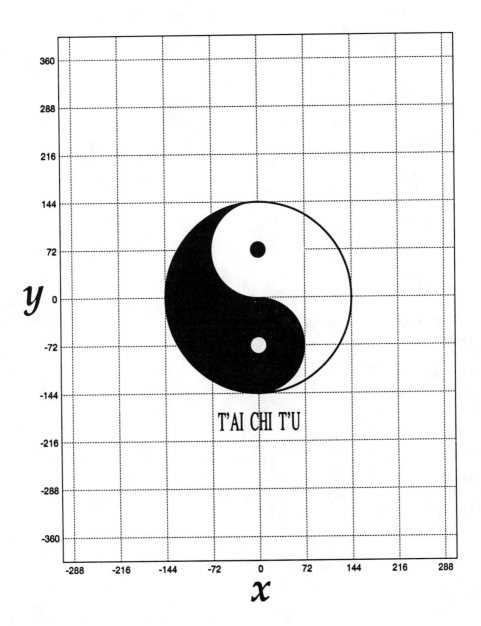

T'AI CHI T'U

# Tao Steps

```
306 396 translate

% Stage one
0 0 144 90 270 arc  % Black semicircle
fill

% Stage two
0 -72 72 0 360 arc  % Lower black circle
fill

% Stage three
gsave                % Draw two white circles
    1 setgray
    0 72 72 0 360 arc    % Upper white circle
    fill
    0 -72 12 0 360 arc  % White dot
    fill
grestore

% Stage four
0 72 12 0 360 arc    % Black dot
fill
0 0 144 0 360 arc    % Black encircle
stroke

/Times-Roman findfont 20 scalefont setfont
-60 -200 moveto
1 2 scale
(T'AI  CHI  T'U) show

showpage
```

You don't need to use *closepath* to finish the semicircle in stage one. The interpreter closes the path implicitly when you use the *fill* operator.

A separate program (not shown) was used to construct the four stages cumulatively in a smaller scale.

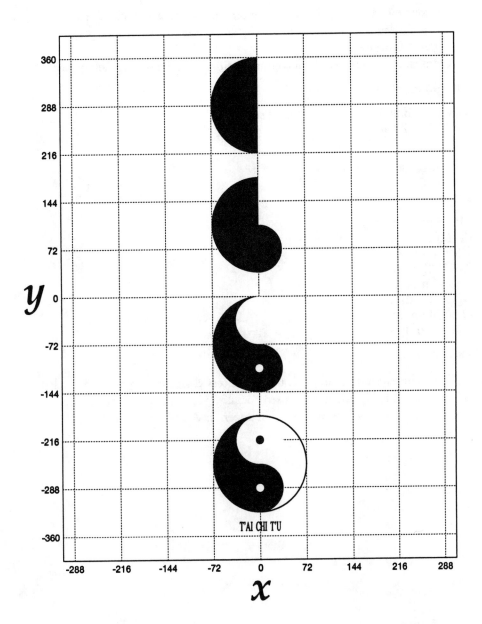

T'AI CHI T'U

# Semicircle

In the course of drawing the Tao symbol, we created a semicircle using *arc*, starting at 90 degrees, moving counter-clockwise from the horizontal plane, and ending at 270 degrees.

A semicircle with the cardinal compass points is shown on the facing page.

```
306 396 translate

/Helvetica-Bold findfont 24 scalefont setfont
0 0 72 90 270 arc
fill

.1 setlinewidth
0 0 144 0 360 arc
stroke

110 -5 moveto
(0/360\312) show     % See note below
-15 138 moveto
(90\312) show
-165 -5 moveto
(180\312) show
-20 -150 moveto
(270\312) show

showpage
```

Note: The expression "\nnn" is used to access characters from the expanded character set. In this instance we used "octal" \312, which gives us the degree symbol. These octal values are shown in appendix A.

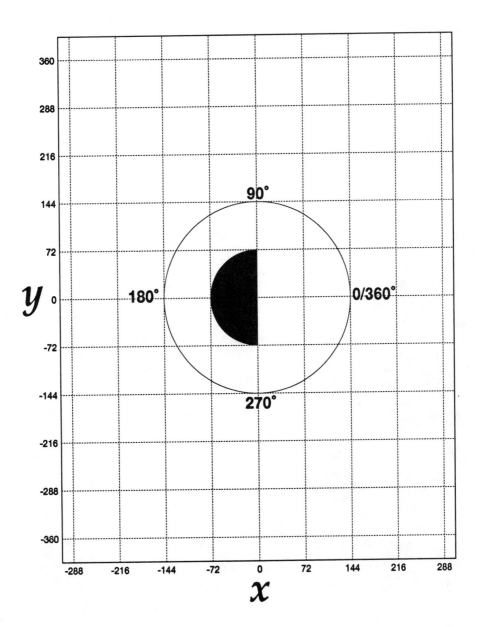

# Pie Wedge

The following instructions create a pie wedge that comprises 20 percent of a circle. The arc begins at 0 degrees and ends at 72 degrees.

```
306 396 translate

/Times-Bold findfont 36 scalefont setfont
2 setlinewidth

0 0 144 0 72 arc      % 360 x .20 = 72
0 0 lineto
closepath
gsave
    fill
grestore
stroke

gsave
    1 setgray
    35 30 moveto
    (20%) show
grestore

gsave
    /Helvetica-Bold findfont 24 scalefont setfont
    150 -5 moveto
    (0\312) show
    35 144 moveto
    (72\312) show
grestore

showpage
```

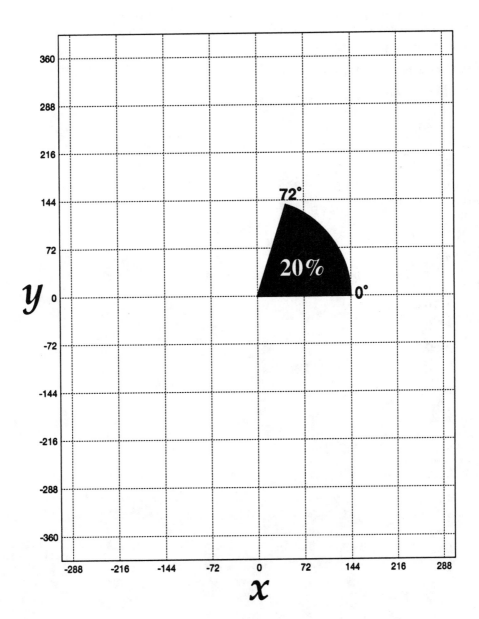

# Pie Wedge 2

Assuming the *showpage* on the previous page had not been issued, we can now add the following instructions to the sample on the preceding page, to add a second pie wedge to the drawing.

```
% Continued from previous sample

0 0 144 72 198 arc   % 360 x .35 = 126 + 72 = 198
0 0 lineto
closepath
gsave
    .9 setgray
    fill
grestore
stroke
-90 40 moveto
(35%) show

gsave
    /Helvetica-Bold findfont 24 scalefont setfont
    -200 -50 moveto
    (198\312) show
grestore

showpage
```

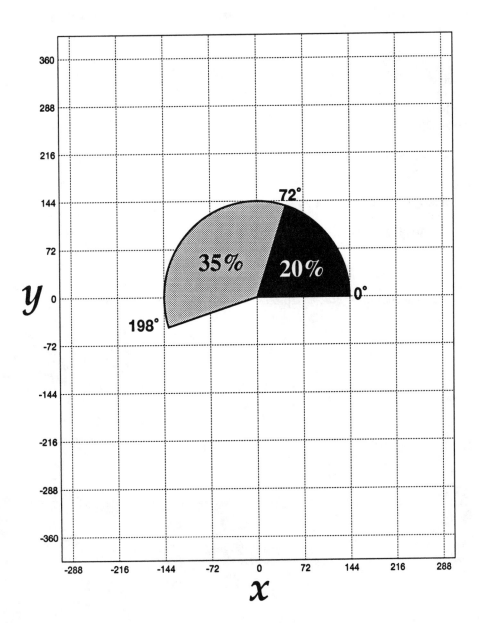

# Pie

Again assuming that no *showpage* has been issued, we can now complete the pie with the third and final wedge by adding the following instructions.

```
% Continued from previous sample

newpath
0 0 144 198 360 arc       % 360 x .45 = 162 + 198 = 360
0 0 lineto
closepath
stroke
-20 -80 moveto
(45%) show
gsave
    /Helvetica-Bold findfont 24 scalefont setfont
    150 -5 moveto
    (0/360\312) show
grestore

showpage
```

Note that *(0/360\312) show* replaces *(0/312) show* from page 5-12.

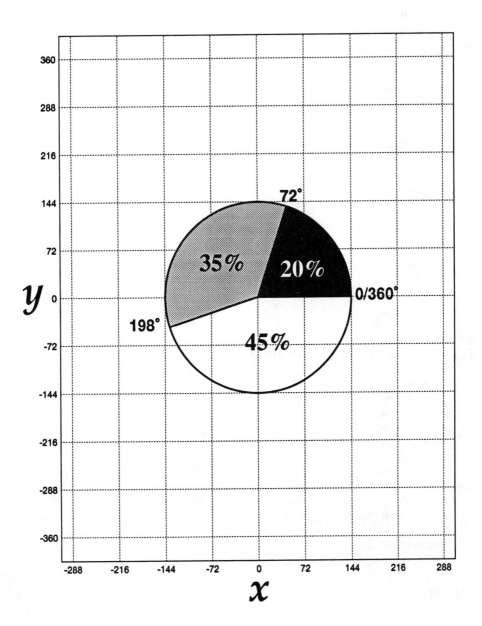

# Pie Slice

The versatility of PostScript makes it very easy to "slice" a piece of pie to emphasize any of the pie wedges. We accomplish this by adding a *gsave/grestore* around the wedge, and using *translate* to reposition the pie slice.

```
306 396 translate
/Times-Bold findfont 36 scalefont setfont
2 setlinewidth

gsave                           % added
    25 20 translate             % added
    0 0 144 0 72 arc            % 360 x .20
    0 0 lineto
    closepath
    gsave fill grestore
    stroke
    gsave
        1 setgray
        35 30 moveto
        (20%) show
    grestore
grestore % added

gsave
    0 0 144 72 198 arc          % 360 x .35
    0 0 lineto
    closepath
    gsave .9 setgray fill grestore
    stroke
    -90 40 moveto
    (35%) show
grestore

gsave
    newpath
    0 0 144 198 360 arc         % 360 x .45
    0 0 lineto
    closepath stroke
    -20 -80 moveto
    (45%) show
grestore

showpage
```

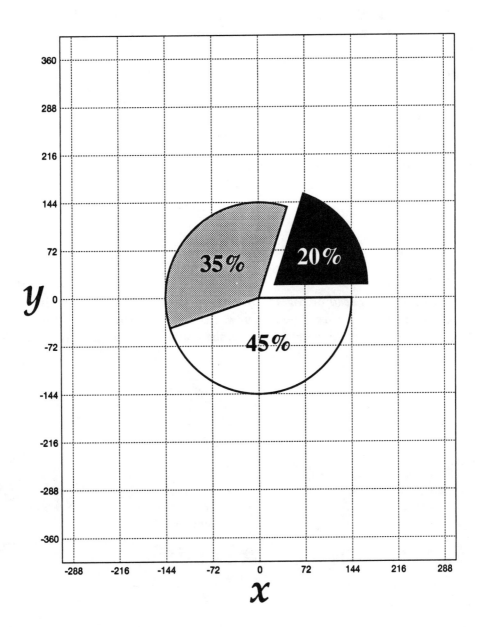

# *Pie Slice with Labels*

Finally, we can add labels to our pie. Assuming that no *showpage* was issued in the previous sample, we can add the following instructions to produce the final image at right.

```
gsave
    /Helvetica findfont 24 scalefont setfont
    150 110 moveto
    (FEES) show
    -215 150 moveto
    (SALES TAXES) show
    -90 -180 moveto
    (INCOME TAXES) show
grestore

-175 250 moveto
2 2 scale
(REVENUE) show

showpage
```

Note the use of *newpath* on pages 5-16 and 5-18. Because there is no explicit *moveto* preceding the *arc* instruction, an unwanted line will be drawn from the text to the new arc. Try this program without the *newpath* to see what happens.

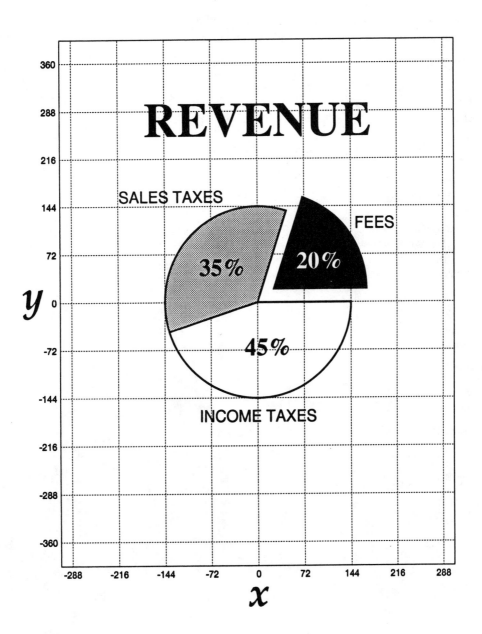

# Transforming Circles into . . .

You can easily transform circular shapes into elliptical shapes by scaling them nonuniformly. First, create four shaded circular shapes.

```
306 396 translate

0 252 translate
0 0 72 0 360 arc
stroke

0 -180 translate
0 0 72 0 360 arc
fill

0 -180 translate
gsave
     0 0 72 0 360 arc
     .5 setgray
     fill
grestore

0 -180 translate
0 0 72 0 180 arc
closepath
gsave
     .9 setgray
     fill
grestore
stroke

showpage
```

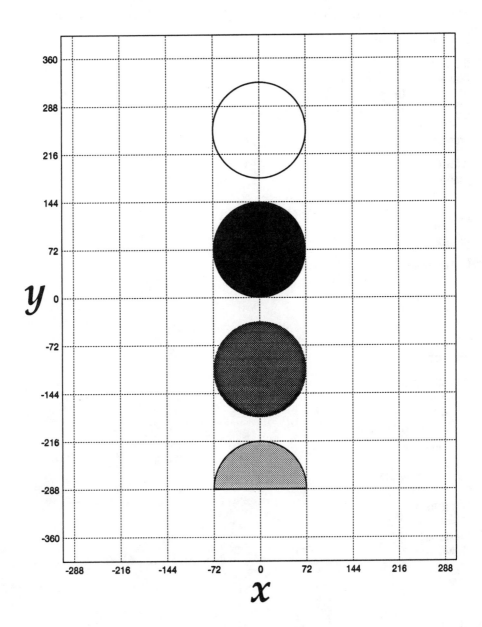

# Ellipses

Then we use *scale* to stretch the four circular shapes into various elliptical shapes.

```
306 396 translate

0 252 translate
gsave
    .5 1 scale
    0 0 72 0 360 arc
    stroke
grestore

0 -180 translate
gsave
    2 1 scale
    0 0 72 0 360 arc
    fill
grestore

0 -180 translate
gsave
    .25 .50 scale
    0 0 72 0 360 arc
    .5 setgray
    fill
grestore

0 -180 translate
gsave
    4 1 scale
    0 0 72 0 180 arc
    closepath
    gsave
        .9 setgray
        fill
    grestore
    stroke
grestore
showpage
```

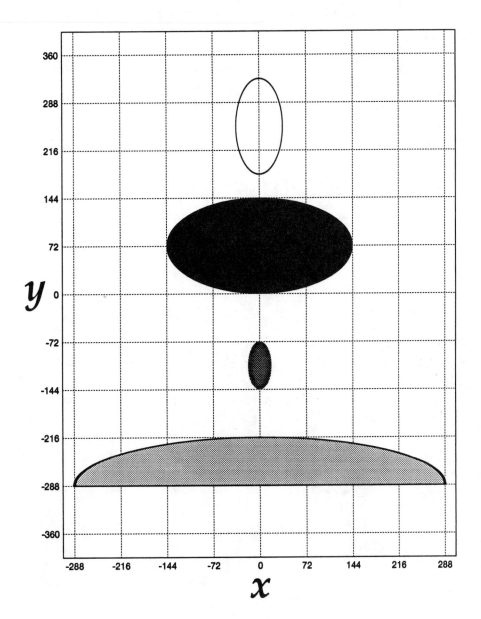

# Atom

We can combine *arc* and *scale* with *rotate* to change the orientation of each ellipse.

306 396 translate

```
gsave
    0 rotate
    .33 1 scale
    0 0 144 0 360 arc
    stroke
grestore

gsave
    60 rotate
    .33 1 scale
    0 0 144 0 360 arc
    stroke
grestore

gsave
    -60 rotate
    .33 1 scale
    0 0 144 0 360 arc
    stroke
grestore

showpage
```

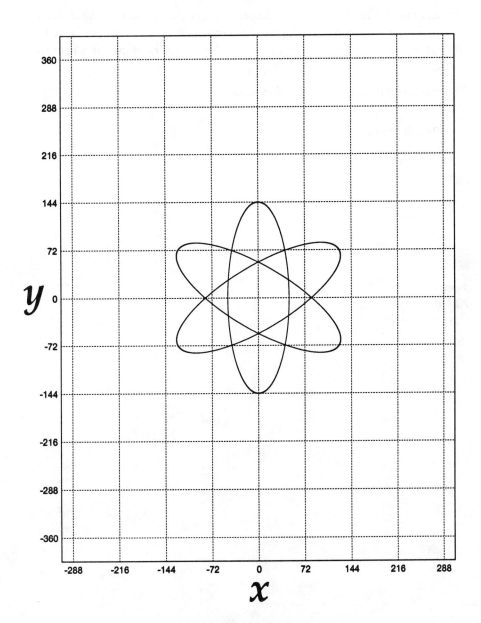

# Ellipses with Text

You can draw an ellipse at any location specified in a *translate* instruction. Always use 0, 0 for the x/y coordinates for the *arc* operator when drawing ellipses. Otherwise, the *scale* operator used for the ellipse will relocate the ellipse elsewhere on the page.

```
/Times-BoldItalic findfont 72 scalefont setfont

gsave
    204 666 translate
    2 .9 scale
    0 0 72 0 360 arc fill
grestore

gsave
    204 666 translate
    2.1 1 scale
    0 0 72 0 360 arc stroke
grestore

1 setgray
72 648 moveto
(Typeface) show

showpage
```

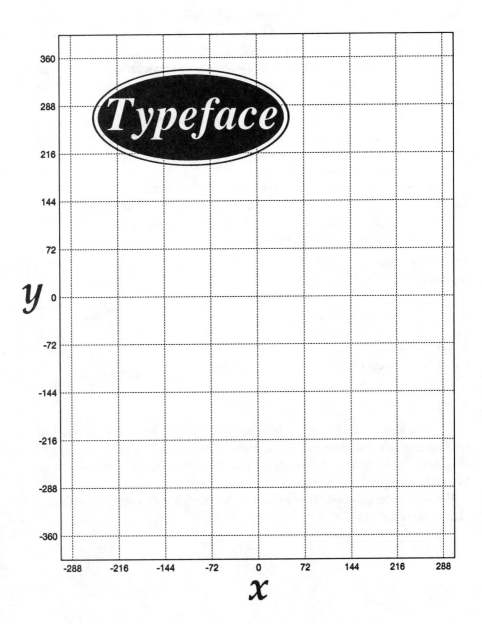

# arcto

The *arcto* operator connects two line segments with a circular arc of any radius and angle. It accomplishes this by adding an arc to the end of one line segment, from which another line can be appended.

This makes *arcto* ideal for connecting two line segments with rounded corners which can then be extended to form either a rectangle with rounded corners or two parallel lines connected with rounded ends.

The five operands required by *arcto* are the x and y coordinates tangent to the arc on both the first and the second line, and the radius of the arc. We use the *clear* operator here to discard some residual information generated by the Post-Script interpreter after executing *arcto*.

Whether or not the arc is preceded by a straight-line segment is determined by the distance between the points and the radius of the arc. Arcs both with and without straight line segments are used in the following example, in which two parallel lines are connected by curved ends.

```
108 108 translate
newpath

0 36 moveto
0 72  216 72  36 arcto clear
216 72  216 0  36 arcto clear
216 0  0 0  36 arcto clear
0 0  0 72  36 arcto clear
stroke

showpage
```

The rounded-corner box at the bottom is what results from this sample. The top four examples show the individual steps for each *arcto*. Those four steps, and the gray lines, tick marks, and coordinates on the bottom example were generated by another program (not shown).

For an excellent discussion of *arcto*, see the *PostScript Programmer's Reference Guide*, pages 160–162.

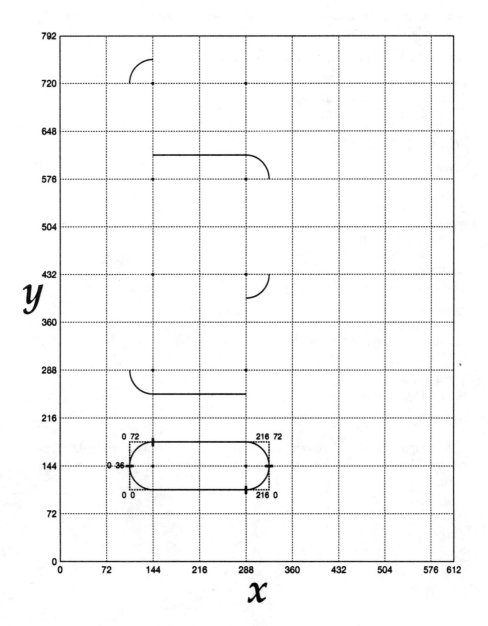

# Round Box with Text

You can combine rounded boxes created using *arcto* with text to create the familiar effect at right.

/Times-BoldItalic findfont 72 scalefont setfont

```
76 424 moveto
76 472  528 472  48 arcto clear
528 472  528 376  48 arcto clear
528 376  76 376  48 arcto clear
76 376  76 472  48 arcto clear

gsave
    fill        % Black box
grestore

gsave
    12 setlinewidth
    stroke    % Extra black
grestore

1 setgray
gsave
    4 setlinewidth
    stroke    % White ring inside
grestore

100 400 moveto
(ROUNDBOX) show

showpage
```

In chapter 7, we will convert this routine to a generalized procedure that creates a similar rounded box around any string of text of any size and typeface.

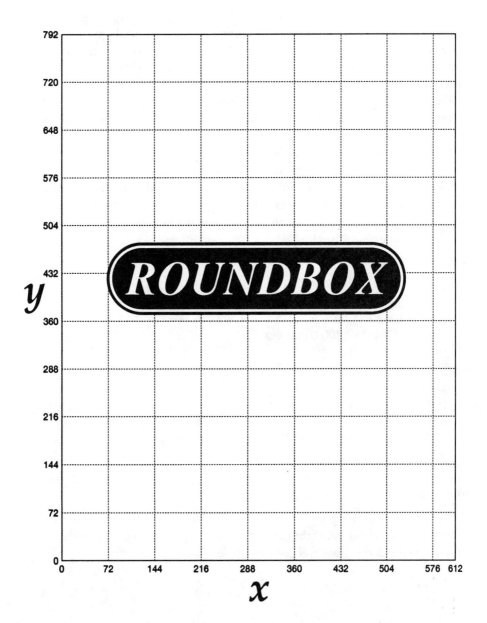

# curveto

The *curveto* operator is the foundation of the PostScript language; it gives you access to the Bézier curves discussed in chapter 2. This powerful operator adds a Bézier curve section to the current path between the current point and the end point of the curve, using two external control points to define the shape of the curve.

The accompanying drawing shows two basic shapes that can be created with *curveto,* together with the control points that give the curve what are referred to as its "motion and direction."

The *curveto* operator requires an initial current point (here defined by a *moveto*) and six operands that are shown successively in the accompanying sample. The initial *moveto* establishes the beginning of the curve, and the last set of coordinates establishes the end of the curve. The other two sets of x/y coordinates are the control points that are represented in the drawing as points on dashed lines outside of the curve.

```
306 396 translate

gsave
    0 144 translate
    -200 0 moveto
    -100 100 100 150 200 0 curveto
    stroke
grestore

gsave
    0 -144 translate
    -200 0 moveto
    -100 100 100 -150 200 0 curveto
    stroke
grestore

showpage
```

Notice how changing only one number (150) from positive to negative completely alters the shape of the curve. We used a separate program (not shown) to generate the dotted lines and coordinates for the example at right.

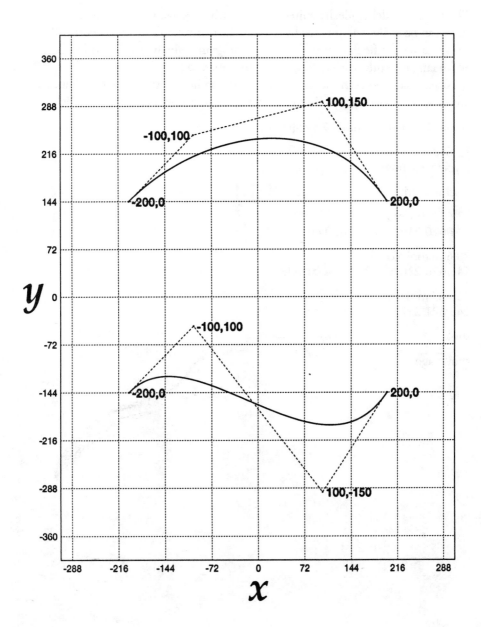

# Brush Stroke

The Bézier model is ideally suited for use in interactive graphics, because the curve can be easily manipulated by moving the control points with a mouse. But *curveto* is very difficult to use directly in a program, which is why existing PostScript language tutorials say little about this operator.

Nevertheless, you can use *curveto* to perform some functions that could not be done any other way, such as simulating a brush stroke under text, as shown below.

```
/Times-BoldItalic findfont 72 scalefont setfont

72 648 moveto
(Typeface) show

4 setlinewidth

77 605 moveto
144 620 216 630 325 620 curveto

78 606 moveto
145 620 216 632 327 624 curveto

78 607 moveto
145 621 217 634 329 626 curveto

stroke

showpage
```

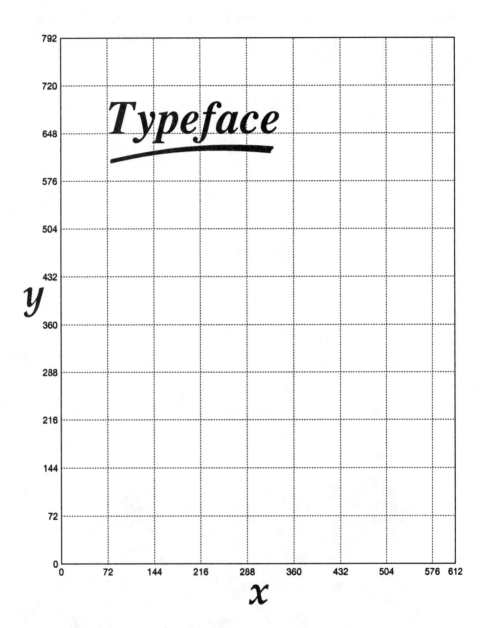

# Sine Wave

There is, however, one area in which *curveto* is easier to use directly than it is interactively: for creating symmetrical designs where a single *curveto* that creates the simple sine wave at right is repeated many times.

306 396 translate

0 0 moveto
72 72 72 -72 144 0 curveto
stroke

showpage

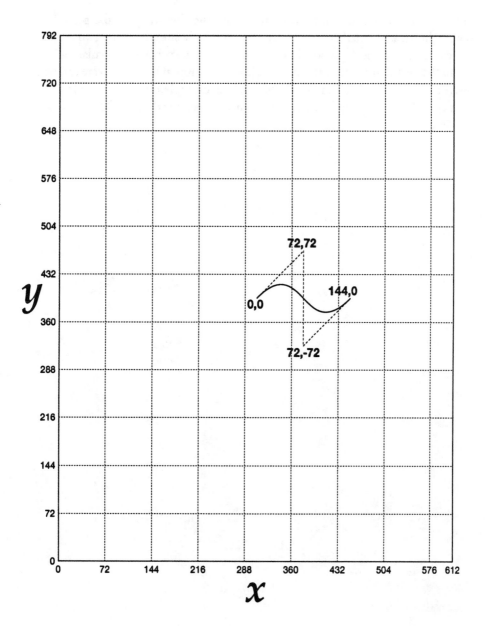

# Symmetrical Designs

The accompanying drawing was created from the sine wave on the preceding page (shown as the darker curve in the example opposite), by using two "repeat loops" to symmetrically reposition and reflect the sine wave in a circular path.

In the next chapter, we will show you how to use repeat loops to create this and even more elaborate symmetrical designs. The example opposite, for instance, was completed by filling it with a new painting operator that will be introduced in chapter 6.

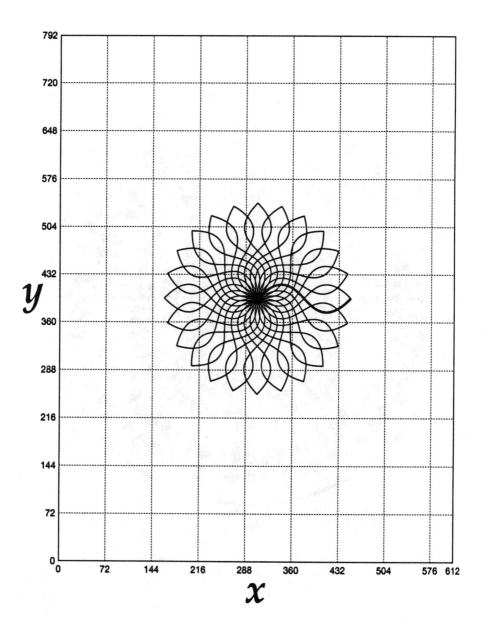

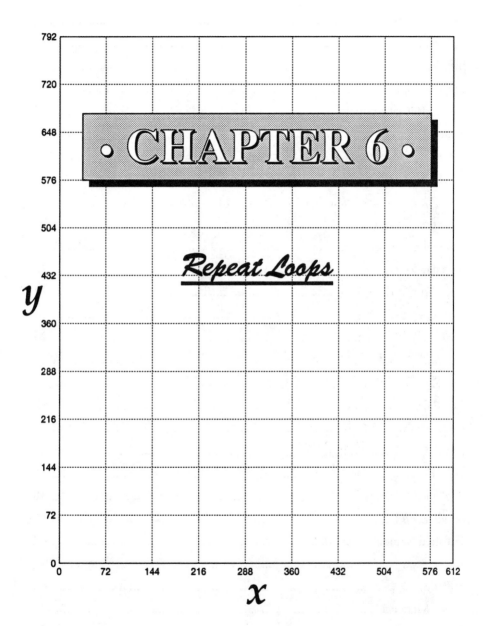

# CHAPTER 6

## *Repeat Loops*

# Chapter 6

# Repeat Loops

As everyone knows, computers are very good at repetitive tasks—mundane work such as invoicing or mail-merging that can drive humans to distraction. But armed with a page description language, computers can perform another kind of repetitive work that is unlike anything we normally associate with computing.

We are speaking of using PostScript repeat loops to create symmetrical designs that are so intricate that they would be almost impossible to do by hand, at least with anything approaching PostScript's speed and accuracy.

Symmetrical designing is one application that you can do better with just a few simple lines of PostScript code than using even the most sophisticated drawing software presently available. The symmetrical design at the end of the last chapter, for instance, was created with a simple repeat loop.

In this chapter we will describe what could be called the most creative aspect of page description languages. If it is not the most creative, it is without question the most fun. We will cover the two most common types of loops: those that use the *repeat* and *for* operators. And we will also introduce a new painting operator that makes these intriguing visual effects possible.

# *repeat*

The repeat loop below replaces a series of nine instructions on page 4-20 that were so tedious that after showing only three of the series to convey the idea, we used "Etc." to save time and space.

All you require is a PostScript procedure—a set of PostScript instructions surrounded by braces—preceded by a number representing the number of times it is to be executed, and followed by the *repeat* operator.

Enclosing procedures in braces is a PostScript convention that has many uses, as we shall see in the pages that follow.

```
/Times-BoldItalic findfont 72 scalefont setfont

72 648 translate

9 {
    0 0 moveto
    (Typeface) show
    0 -72 translate
} repeat

showpage
```

This is the familiar Times-BoldItalic "Typeface" shown at coordinates 72, 648, repeated on eight successive lines. The *0 -72 translate* instruction on the last line of the procedure repositions each successive line every time the loop is repeated.

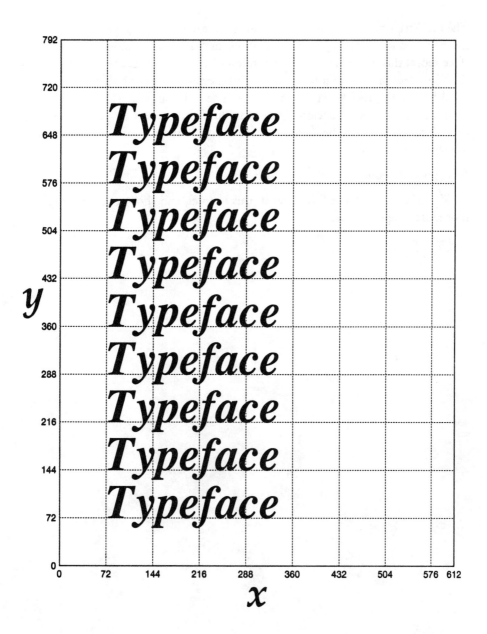

# Infinity

The PostScript procedure that we used to "grid" each example page appearing in this book reduces each page to one-half its normal size prior to showing the page. If we repeat this procedure a sufficient number of times using *repeat,* the results disappear into infinity, and become so small they are unrecognizable.

Although the procedure to be repeated can be very complex, it's easy to create a repeat loop. Here we enclose "grid procedure" in a repeat loop. The actual procedure is too long to be shown here, so please do not attempt to execute the following instruction.

6 {..."grid procedure"...} repeat

We discuss grids more fully later in this chapter, and show a complete grid procedure in appendix B.

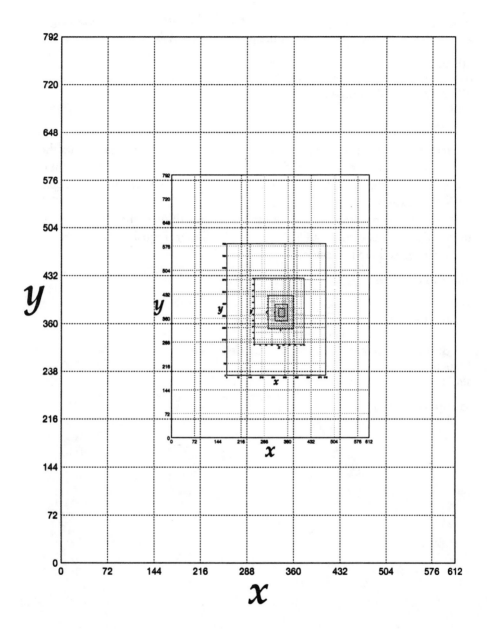

# div

In the preceding chapter, page 5-38, we showed the instructions for drawing a 2-inch sine wave from the center of the page using *curveto*.

```
306 396 translate
0 0 moveto
72 72 72 -72 144 0 curveto
stroke
showpage
```

Here, we integrate the same instructions into a repeat loop that repeats the sine wave 16 times, rotated around a circle. The instruction for rotating around the circle uses the *div* (divide) operator to divide the circle into 16 equal 22.5-degree segments.

The *div* operator is executed at the end of each repetition of the repeat loop, so the rotational effect is cumulative. Note that the divisor is equal to the number of times the repeat loop is executed.

```
306 396 translate

16 {
    0 0 moveto
    72 72 72 -72 144 0 curveto
    360 16 div rotate              % 22.5 degrees each
} repeat
stroke

showpage
```

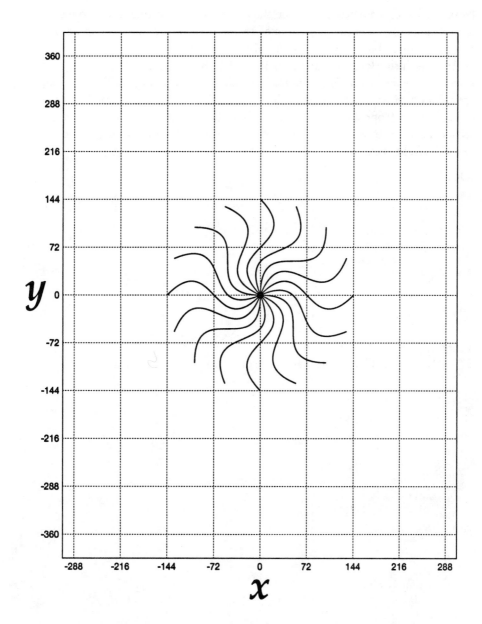

# Nested Repeat Loops

Next, we "nest" the repeat loop from the preceding page within a second repeat loop that causes the entire procedure of 16 rotations of the sine wave to be executed two times, but with a different twist.

After the inside loop has run once, producing the first series of 16 rotated sine waves, we use the *-1 1 scale* instruction to produce a mirror image of the first pass, the second time through the repeat loop. (Negative scaling is explained on page 4-12.) The *scale* operator has no effect when it's encountered at the end of the second pass, because all path construction operations are finished and we are ready to stroke the path.

```
306 396 translate

2 {
    16 {
        0 0 moveto
        72 72 72 -72 144 0 curveto
        360 16 div rotate
    } repeat
    -1 1 scale
} repeat
stroke

1 setgray
0 0 10 0 360 arc fill % Add small white circle in center

showpage
```

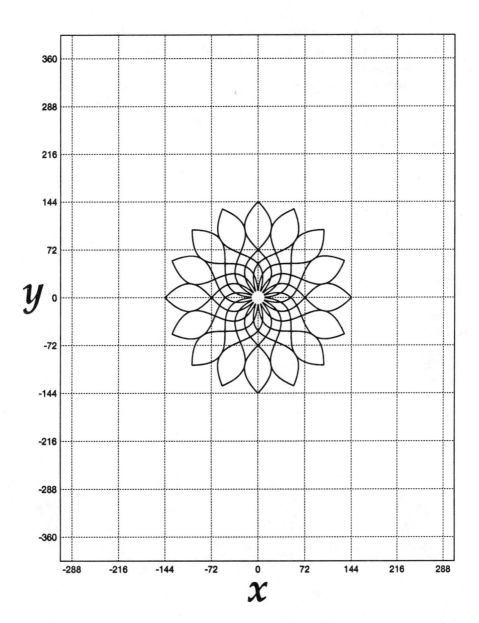

# eofill

The instructions below are exactly the same as those on the preceding page, except for the *eofill* (even-odd fill) operator, which alternately fills points on the current path according to the even/odd rule (see the example on page 6–41, and the Red book, pages 70–71).

As you can see, this single operator transforms the basic design from an interesting line drawing into a finished symmetrical design. And we accomplished this with less than a dozen simple instructions.

```
306 396 translate

2 {
    16 {
        0 0 moveto
        72 72 72 -72 144 0 curveto
        360 16 div rotate
    } repeat
    -1 1 scale
} repeat
eofill

1 setgray
0 0 10 0 360 arc fill

showpage
```

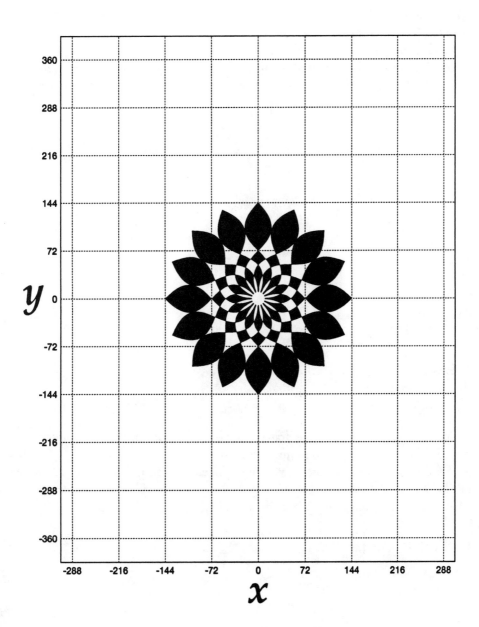

# Increasing Repetitions

We can make this basic design even more intricate by simply increasing the number of repetitions of the "inside" loop.

The instructions below are exactly the same as those on the preceding page, except that we doubled the number of repetitions and the divisor for the rotations, from 16 to 32. We also added three rings around the design to enhance its appearance.

```
306 396 translate

2 {
    32 {
        0 0 moveto
        72 72 72 -72 144 0 curveto
        360 32 div rotate
    } repeat
    -1 1 scale
} repeat
eofill

0 0 150 0 360 arc stroke
0 0 160 0 360 arc stroke
3 setlinewidth
0 0 155 0 360 arc stroke

1 setgray
0 0 10 0 360 arc fill

showpage
```

We used 64 repetitions in the drawing opposite the title page of this chapter, page 5-42, to achieve an even more intricate design.

If this sample won't execute on your interpreter, you can try moving *eofill* to just below the *-1 1 scale* instruction. The resulting output will be different from what you see here, but it will probably execute.

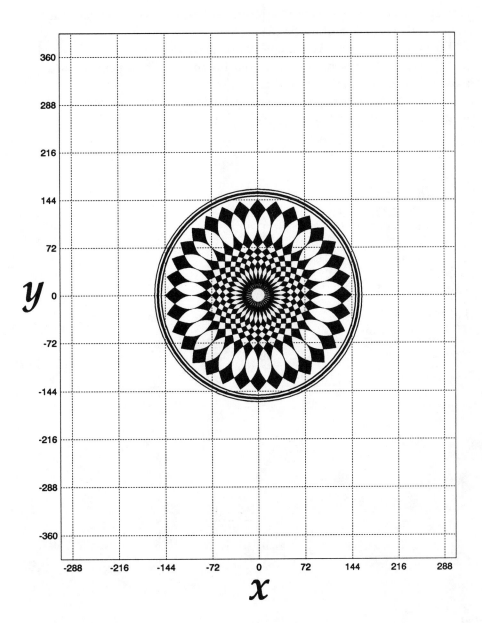

# Redefining the Sine Wave

Here again, small changes in the basic instructions shown on the preceding pages cause a radical alteration of the finished design.

The basic change here is very simple. We doubled the x coordinate for the end point operand of the *curveto* operator from 144 to 288. This lengthens the descending portion of the sine wave.

Also, to eliminate overlapping we changed the number of repetitions and the rotational divisor from 32 to 24.

```
306 396 translate

2 {
    24 {
        0 0 moveto
        72 72 72 -72 288 0 curveto
        360 24 div rotate
    } repeat
    -1 1 scale
} repeat
eofill

1 setgray
0 0 10 0 360 arc fill

showpage
```

# for

A PostScript for loop is similar to a repeat loop; it has numeric operands preceding a procedure enclosed in braces, followed by a PostScript *for* operator. But where the repeat loop has a single numeric operand that specifies the number of times the procedure is to be repeated, the *for* operator requires three numeric operands that convey more precise information to the PostScript interpreter regarding how many times the loop is to be repeated.

The procedure for drawing the three ellipses on the next page—the portion of the instructions enclosed in left and right braces—is exactly the same as the three instructions on page 5-26, except that the degrees of rotation for each ellipse are not specified. In fact, the *rotate* operator appears to have no operand at all!

```
306 396 translate

-60 60 60 {
    gsave
        rotate
        .33 1 scale
        0 0 144 0 360 arc
        stroke
    grestore
} for

showpage
```

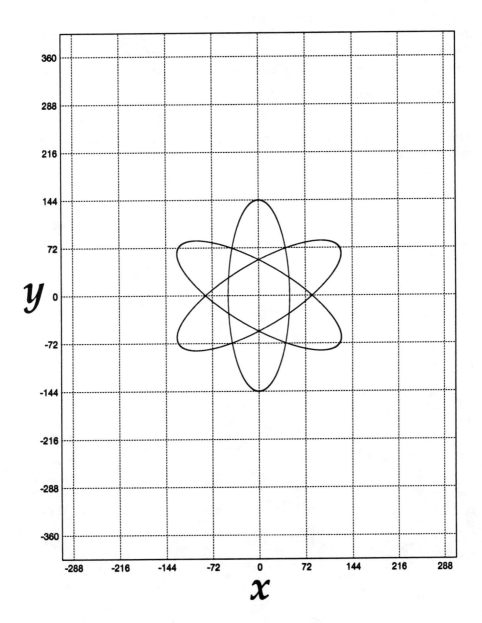

# For Loop Operands

In keeping with PostScript's requirement for placing operands before the operator, the *for* operator is preceded by four operands. These four operands are: an *initial value*, an *increment*, a *limit*, and, finally, a *procedure* enclosed in braces. The for loop on the preceding page, for instance, was as follows.

-60 60 60 {...procedure...} for

This tells the interpreter to start with an *initial value* of -60, repeat the procedure and *increment* this value each time by 60 until the *limit* of 60 is reached, and then go on to the next instruction in the page description, which in this case is *showpage*.

# Control Variable

In all for loops, the PostScript interpreter uses a number called a "control variable" to keep track of how many times the loop has been repeated. In the sample at left, the initial value of the control variable is -60, as determined by the first operand, then 0, and finally 60, as the initial value is incremented by the second operand (the increment) each time through the loop. When the control variable exceeds the third operand (the limit) the interpreter stops repeating the loop.

Notice that this number (-60 then 0 then 60), which represents the value of the control variable each time through the loop, corresponds to the degrees of rotation required for the *rotate* operator in the program on page 5-26. It is this number that is used as the operand for the *rotate* operator each time through the loop. The program does not supply the operator; it is generated by the interpreter.

Thus the control variable performs a second function, in addition to keeping track of the for loop. It is used in the logic of the page description—in this case, determining the degrees of rotation for each ellipse.

# Circular Text

In the instructions below, each new control variable becomes the operand for the ensuing *rotate*. The first loop is rotated 20 degrees, the second 40 degrees, and so on. Each *rotate* is enclosed in a *gsave/grestore*, so the effect is not cumulative. Notice that the limit is 340 instead of 360 degrees, so that the last space is left for writing the name "on top" of the other names created in the loop.

```
/Helvetica-BoldOblique findfont 48 scalefont setfont

165 400 translate
.5 setlinewidth

20 20 340 {
    gsave
        rotate 0 0 moveto
        (Smith) true charpath stroke
    grestore
} for

0 0 moveto
(Smith Consulting) true charpath
gsave
    1 setgray
    fill
grestore
stroke

200 -50 moveto
(Group) true charpath
gsave
    1 setgray
    fill
grestore
stroke

showpage
```

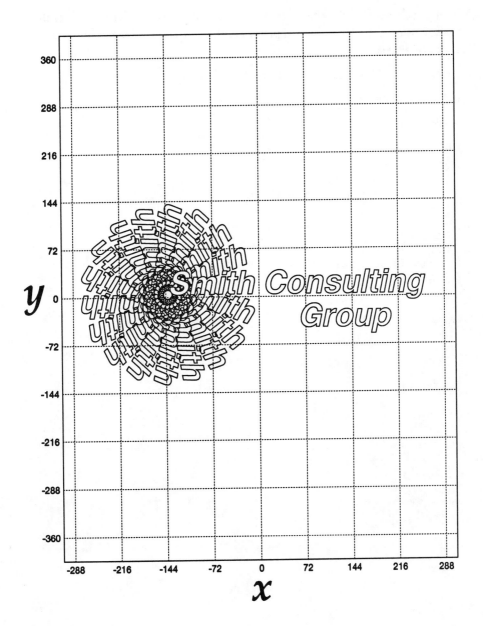

# Designing with Text

We arbitrarily selected the character string (OOOllllll) to see what would result (the "bar" is ASCII 124). It looked pretty good, so we show it here in hopes that it may give you some ideas.

```
/Helvetica-BoldOblique findfont 48 scalefont setfont

306 396 translate

.5 setlinewidth

10 10 360 {
    gsave
        rotate 0 0 moveto
        (OOOllllll) true charpath stroke
    grestore
} for

0 0 205 0 360 arc stroke
0 0 215 0 360 arc stroke
3 setlinewidth
0 0 210 0 360 arc stroke

showpage
```

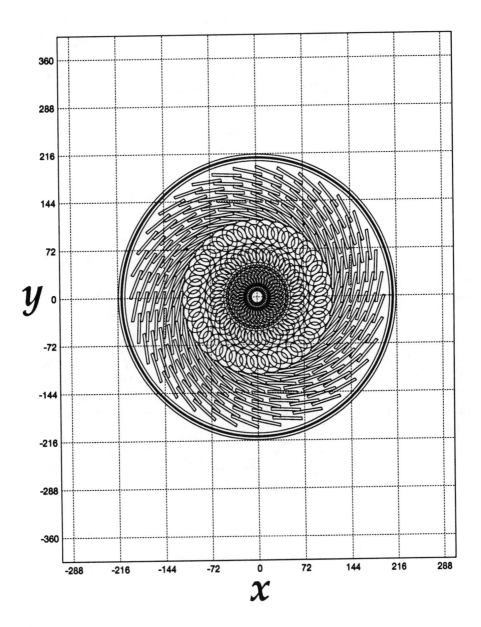

# Grid Lines

Of course for loops can do things other than making pretty designs. The for loop below creates the vertical lines used in this book to produce the visual page grids for displaying the examples at one-half scale. Here's how we start the grid.

The control variable here becomes the x coordinate for the ensuing *moveto* instruction (*0 0 moveto, 72 0 moveto, 144 0 moveto,* etc.).

```
612 4 div 792 4 div translate
.5 .5 scale
.9 setgray

0 72 612 {
    0 moveto % Control variable is value of x
    0 792 rlineto
    stroke
} for

0 setgray
0 0 moveto
612 0 rlineto 0 792 rlineto -612 0 rlineto
closepath stroke
showpage
```

Note how we use the PostScript *div* operator to initially position the lower-left corner of the half-size grid one-quarter of a page right and up from the page origin. Note also how we scale the page to half-size with *.5 .5 scale,* which is the same way we create the visual page grid (see appendix B). Finally, we draw a surrounding box from that location (*0 0 moveto*), after the vertical lines have been rendered by the loop.

# exch

The instructions for creating horizontal grid lines are identical to those used in the previous program for creating vertical grid lines, except in three respects. The first difference is the obvious change in the limit to 792, which represents the 11-inch top of the page. Secondly, we use *612 0 rlineto* to draw the horizontal lines. The other difference is the change in the first line in the for loop, from *0 moveto* to *0 exch moveto*.

We use the PostScript *exch* (exchange) operator to exchange the positions of the x and y values for *moveto*.

As a new control variable is generated by the interpreter each time through the loop, we exchange the position of the control variable and the 0 used as the operands for *moveto*, so that the x/y operands are in the proper order—0, 72; 0, 144; etc., instead of 72, 0; 144, 0, as they were in the previous example.

```
612 4 div 792 4 div translate
.5 .5 scale

.9 setgray

0 72 792 {
    0 exch moveto % Exchange value of y with 0
    612 0 rlineto
    stroke
} for

0 setgray
0 0 moveto
612 0 rlineto 0 792 rlineto -612 0 rlineto
closepath stroke

showpage
```

# def

Another way to use the PostScript control variable is to define it as a "named" variable using the PostScript *def* (define) operator.

As we saw in chapter 2, PostScript uses a forward slash as a special character to define a literal name, e.g., "/Times-BoldItalic." Here, the instruction */y exch def* defines a literal name *y* with a value of the control variable.

Each new control variable (72, 144, etc.) becomes the value of the variable *y* each time through the loop. This is done by exchanging the position of the variable name *y* with this value to get them in the proper order, and then defining the variable—*/y 72 def, /y 144 def,* etc., each time through the loop. Each new control variable then becomes the value for *y* in each *0 y moveto,* giving us a new point from which to draw each successive vertical grid line.

```
612 4 div 792 4 div translate
.5 .5 scale
.9 setgray

0 72 792 {
    /y exch def      % Define each control variable as y
    0 y moveto        % Start each line at new y value
    612 0 rlineto stroke
} for

0 setgray
0 0 moveto
612 0 rlineto 0 792 rlineto -612 0 rlineto
closepath stroke
showpage
```

There is never a space between a slash and the next character in any defined name (as in */y*), but it may sometimes look that way when you see it in print.

# CVS

Capturing the control variable provides the additional advantage of being able to use it for other purposes, such as showing the numerical value of the variable adjacent to the grid line.

We accomplished this with the PostScript *cvs* (convert to string) operator, which converts the numeric variable *y* to a character string so we can display the string with the PostScript *show* operator. The *cvs* operator requires two operands—the object being converted (in this case, the variable *y*), and an "empty string" into which the result of the conversion is placed (defined here as *str*, which can hold up to four characters).

```
612 4 div 792 4 div translate

/str 4 string def % Empty string 4 chars long

/Helvetica-Bold findfont 14 scalefont setfont
.5 .5 scale
.9 setgray

0 72 792 {
    /y exch def
    0 y moveto 612 0 rlineto stroke
    gsave
        -30 y moveto
        0 setgray
        y str cvs       % Convert y value to string
        show            % Show each value
    grestore
} for

0 setgray
0 0 moveto
612 0 rlineto 0 792 rlineto -612 0 rlineto
closepath stroke
showpage
```

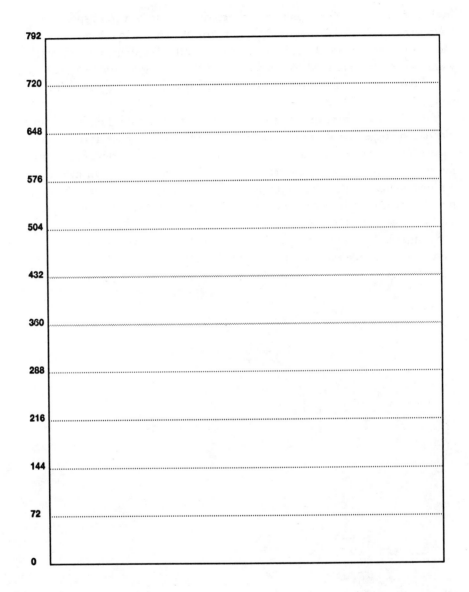

# Mandalas

In the remainder of the chapter we will describe how to construct special symmetrical designs called "mandalas," the Sanskrit word for both circle and center. Mandalas have a mystical significance in the Hindu, Buddhist, and other religions, where they are used for meditation. After staring at some of these extraordinary designs for longer than we perhaps should, we can testify to their effectiveness.

We got the idea for using PostScript to create these mystical designs from a mandala on page 114 of *Mandalas* by José and Miriam Argüelles. It is shown on page 6-39. The authors explain how all mandalas consist of a series of concentric forms (here circles) that have three things in common: a center, symmetry, and cardinal points—in this case, around the perimeter of the circle. The same structural law is at work in flat representations of chemical elements, snow crystals, and the cross section of a twig.

Symmetrical designing with for loops is something that you can do very easily with PostScript code, as you will see in the following pages.

# mul

In the sample programs that follow, we use the variable $c$ to define the number of circles that radiate from a point on the perimeter of the mandala. The radius of the mandala is 100 in the next few examples, but it could be any size.

The variable is used not only as the limit of the for loop, but also as the divisor in the first line of the loop. The line that reads *100 c div mul* (multiply), multiplies the control variable by the radius divided by $c$, to determine the radius of each radiating circle.

Don't worry too much about how this math is done, as this will be discussed in the next chapter. Concentrate on the way we use the for loop to draw the radiating circles that comprise the mandalas.

# dup

The result of the computation on the previous page determines not only the radius of each radiating circle each time through the loop (as *c* increases), but also the x coordinate for the ensuing *arc* operation. Therefore, we duplicate this number with *dup* (duplicate). The *0 exch* then puts the x, y, and radius in the proper order, and the *-180 180 arc* uses these operands to draw the radiating circles from the perimeter of the mandala (*10 0 10 -180 180 ... 100 0 100 -180 180*).

```
306 396 translate

/c 10 def

-90 rotate % Start at top

-100 0 translate
0 0 moveto
1 1 c {
    100 c div mul
    dup 0 exch
    -180 180 arc
} for
stroke

showpage
```

Note that we use *-180 180* instead of *360 360* to draw each circle from the perimeter.

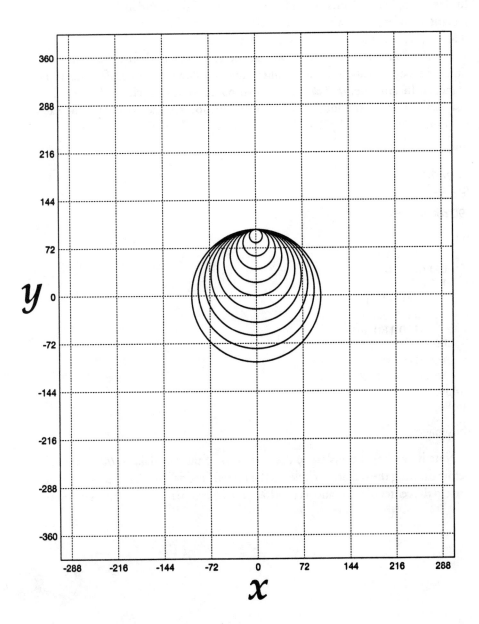

# Nested Loops

In this example the points around the perimeter of the mandala from which the radiating circles are drawn are determined by a repeat loop, in which the for loop that executes the radiating circles is nested.

For this "outside" repeat loop, we use the variable $p$ to define the number of times the loop repeats, and the number of points along the circumference of the mandala. In this case, /p 2 def defines two points along the circumference. The last instruction in the loop, 360 p div rotate, locates the perimeter for each rotation—360 divided by 2, or 180, in this case.

```
306 396 translate

/c 10 def
/p 2 def

-90 rotate    % Start at top

p {
    -100 0 translate
    0 0 moveto
    1 1 c {
        100 c div mul
        dup 0 exch
        -180 180 arc
    } for
    100 0 translate
    360 p div rotate
} repeat
stroke

showpage
```

Note how we first translate to the perimeter of the mandala (*-100 0 translate*) before drawing the radiating circles in the nested "inside" loop, and then translate back to the center of the mandala (*100 0 translate*) before rotating to the next point.

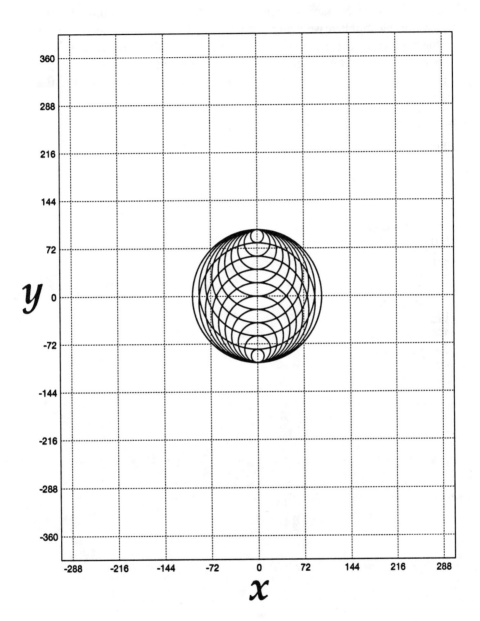

# Argüelles Mandala

The instructions for this sample program are exactly the same as those for the previous example. But here we change the value of $p$ from 2 to 4, to radiate circles from four points around the circumference of the mandala. (Note that we have also changed the initial value of the inside for loop operands from 1 to 2, to create a larger first circle on the perimeter, in order to conform to the mandala in the Argüelles book.)

```
306 396 translate

/c 10 def
/p 4 def

-90 rotate

p {
    -100 0 translate
    0 0 moveto
    2 1 c {
        100 c div mul
        dup 0 exch
        -180 180 arc
    } for
    100 0 translate
    360 p div rotate
} repeat
stroke

showpage
```

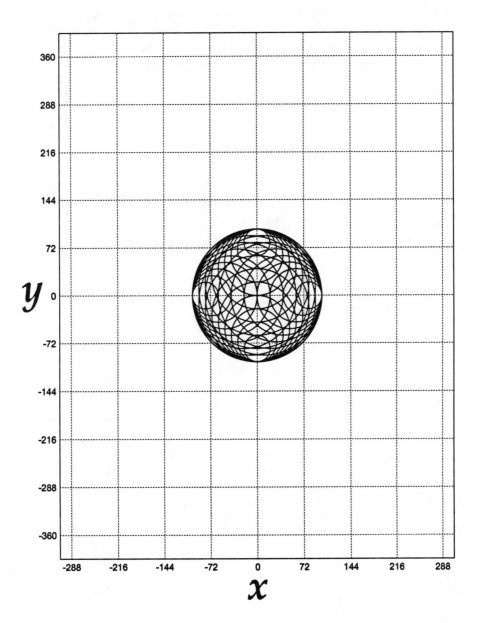

# Single eofill

Before we use *eofill* to paint the mandala, we want to show you how a single series of radiating rings appears when painted by *eofill*. Here again we are using 2 for the initial value of the loop operands. Otherwise, this sample is the same as the first mandala on page 6-35, except for *eofill* replacing *stroke*.

```
306 396 translate

/c 10 def

-90 rotate

-100 0 translate
0 0 moveto
2 1 c {
    100 c div mul
    dup 0 exch
    -180 180 arc
} for
eofill

showpage
```

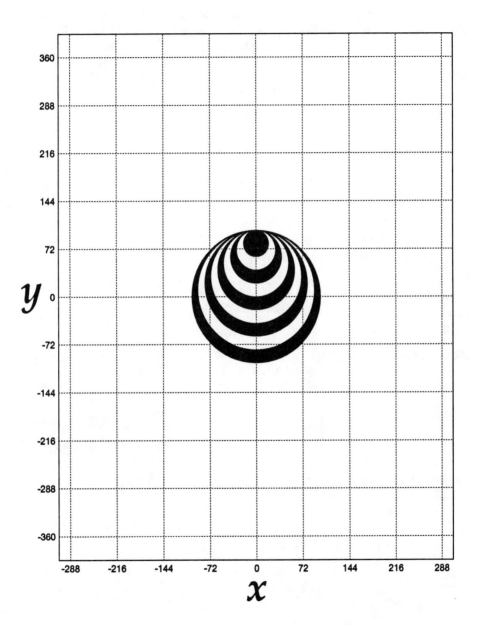

# Finished Mandala

We now create our first finished mandala, completing it with the *eofill* operator. The instructions are exactly the same as those on page 6-39, except *eofill* replaces *stroke,* and the initial value of the nested loop is again 2.

```
306 396 translate

/c 10 def
/p 4 def

-90 rotate

p {
    -100 0 translate
    0 0 moveto
    2 1 c {
        100 c div mul
        dup 0 exch
        -180 180 arc
    } for
    100 0 translate
    360 p div rotate
} repeat
eofill

showpage
```

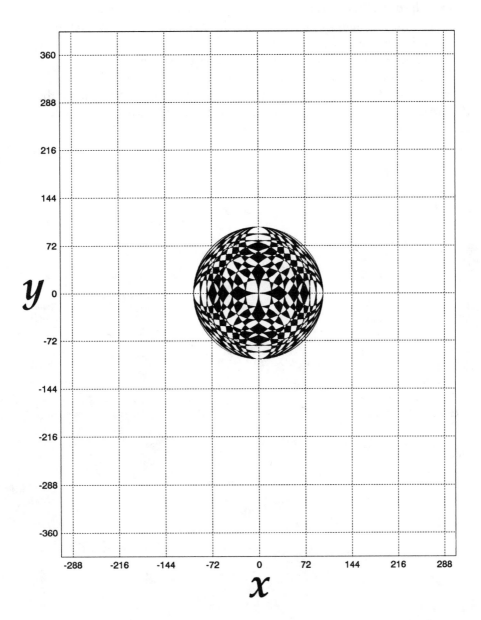

# neg

Some of the drawings in this chapter result in a substantial number of individual line segments. The number may exceed the limits of the PostScript interpreter you are using, which may then fail to print. If this happens, you can reduce the size of the design by reducing the radius, as we have done here.

To reduce the radius we define a new variable with */r 50 def,* and replace the old radius of 100 with *r* in three separate instructions below. We then use the PostScript *neg* (negative) operator, on the line that formerly read *-100 0 translate,* to change the sign of the radius to be negative.

```
108 684 translate

/c 10 def
/p 4 def
/r 50 def

-90 rotate

p {
     r neg 0 translate
     0 0 moveto
     2 1 c {
         r c div mul
         dup 0 exch
         -180 180 arc
     } for
     r 0 translate
     360 p div rotate
} repeat
eofill

showpage
```

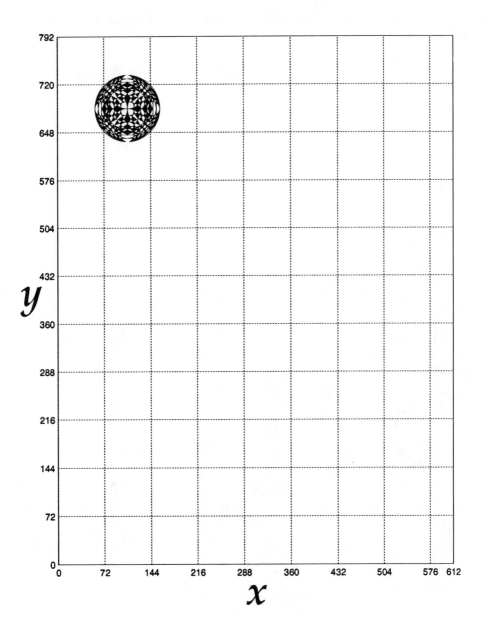

# setflat

Another way to reduce the number of line segments is to use the PostScript *setflat* operator (always enclosed within a *gsave/grestore*). This operator flattens curved lines, to reduce the number of line segments (see the Red book, page 215). Start at *20 setflat* and increase the number by 20 until you reach 100. If the design still will not print, then reduce the radius, or use *stroke* instead of *eofill*.

```
306 396 translate

/c 8 def
/p 6 def
/r 200 def

-90 rotate

p {
    r neg 0 translate
    0 0 moveto
    2 1 c {
        r c div mul
        dup 0 exch
        -180 180 arc
    } for
    r 0 translate
    360 p div rotate
} repeat

gsave
    20 setflat
        eofill
grestore

showpage
```

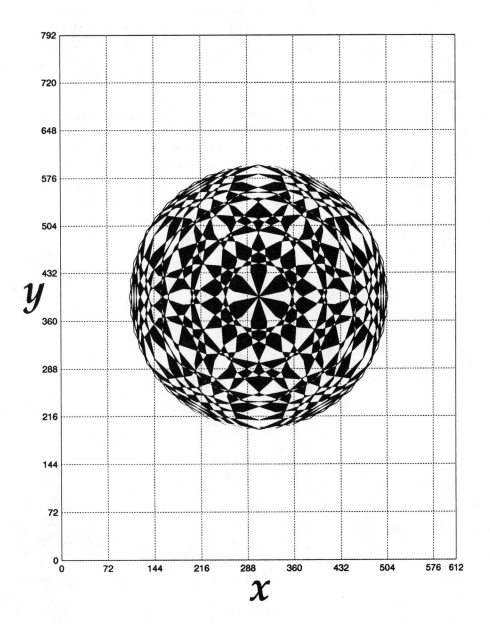

# Giant Mandala

The interpreter we use to produce these mandalas provides for a substantial number of line segments. Although we used a *20 setflat* in the previous drawing, we were still able to double the radius to 200 to produce a larger design.

Here we increase the radius to a whopping 1800—beyond the limits of most PostScript interpreters—to produce the design used for the cover of this book. We'll close the chapter by showing you how it is done.

The instructions are the same as those for the preceding drawing, except that */r 200 def* has been changed to */r 1800 def*, to increase the radius of the outside perimeter ninefold. Obviously, a substantial portion of the mandala is off the page.

You might be interested to know that we did not attempt this until the firm that designed the cover showed us their idea, with the mandala enlarged photographically to use as the background. We were not sure we could do it because of the demands placed on the interpreter. But, as you can see, it worked very nicely, and provided us with a new use for these mandalas that we had not envisioned.

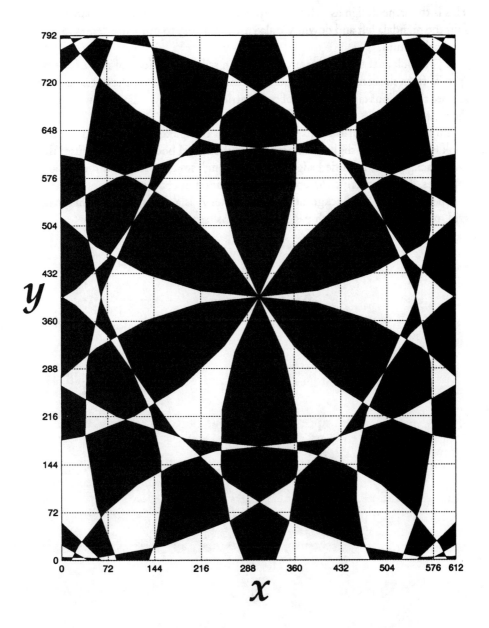

$y$

$x$

# Background Design

This is the same design as before, except that here we add *-378 -128 translate* to shift the mandala left and down. We also use *.95 setgray* to mute the design for use as a background.

If you look at the design carefully, you can still see portions of two of the six "petals" from the center of the mandala, in the lower-left side of the page. You can also see the various circular paths of concentric rings as they radiate outward from the center.

On the last page of this chapter, we show a completed cover design for this book (which may be slightly different from the actual book cover) that uses this same background, modified slightly by "clipping" small portions of the left and top sides. The PostScript *clip* operator is explained in chapter 8.

The grid used as a background for the letter A is a different size visual page grid, used for 11-by-17-inch page descriptions (see appendix B).

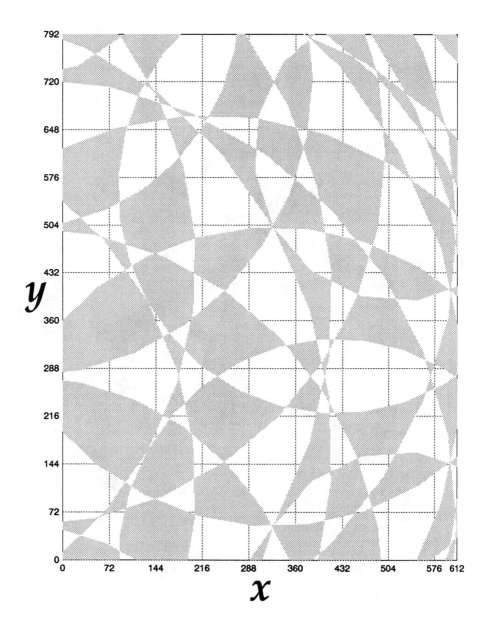

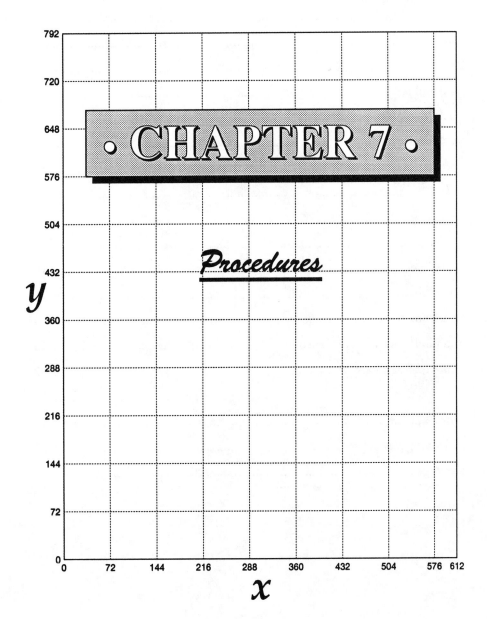

# CHAPTER 7

## *Procedures*

# Chapter 7

# Procedures

As you saw in the previous chapter, a procedure is a group of PostScript instructions enclosed in braces that performs some specific function. Procedures make PostScript programs more compact, more readable, and easier to modify. You can define your own procedures and use them whenever you need them.

It is not necessary that you understand how to write procedures to use PostScript effectively, but you will find that they are very useful for performing repetetive tasks.

Procedures can save you time and make using the language much more enjoyable, particularly if you will be doing the same kinds of things more than once. And understanding procedures will greatly enhance your proficiency with the language and your ability to decipher PostScript code developed by others.

In this chapter we show you procedures for performing a few common tasks such as drawing rectangles, changing fonts, and centering text. We also demonstrate how to use "stack manipulation" and "program control" operators to make your PostScript programs more efficient.

# Circle

Procedures don't have to be complex to be effective. Let's say that you want to draw a shaded 2-inch diameter circle in the center of the page. Instead of writing the instruction for drawing the same circle three times, you can create a specialized procedure that draws the circle, and then give that procedure a name. Then you simply call the procedure by name each time you want to draw a circle, in the same way you use a PostScript operator.

We use *def* to define a named procedure just as we used it to define named variables, except procedures are always enclosed in braces. The procedure is not executed when you define it. Execution is deferred until you call it by name in your program.

```
/circle {0 0 72 0 360 arc} def

306 396 translate

gsave
    10 -10 translate
    circle
    fill        % Shaded black circle
grestore

circle
gsave
    1 setgray
    fill        % White circle
grestore
stroke          % Circle outline

showpage
```

Notice how we call the procedure by name each time we want to use it—first to draw the shaded circle, then to draw the filled white and outlined circles.

You can speed the execution of your procedures by using the PostScript *bind* operator in conjunction with *def,* as follows (see the Red book, page 124).

```
/circle {0 0 72 0 360 arc} bind def
```

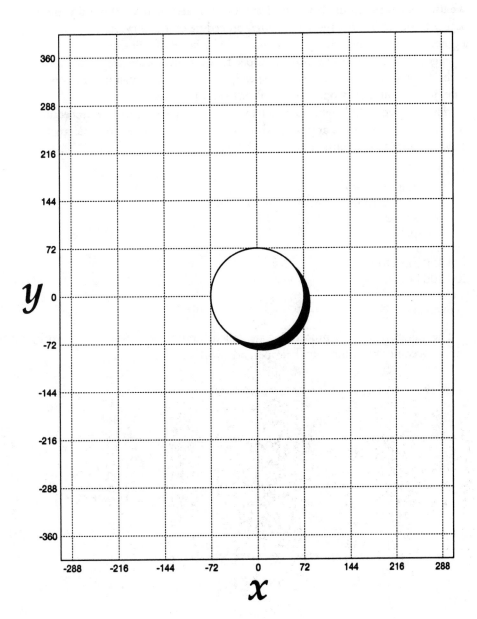

# Box

We use the *box* procedure below to draw the same rectangle we showed you on page 3-8. But unlike the specialized *circle* procedure on the previous page, this is a generalized procedure that you can use to draw boxes of any size.

In generalized procedures you don't specify the values inside the procedure as in the previous example. Rather, you specify the values when you use the procedure, just as you specify operands for PostScript operators.

Here, we specify the height and width of the box when we use the *box* procedure. You can give a procedure any name you like. We used "box" for this rectangle-drawing procedure because it's short and descriptive.

```
/box {
    exch dup 0 rlineto
    exch 0 exch rlineto
    neg 0 rlineto
    closepath
} bind def
100 400 moveto
200 300 box
stroke
showpage
```

The values used with procedures are called "arguments." Arguments work with procedures the same way that operands work with operators.

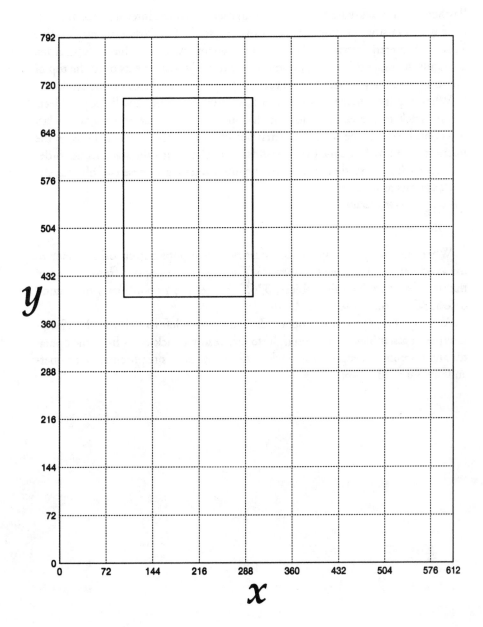

# Push and pop

PostScript is a "stack-based" language. This means that the interpreter communicates with a PostScript program by means of a stack. The PostScript stack is like a stack of cafeteria trays. As the interpreter encounters new objects (operators, operands, names, etc.) from a program, it "pushes" these objects onto the top of the stack. Each new object pushes earlier objects further down on the stack.

When the interpreter encounters a PostScript operator, it will "pop" objects off the stack to use as operands for the operator. Like cafeteria trays, the last object pushed onto the stack is the first object popped off the stack. Thus, in the instruction *36 576 moveto,* the operands are pushed onto the stack in the order encountered: 36 first, then 576. After the interpreter reads these two objects, the stack appears as follows.

576 —— *top of stack*
36

When the interpreter then encounters *moveto,* it pops objects off the stack to use as operands for the *moveto* operator. The objects are popped from the top of the stack in order. The first object, 576, becomes the Y coordinate; the second object, 36, becomes the X coordinate.

Although programs supply operands reading from left to right, the PostScript interpreter assembles them from right to left, reading backwards from the operator and popping objects off the stack until the operator's requirements for operands are satisfied.

# Stack Manipulation

The PostScript language contains several operators for manipulating objects on the stack. We encountered three of the most commonly used stack manipulation operators—*exch, dup,* and *neg*—in the previous chapter.

The most widely-used stack operator, *exch,* simply exchanges the positions of the two topmost objects on the stack; *dup* duplicates the object on the top of the stack and places the copy on the top of the stack; and *neg* changes the sign of the object on the top of the stack, from positive to negative or vice versa.

On the next page, we will step through our new box-drawing procedure, showing what the interpreter does with each element it encounters, beginning with the line that reads *200 300 box.* You will see how the three stack-manipulation operators discussed above position each object on the stack in the proper sequence, to be used as operands for the path construction operators that draw the four sides of the box.

When asterisks appear next to objects on the stack, this means that the two objects are about to be popped off the stack and used as operands for the *rlineto* operator that follows.

# Stack Example

/box {exch dup 0 rlineto exch 0 exch rlineto neg 0 rlineto closepath} def
200 300 box

| Object | Stack | Explanation |
|---|---|---|
| *200* | 200 | width pushed onto stack |
| *300* | 300<br>200 | height pushed onto stack |
| *exch* | 200<br>300 | top two elements exchanged |
| *dup* | 200<br>200<br>300 | top element duplicated |
| *0* | 0*<br>200*<br>200<br>300 | pushed onto stack |
| *rlineto* | 200<br>300 | side one operands consumed |
| *exch* | 300<br>200 | top two elements exchanged |
| *0* | 0<br>300<br>200 | pushed onto stack |
| *exch* | 300*<br>0*<br>200 | top two elements exchanged |
| *rlineto* | 200 | side two operands consumed |
| *neg* | -200 | number changed to negative |
| *0* | 0*<br>-200* | pushed onto stack |
| *rlineto* | empty | side three operands consumed |
| *closepath* | empty | side four complete |

* Will be popped off the stack and consumed by the *rlineto* operator.

# exch def

In the previous chapter, we used the instruction */y exch def* to capture the control variable pushed onto the stack by the PostScript interpreter. And we showed how to define a variable with an instruction like */c 10 def.* This could just as easily have been written *10 /c exch def,* to place the number at the beginning of the line where it could be more easily modified by the programmer.

The *exch* operator simply exchanges the position of the two topmost objects on the stack to get them in the proper order for the interpreter. When the "value" precedes the "name," whether it is written that way (as in *10 /c exch def*) or whether the interpreter pushes the value onto the stack first, it is necessary to exchange their order so that the value is on the top of the stack and its name below when they are consumed by the *def* operator.

We can use this same principle to save the tedium of always having to type the three operators necessary to select a font. Based on an example shown on page 16 of the Green book, the following procedure exchanges the point size with the typeface located by the *findfont* operator, to define a default font for your program.

/font {findfont exch scalefont setfont} bind def

Using this procedure, you can select fonts with an instruction like the following.

72 /Times-BoldItalic font

# index

We can make our box-drawing procedure even more efficient by using an operator that is made to order for drawing rectangles. Here, we replace *exch dup* on the first line with *1 index*. Instead of duplicating the object on the top of the stack, *1 index* counts down the number specified by the *index* operand (1 from the top, in this case) and copies that object onto the top of the stack.

Using *index*, we can more efficiently arrange the objects on the stack in the proper order (x, y, x) for drawing each line of the box. We have thereby eliminated the need for the *exch* on the second line in the previous procedure, effectively shortening the procedure by one operator, and making it easier to understand.

```
/box {
        1 index 0 rlineto      % Get duplicate of x
        0 exch rlineto         % Exchange y and 0
        neg 0 rlineto          % Reverse sign of x
        closepath
} bind def

gsave
        10 -10 translate
        36 576 moveto
        540 100 box
        fill
grestore

36 576 moveto
540 100 box
gsave
        .95 setgray
        fill
grestore
stroke

showpage
```

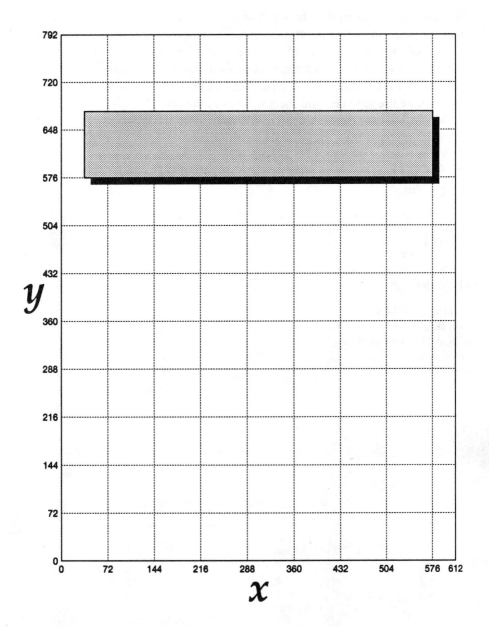

# Centering Text

We have already learned that the width of any character is the distance between the beginning and ending points of origin. The PostScript *stringwidth* operator pushes onto the stack the sum of all these widths for all characters in a string. (Actually, the values for both x and y are pushed onto the stack, but because y is meaningless for languages like English that read characters horizontally in an x direction, we use *pop* to discard the y value from the stack.)

The *dup* operator pushes a copy of the string onto the top of the stack, and *stringwidth* replaces the string with its width values.

Notice how the location of x is given as the center of a portrait page (306 = 612 / 2), and how the string must be specified prior to using *center* to obtain the string width.

```
/font {findfont exch scalefont setfont} bind def

/center {
    dup stringwidth pop
    2 div neg 0 rmoveto
} bind def

72 /Times-Bold font
306 603 moveto
(CHAPTER) center show
showpage
```

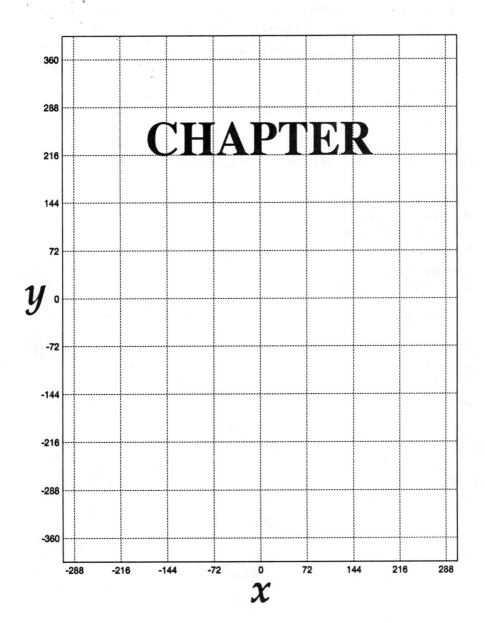

# Center

In the sample below, we add the text to the boxes created in the example on page 7-10. (The code for drawing the boxes is not shown.)

```
/font.{findfont exch scalefont setfont} bind def

/center {
    dup stringwidth pop
    2 div neg 0 rmoveto
} bind def

72 /Times-Bold font
/title (\267 CHAPTER 7 \267) def      % \267 is a bullet

gsave
    3 -3 translate
    306 603 moveto
    title center show
grestore

306 603 moveto
title center true charpath
gsave
    1 setgray
    fill
grestore
.5 setlinewidth
stroke

showpage
```

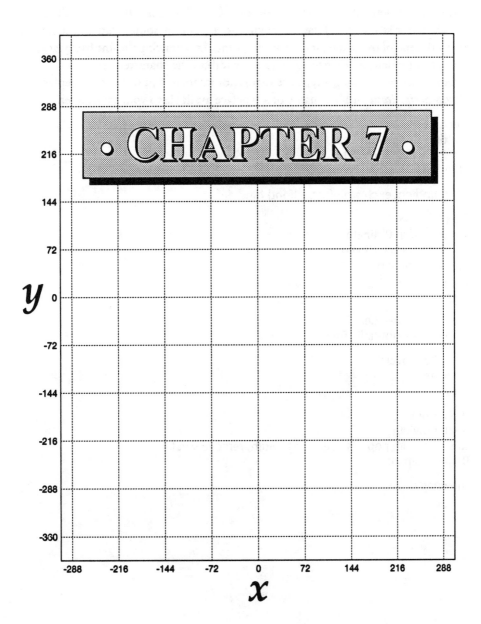

# Underline

The routine below shows how to use *stringwidth* to draw a line the same width as any character string. It's done by moving to a position some relative distance below the end of the string (at the current point), and drawing the line backwards (from right to left) a distance equal to the width of the character string.

Note that we are using a typeface that is not internal. You will need to replace */Brush-Script-Italic* with the name of a typeface available to your interpreter.

```
/center {
    dup stringwidth pop
    2 div neg 0 rmoveto
} bind def

/font {findfont exch scalefont setfont} bind def

/box {
    exch dup 0 rlineto
    exch 0 exch rlineto
    neg 0 rlineto
    closepath
} bind def

/str (Procedures) def
48 /Brush-Script-Italic font

306 432 moveto
str center
show

0 -12 rmoveto
5 setlinewidth
str stringwidth pop    % Get string width, remove y value
0 rlineto stroke

showpage
```

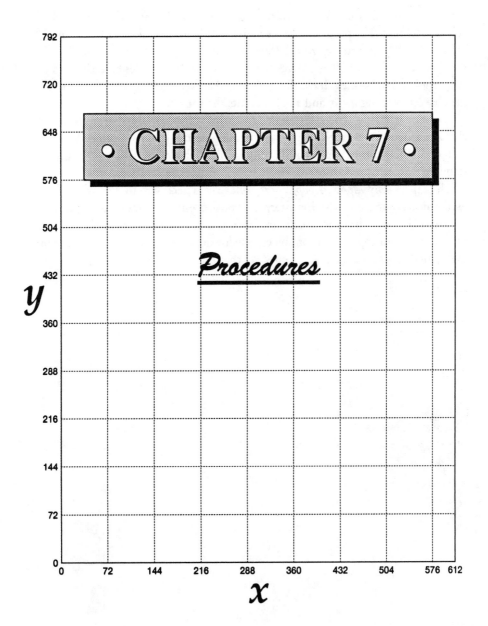

# · CHAPTER 7 ·

## Procedures

# Roundbox

Here is the routine we promised in chapter 5, for drawing an elaborate rounded box around text. The program uses certain variable information that you supply, such as the character string (*ROUNDBOX*), typeface, point size, and location for x and y. Then, the *roundbox* procedure computes other variables based on similar properties of all typefaces, draws the straight and curved line segments surrounding the characters using *arcto,* and finally, paints the roundbox.

You can use this procedure with any string of either upper- or lowercase characters in any typeface or any size, by changing the last instruction. We have included a diagram in the example on page 7-21 that will assist you in understanding how the procedure works.

The repeat loop */4pop {4{pop}repeat } bind def* is necessary to discard four unused objects that the PostScript interpreter pushes onto the stack each time *arcto* is executed. Note that the procedure *4pop* is a repeat loop enclosed within a procedure, requiring two sets of braces: one for the *{pop}* instruction, and one for the named procedure *4pop {. . .} bind def* that executes the repeat loop.

# Roundbox Routine

```
%%%%%%%% USER SUPPLIED INFORMATION %%%%%%%%%%%
(ROUNDBOX) /name exch def
72 /pt exch def
/Times-BoldItalic findfont pt scalefont setfont
100 /x exch def
600 /y exch def
%%%%%%%%%%%%%%%%%%%%%%%%%%%%%%%%%%%%%%%%

/center {dup stringwidth pop 2 div neg 0 rmoveto} bind def
/pop4 {4{pop}repeat} bind def

/roundbox {
        /pt exch def
        /s exch def

        currentpoint              % Puts current x and y coordinates on stack
        /y exch def
        /x exch def
        /sw s stringwidth pop def  % Width of name
                                   % Comments assume a 72-point font
        /q pt 3 div def            % q for quarter is 1/3 pt size, or 24
        /radius q 2 mul def        % Radius is twice q, or 1/2 height, or 48
        /xleft x q sub def         % 1/4 left of x
        /xright x q add sw add def % xright is x + stringwidth sw + q on right
        /ycenter y q add def       % Center of radius is 1 q above baseline y
        /ytop y pt add def         % ytop is 3 q above baseline
        /ybottom y q sub def       % ybottom is 1 quarter below baseline
        xleft ycenter moveto       % 1 q left and up from baseline

        xleft ytop xright ytop radius arcto pop4
        xright ytop xright ybottom radius arcto pop4
        xright ybottom xleft ybottom radius arcto pop4
        xleft ybottom xleft ytop radius arcto pop4
} def
```

# Roundbox Routine Continued

```
x y moveto
name pt roundbox
% Name center pt roundbox        % Replace above with this to center
% Change /x to the halfwidth of page, e.g., 306 for 8.5 inches
gsave
        fill % Black background
grestore
gsave
        pt 6 div setlinewidth          % Add 12 pt more black around
        stroke
grestore
gsave
        1 setgray
        pt 6 div 3 div setlinewidth    % 4 pt white ring inside black
        stroke
grestore
gsave
        1 setgray
        x y moveto
%   0 pt 12 div rmoveto                % Use if name string contains descenders
        name show
grestore

showpage
```

For names with descenders, enable the line *0 pt 12 div rmoveto* above, by removing the leading "%" comment character.

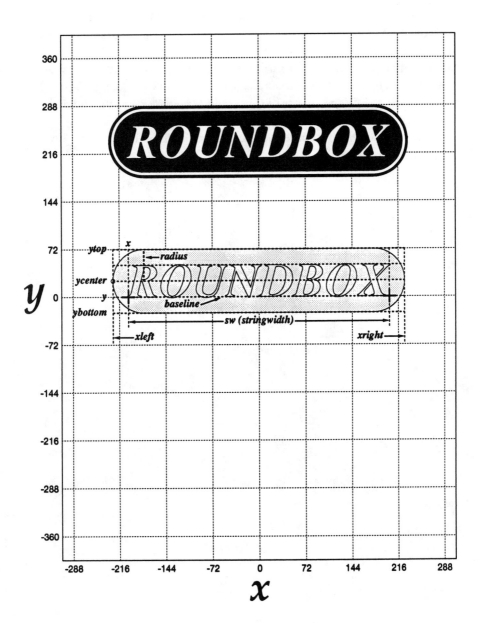

# Centered Roundbox

The preceding program positions the roundbox at any location specified for $x$ in *100 /x exch def.* Since the center procedure is included in the program, you can use it to center the round box.

Simply define the variable $x$ to be half the width of the area in which you want the roundbox to be centered. For example, to center on an 612-point (8.5- inch) page, use *306 /x exch def* and replace the line *name pt roundbox* near the end of the program with the line *name center pt roundbox.*

In the example on the next page, we also changed slightly the way the round-box is painted (not shown).

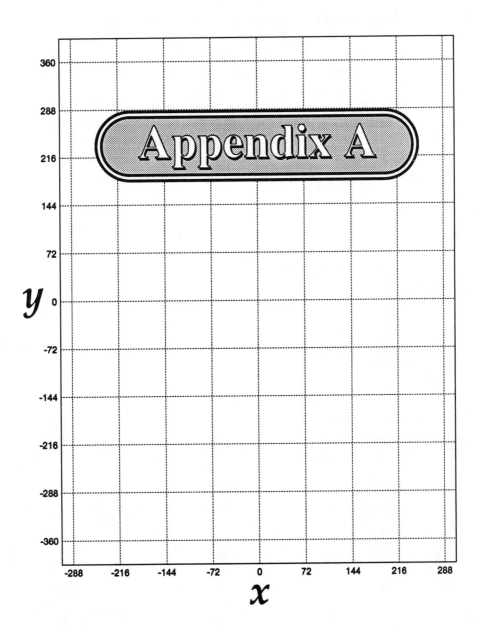

# *if*

Because PostScript is a programming language as well as a page description language, it contains "conditional" operators that execute certain procedures only *if* a certain condition is true. Here, we show the for loop from the procedure for drawing horizontal grid lines on page 6-30, which includes the instructions for showing the string values for each line using the *cvs* operator.

The line *y 0 eq {(   ) show} if,* with four spaces in the parentheses, will show the four spaces prior to showing the number only if the number equals (*eq*) 0. Likewise, the following line adds two spaces only if the number is 72. This is a quick and dirty way to right-align numbers of unequal length, as in the example opposite. A more elegant method of right-aligning numbers is shown in appendix B.

```
/s 3 string def

0 72 792 {
    /y exch def
    0 y moveto 612 0 rlineto stroke
    gsave
        -30 y 3 sub moveto % y minus 3 places number on the line
        0 setgray
        y   0 eq {(   ) show} if
        y 72 eq {( )  show} if
        y s cvs show
    grestore
} for
```

Note that the line *-30 y 3 sub moveto* places the numbers 30 points left of each grid line and 3 points below. This aligns the numbers adjacent to each line instead of on the same baseline.

# ifelse

Here we have a similar conditional operator, *ifelse,* that executes procedure 1 *if* the results of a comparison are true, *else* it executes procedure 2.

In this example, the control variable is compared to the number 1, and if the control variable is less than or equal to (*le*) 1, then it prints the numeral 1 (octal 266) from the ZapfDingbats character set (see appendix A); otherwise it prints the numeral 2 (octal 267). Because the control variable is first 1 and then 2, each number is printed.

```
/ZapfDingbats findfont 288 scalefont setfont

1 1 2 {
    1 le
        {190 504 moveto (\266) show}
        {190 72 moveto (\267) show}
    ifelse
} for

showpage
```

In addition to *le* (less than or equal to), PostScript can test for *lt* (less than), *eq* (equal to), *ge* (greater than or equal to), *gt* (greater than), *ne* (not equal), and other logical comparisons.

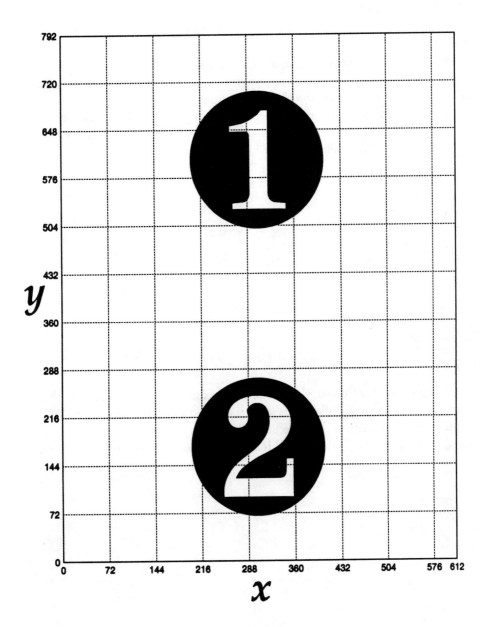

# Redefining showpage

Not only does PostScript allow you to define your own procedures, you can also redefine internal PostScript operators to perform a different function than they normally would.

For instance, we can redefine *showpage* to include additional steps that print a message on the top of each page. Then we execute a normal *showpage* by using the original definition for *showpage* that is contained in "systemdict," the internal PostScript dictionary that contains the PostScript operators. The message could be anything: a company name and address, a logo, a background, or, in this case, a message "from the desk of ..." printed at the top of the page.

```
serverdict begin 0 exitserver

/showpage {
    gsave
        /Palatino-BoldItalic
        findfont 16 scalefont setfont
        72 720 moveto
        (from the desk of Ross Smith . . .)
        show
    grestore
    systemdict begin
    showpage
    end
} bind def
```

After each job is executed, the PostScript interpreter is reset to the state that existed at the beginning of the job. This is referred to as the "server loop." To make permanent changes that affect all subsequent jobs until the interpreter is reset, it is necessary to "exit" from this server loop, as we have done above with *serverdict begin 0 exitserver.* (Server loops are explained in appendix B.)

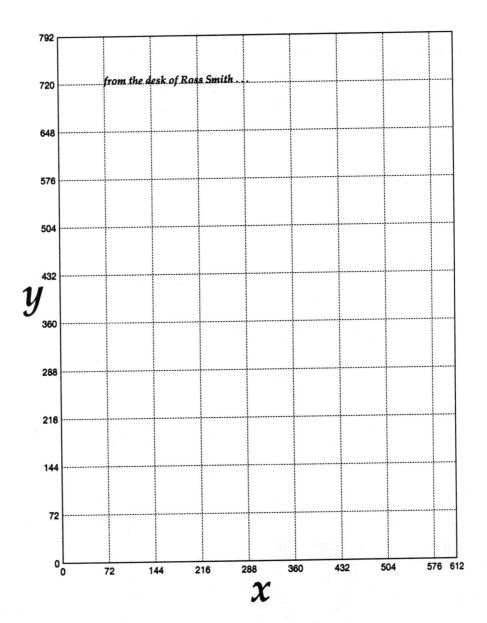

from the desk of Ross Smith....

# showpage

There are two ways to undo the results of the procedure on the preceding page. If you have a PostScript printer you can either reinitialize your PostScript interpreter by turning your PostScript printer off and on, or if the interpreter is loaded from software, you can reload it.

Or, you can use the following instructions to redefine *showpage* so it executes normally, by using the original definition from systemdict.

```
serverdict begin 0 exitserver

/showpage {
    systemdict begin
    showpage
    end
} bind def
```

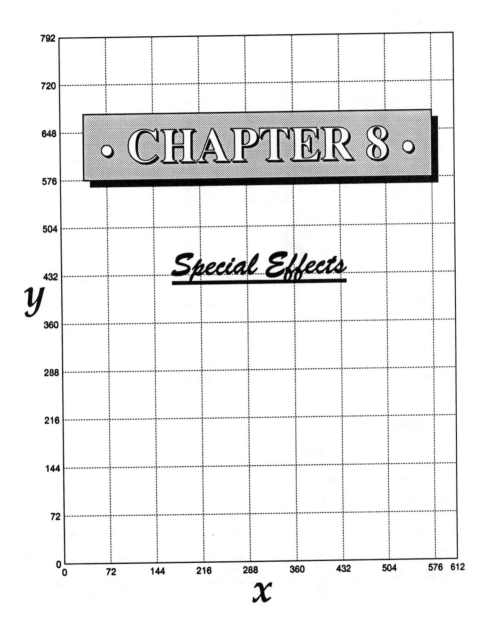

# CHAPTER 8

## Special Effects

# Chapter 8

# Special Effects

In this final chapter it's appropriate that we discuss some of the advanced features of PostScript to provide a complete treatment of the language.

Space does not permit us to do more than touch on these features, giving you an idea of what can be done. In most cases we do not include the detailed explanations necessary for you to gain complete understanding of the principles involved. But we will tell you where you can learn more about them.

Many of the examples in this section demonstrate only the code that relates to the feature described, particularly when other instructions necessary to produce the accompanying example have been covered elsewhere in the book.

We will start by showing you how to achieve more subtle shading effects using shades of gray generated by for loops, and how to create shadows with the current transformation matrix. Then we will discuss circular text, halftone screens, clipping paths, synthetic imaging, and finally, conclude with a brief introduction to color using the RGB and HSB models, and color imaging and separations using the new CMYK model.

# Gray Shading

You can use a for loop to decrement the shades of gray from 1 to 0 (white to black), using the control variable as the operand for *setgray*. Note how *1 -.05 translate* moves right and down each time through the loop.

```
/font {findfont exch scalefont setfont} bind def
/name {0 0 moveto (SMITH) true charpath} bind def

72 /Times-Bold font

gsave
    52 674 translate
    1 -.05  0 {
        setgray
        name fill
            1 -.5 translate
    } for

    name
    gsave
        1 setgray
        fill
    grestore
    .5 setlinewidth
    stroke
grestore

75 650 moveto
17 /Palatino-Bold font
2 1 scale
(consultingroup) show

showpage
```

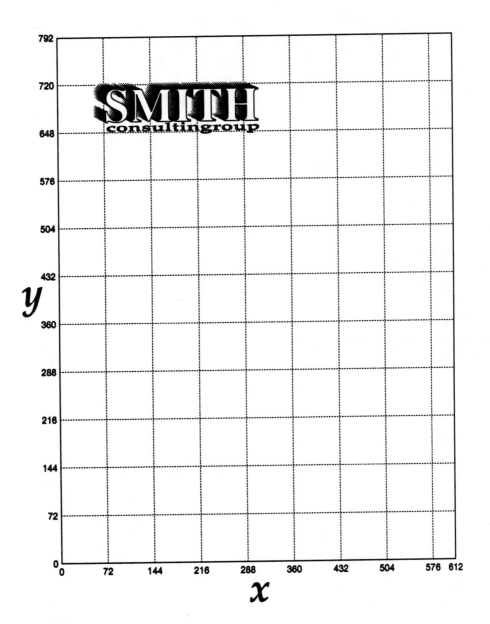

# Shading and Sizing

This is a variation on the gray-shading theme, using the *center* procedure to position each line. Note how the point size is incremented by .5 each time through the loop (from 48 to 98 in this case), and the position on the Y axis decremented 1 point with *0 -1 translate.*

```
/center {dup stringwidth pop 2 div neg 0 rmoveto} bind def
/font {findfont exch scalefont setfont} bind def
/ptsize 48 def

306 396 translate
0 100 translate % Times through loop

1 -.01 0 {
    setgray
    ptsize /Times-Bold font
    0 0 moveto
    (PostScript) center show
    0 -1 translate
    /ptsize ptsize .5 add def
} for

0 0 moveto
(PostScript) center true charpath
gsave
    1 setgray
    fill
grestore
stroke

showpage
```

On some interpreters, this program may take a long time to print.

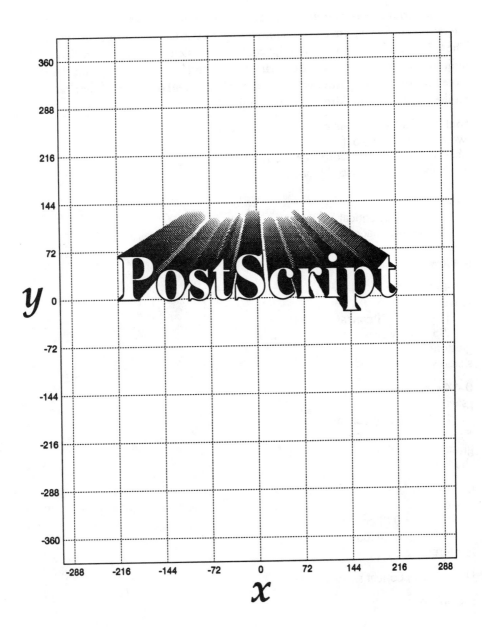

# concat

The PostScript *concat* (concatenate) operator is a powerful way to quickly create interesting shadowing effects by manipulating the current transformation matrix. The CTM, the basis of the PostScript coordinate system, is a six-element "array," indicated by the special PostScript characters "[" and "]" (left and right brackets). Note how the fourth position changes both the size and direction of the shadow on the Y axis, and the third position changes the direction of the X axis.

```
/font {findfont exch scalefont setfont} bind def
/word (SHADOWS) def
/shadow {0 0 moveto word show} bind def
96 /Helvetica-Narrow-Bold font
75 648 translate
gsave
      [1 0 1 1 0 0] concat
      .95 setgray shadow
grestore
shadow

0 -144 translate
gsave
      [1 0 1 .5 0 0] concat
      .95 setgray shadow
grestore
shadow

0 -144 translate
gsave
      [1 0 -1 -1 0 0] concat
      .95 setgray shadow
grestore
shadow

0 -144 translate
gsave
      [1 0 1 -3 0 0] concat
      .95 setgray shadow
grestore

[1 0 1 1 0 0] concat shadow

showpage
```

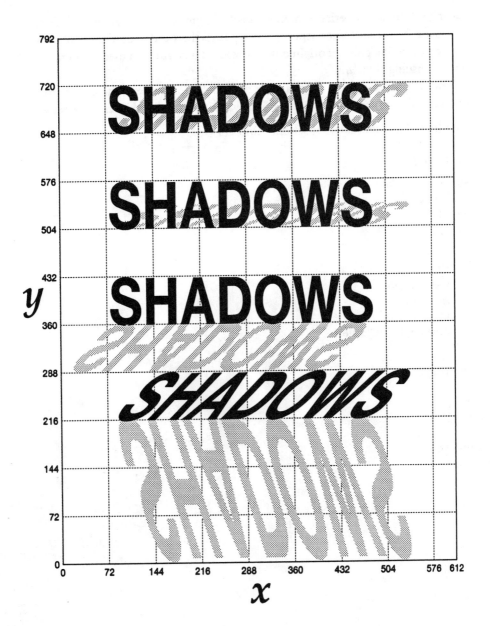

# currentpoint

Placing an alphabetic series of monospaced (nonproportional) text in a circle is easy using the *currentpoint* operator, which pushes the x and y coordinates of each character's ending point of origin onto the stack. These are then used as operands for the ensuing *translate*.

The *put* operator places the character with the ASCII value of the increment *i* into the string *str*. For instance, the ASCII value 65 is replaced with the letter A.

```
/font {findfont exch scalefont setfont} bind def
48 /Courier font
/str 1 string def

306 396 translate
-120 0 translate
90 rotate

65 1 90 {
    /i exch def
    str 0 i put
    0 0 moveto
    str show
    currentpoint translate
    360 26 div neg rotate
} for

showpage
```

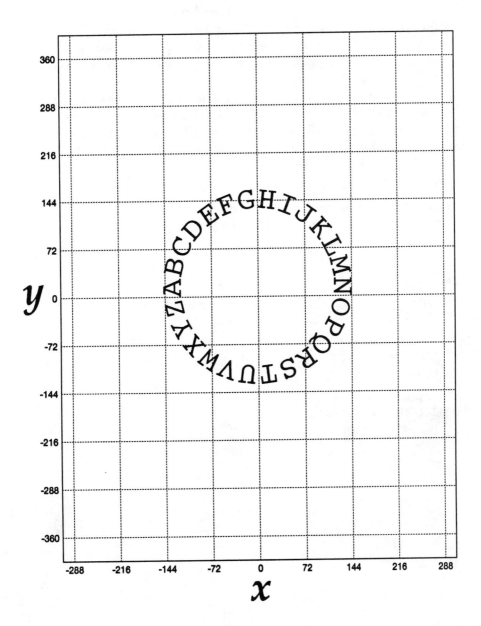

# Circular Text

The best way we have found to fit proportional text to a curve is by using procedures from the Blue book, pages 167–168. These procedures (which are not shown here), *outsidecircletext, insidecircletext, findhalfangle* (with *circtextdict* and *pi*), *outsideplacechar,* and *insideplacechar,* must be copied and added to the code segment below to run this program.

The two procedures *outside-* and *insidecircletext* (that invoke the other procedures) each take three arguments: the point size of the font, the mid-point of the circle (in degrees), and the radius of the arc. Note that when the two strings are of unequal length, the point size of the longer string should be smaller than the shorter string. The rings in the example are arcs connected by line segments (code not shown).

```
/font {findfont exch scalefont setfont} bind def
% Circle-drawing procedures from Blue book (see above)

306 396 translate
2 2 scale

0 0 76 0 360 arc fill        % Black ring
1  setgray                   % Change to white for donut & letters
0 0 55 0 360 arc fill        % Cut out white inside

16 /Times-Bold font
(DESKTOP PUBLISHING)
16 90 60 outsidecircletext

14 /Times-Bold font
(PRESENTATION GRAPHICS)
14 270 70 insidecircletext
```

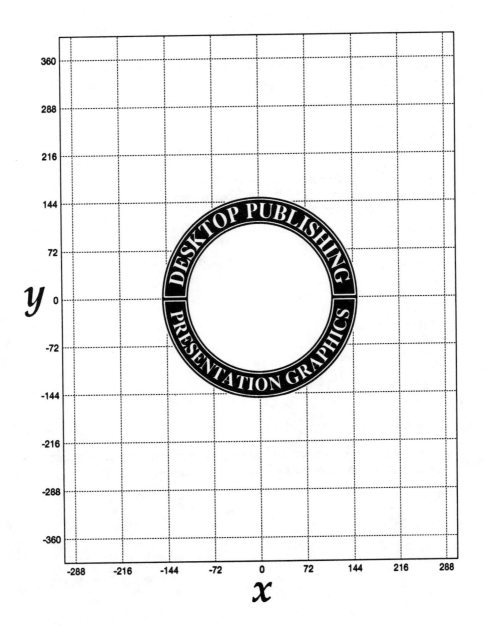

# setscreen: Frequency

Halftone screens used for gray-scale imaging are covered thoroughly in the Orange book (pages 141–191) and the Green Book (pages 131–136). We will discuss the PostScript *image* operator later in this chapter.

Here, we show how to produce certain effects by changing the screen frequency, angle, and spot function (a procedure that determines the shape of the halftone spots).

```
/font {findfont exch scalefont setfont} bind def
160 /Times-Bold font
90 648 translate

currentscreen   % Get frequency, angle, and spot function
/dot exch def    % Assumes default "dot" spot function
pop pop          % Discard frequency and angle

60 -12.5 10 {
    /f exch def
    0 0 moveto
    gsave
        .5 setgray
        f 45 {dot} setscreen
        (DOTS) show
    grestore
    (DOTS) true charpath
    stroke
    0 -144 translate
} for

showpage
```

Note how we use *currentscreen* to obtain the procedure for creating dots, and then use it each time through the loop for each new *setscreen*.

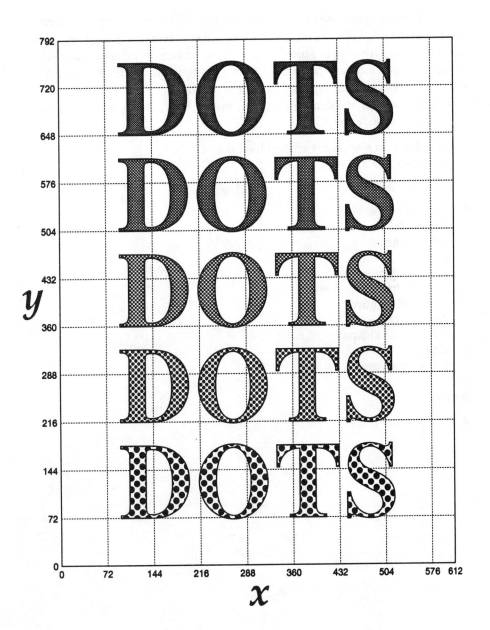

# setscreen: Spot Function

In the previous example, we defined *dot* as the procedure for creating dot screens of various sizes. (Actually, we just used the default spot function pushed onto the stack by *currentscreen*.) To produce line screens, we replace the procedure *dot* with a simple *{pop}* as the third parameter. Amazingly, this converts the shape of the screen from dots to lines! Try it and see for yourself.

In both instances, the same operands are used in the for loop, to alter the size of the dots or lines, respectively.

```
/font {findfont exch scalefont setfont} bind def
160 /Times-Bold font

63 648 translate

60 -12.5 10 {
    /f exch def
    0 0 moveto
    gsave
        .5 setgray
        f 45 {pop} setscreen
        (LINES) show
    grestore
    (LINES) true charpath
    stroke
    0 -144 translate
} for
grestore

showpage
```

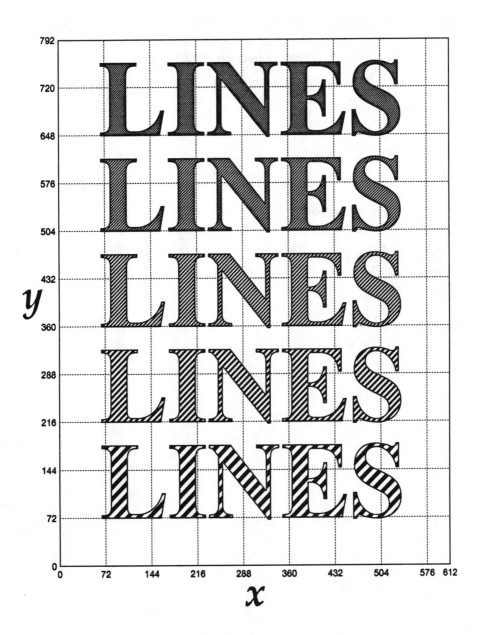

# setscreen: Angle

This is basically the same line-setting loop as the previous example, except that here we set the frequency to 30 and use the loop control variable to decrement the screen angle from 90 to 0 degrees, in intervals of 22.5 degrees.

```
/font {findfont exch scalefont setfont} bind def
160 /Times-Bold font
24 648 translate

90 -22.5 0 {
    /a exch def
    0 0 moveto
    gsave
        .8 setgray
        30 a {pop} setscreen
        (ANGLE) show
    grestore
    (ANGLE) true charpath
    stroke
    0 -144 translate
} for

showpage
```

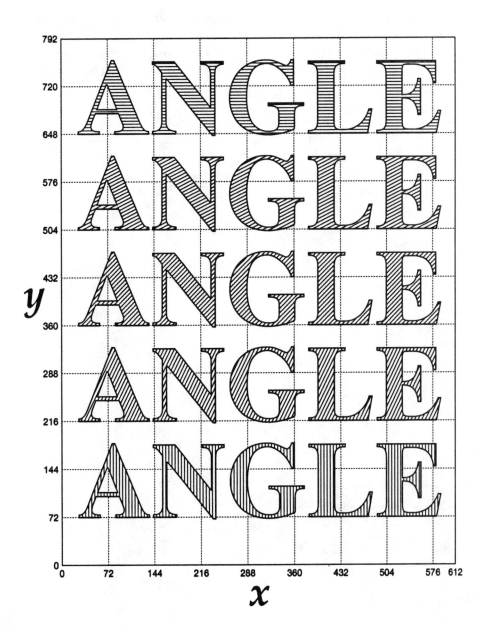

# setscreen: Background

Again we are using the same procedure to change the screen to a line screen, but this time with lines at a 45-degree angle and with a frequency of 30. We then use this as a background to fill the box drawn with our box procedure. Note that *setscreen* is enclosed in a *gsave/grestore*, so that subsequent code will not be affected.

```
/font {findfont exch scalefont setfont} bind def
/box {1 index 0 rlineto 0 exch rlineto neg 0 rlineto closepath} bind def

108 /Times-Bold font
36 576 moveto
540 100 box
gsave
     30 45 {pop} setscreen
     .8 setgray
     fill
grestore
stroke

87 590 moveto
(T I T L E) true charpath
gsave
     1 setgray
     fill
grestore
.5 setlinewidth
stroke

showpage
```

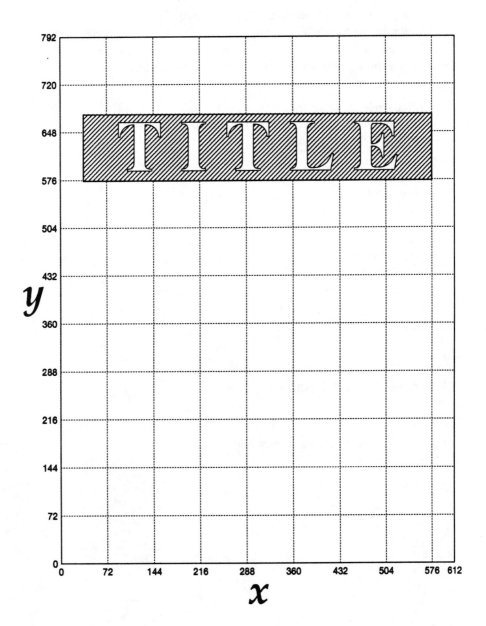

# clip

The PostScript *clip* operator discards unwanted material that is outside of an area—the clipping path—defined in the program, and displays only the material within. The sample shows how this works with the *clip* instruction and without it. (The code without *clip* is not shown, but you can run the program without *clip* to see how it is done.)

```
/font {findfont exch scalefont setfont} bind def
/box {1 index 0 rlineto 0 exch rlineto neg 0 rlineto closepath} bind def
108 /Times-Bold font

/lines {
        .5 setlinewidth
        576 576 translate
        45 rotate
        0 5 450 {
                0 exch moveto
                150 0 rlineto
                -5 0 translate
        } for
}bind def

36 576 moveto
540 100 box
gsave
        clip                 % Establish box as clipping path
        lines stroke         % Then stroke the lines
grestore
stroke

% Include "TITLE" instructions from previous example

showpage
```

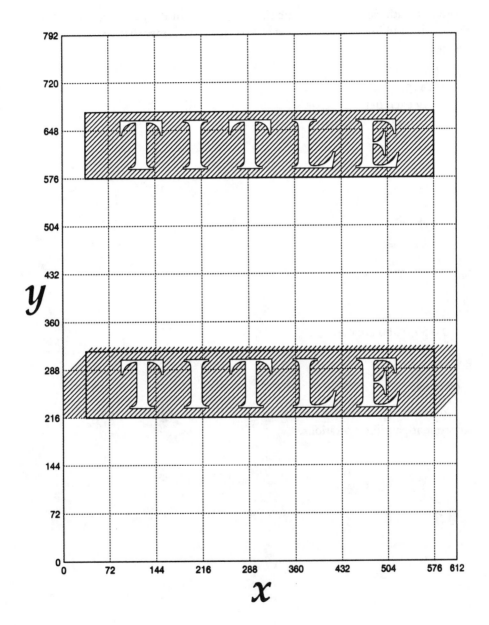

# Clipping Paths

A clipping path can be any graphic shape: a box, as in the previous example; a circle, below; an irregular shape; or even text characters, as we shall see later in the chapter.

```
/lines {
    54 -4 -54 {
        /y exch def
        -72 y moveto
        72 y lineto stroke
    } for
} bind def

305 395 translate
2 2 scale
2 setlinewidth

0 -100 translate
0 0 55 0 360 arc stroke
lines

gsave
    0 200 translate
    0 0 55 0 360 arc clip
    lines
grestore

showpage
```

Note that *clip* should always be enclosed in a *gsave/grestore,* as it effects all subsequent painting operations.

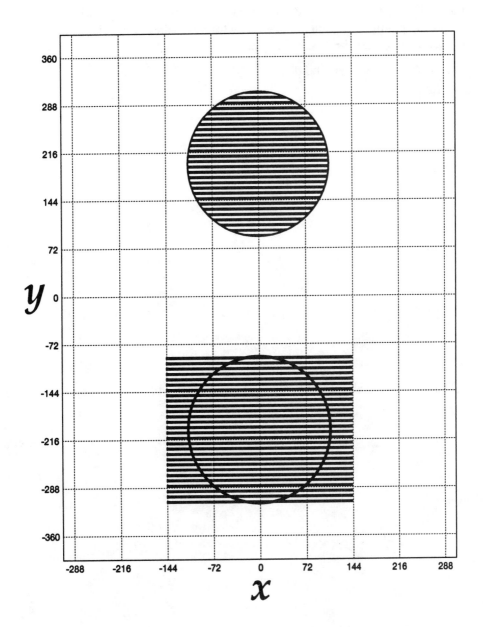

# Highlighting

Using a clipping path, we can transform a simple filled circle into a globe by using a for loop to produce a "highlighting" effect. This creates the illusion of light being reflected from a three-dimensional object.

```
/circle {0 0 50 0 360 arc} bind def

306 396 translate
2 2 scale

.5 setgray
circle
gsave
    fill
grestore
clip

-15 20 translate
1.25 1.25 scale

50 -2.5 2.5 {
    /r exch def
    1 r .01 mul sub setgray
    0 0 r 0 360 arc fill
}for

showpage
```

The bottom example shows how the image would look without the *clip* operator.

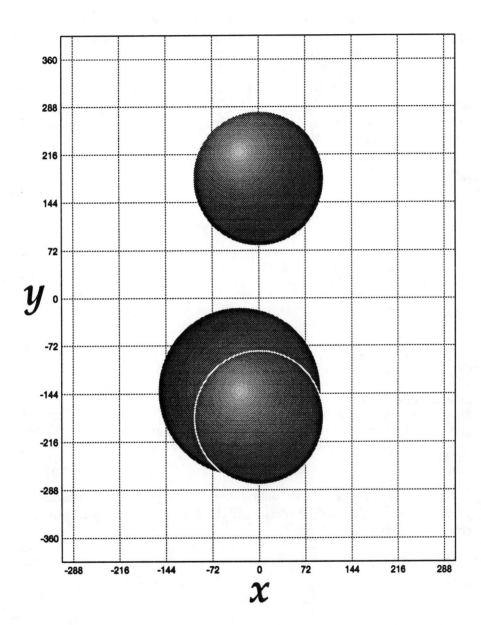

# *image*

PostScript can render scanned images in up to 256 shades of gray, using the *image* operator. You can also use *image* to create "fountain fills"—synthetic images that are filled with progressive gradients of gray values. (See the Green book, pages 123–130, for a complete discussion of the technique.)

Here, the *ffill* procedure generates the data required by the *image* operator. We use *translate* to locate the image origin (indicated by numbers in the accompanying sample), *scale* to size the image, *rotate* to change its origin (if necessary), and two operands to specify the beginning and ending gray values. These can be any numbers between and including 0 and 1.

```
/string256 256 string def

/ffill {
    1 index sub
    exch 255 mul
    0 1 255 {
        string256 exch dup
        4 index mul
        3 index add cvi
        put
    } for
    pop pop
    1 256 8 [1 0 0 256 0 0] {string256} image
} bind def

gsave 72 72 translate 72 72 scale 0 1 ffill grestore
gsave 72 216 translate 216 144 scale 1 0 ffill grestore
gsave 72 648 translate -90 rotate 144 216 scale 0 1 ffill grestore
gsave 360 648 translate -90 rotate 216 144 scale 1 0 ffill grestore

showpage
```

Note that the number of shades of gray that a PostScript device can produce depends on the resolution of the device and the halftone screen frequency. See chapter 10 of the Orange book.

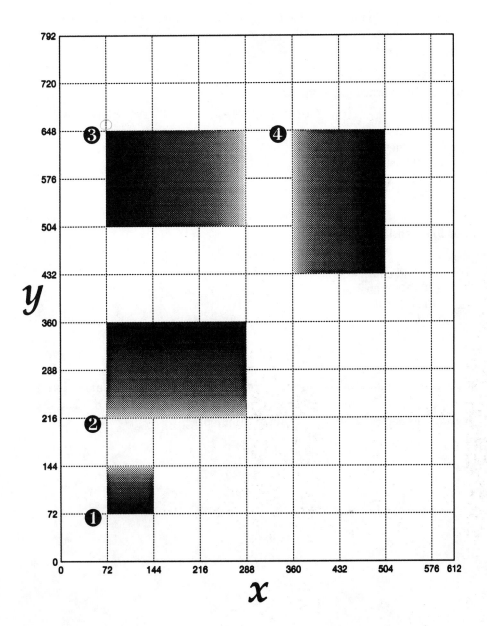

# Clipping Fountain Fills

Synthetic fountain fills are ideal as backgrounds for graphic shapes and large text. In this example we show a 3.33-inch (240-dot) square fountain fill that is clipped to the shape of a diamond of the same width.

```
/string256 256 string def
% Insert "ffill" procedure from previous page here

/diamond {
    -120 0 moveto
    0 120 lineto
    120 0 lineto
    0 -120 lineto
    closepath
} bind def

306 576 translate

gsave
    diamond clip
    -120 -120 translate
    240 240 scale
    0 1 ffill
grestore

showpage
```

The bottom illustration shows the results without clipping. Be sure to insert the instructions for the *ffill* procedure from the previous page into this and the next few examples before attempting to print a page.

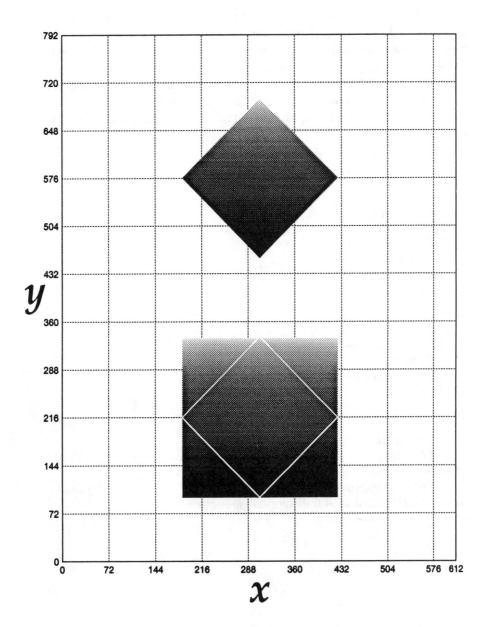

# Gradients

The *ffill* procedure can render a fountain fill for any range of gray values from 0 (all black) to 1 (all white). The number of gradients printed depends on the current halftone screen frequency, the resolution of the raster imaging device, and the range of gray values specified.

Here we show five examples of diamonds that have been clipped in the same way as the previous example, but with each having a different range of gray values. We place these beginning and ending values on the stack before we call the *diamondfill* procedure.

```
/string256 256 string def
% Insert ffill procedure here

/diamond {
    -120 0 moveto
    0 120 lineto
    120 0 lineto
    0 -120 lineto
    closepath
} bind def

/diamondfill {
    diamond clip
    -120 -120 translate
    240 240 scale
    ffill % Uses beginning and ending values below
} bind def

306 396 translate

gsave 0 0 translate .2 .8 diamondfill grestore
gsave -144 216 translate  .8 1 diamondfill grestore
gsave 144 216 translate .9 .6 diamondfill grestore
gsave -144 -216 translate .1 .6 diamondfill grestore
gsave 144 -216 translate .4 0 diamondfill grestore

showpage
```

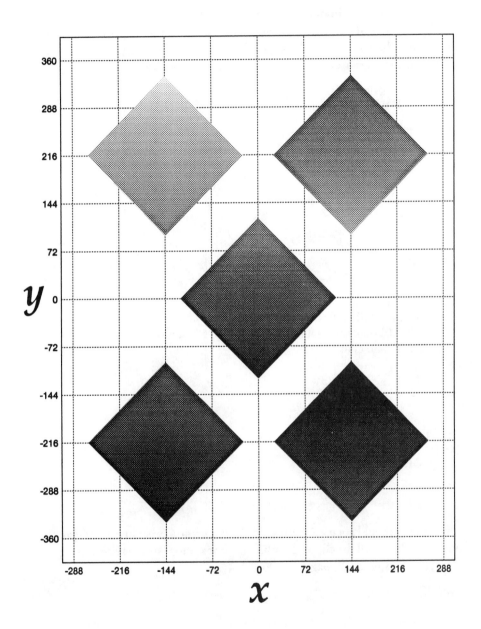

# Fountain-filled Text

Fountain fills can also produce very interesting effects with larger text, particularly when the screen frequency is changed to produce either larger dots or lines. Here we show how to change the screen frequency of a fountain fill and clip the background into a string of text. The code is shown both with and without clipping.

```
/string256 256 string def
% Insert "ffill" procedure here

currentscreen
/spot exch def
pop pop
30 11 {spot} setscreen

gsave
    36 288 translate
    -90 rotate
    144 540 scale
    1 0 ffill
grestore

36 504 moveto
/Helvetica-BoldOblique findfont
[82 0 0 164 0 0] makefont setfont % 82 points, 1 2 scale
(POSTSCRIPT) true charpath
gsave
    stroke
grestore
clip

36 638 translate
-90 rotate
144 540 scale
1 0 ffill

showpage
```

Note that we could not use *scale* to scale the font vertically, because a *gsave/grestore* would have destroyed the clipping path. (For font scaling with *makefont* using the CTM, see the Blue book, pages 94–96.)

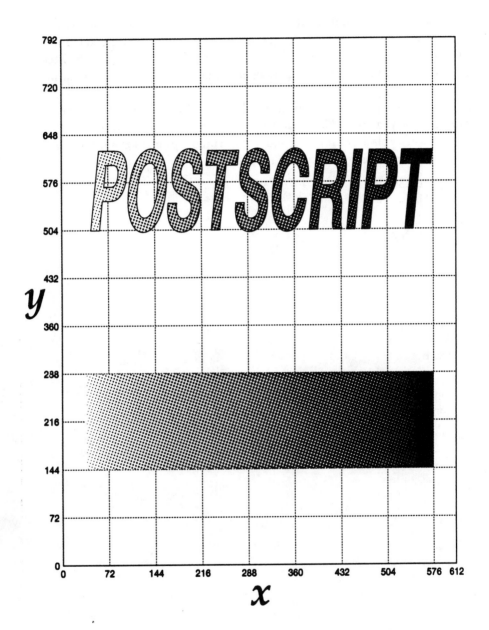

# Circular Text on Fountain Fill

This code sample expands on the earlier somple of circular text shown on page 8-10. Here the *arc* also defines the outside of the clipping path for two fountain fills fading in opposite directions. The white circle inside is filled after the backgrounds are fountain-filled. The text is softened from white (*1 setgray*) in the former example to *.9 setgray* (not shown).

We show only the code segment for doing the fountain fills, using the *ffill* procedure on page 8-26. Note that the two fountain fills are mirror images, with gradients of all black at the center and .5 gray at the top and bottom. The width, 152, is the circumference of the clipping region.

```
/string256 256 str def
% Insert ffill procedure here

/ring {
      0 0 76 0 360 arc clip
      -76 0 translate
      152 76 scale
      0 .5 ffill
} def

306 396 translate
0 -180 translate
2 2 scale

gsave
      ring
grestore

gsave
      1 -1 scale    % Mirror image
      ring
grestore
```

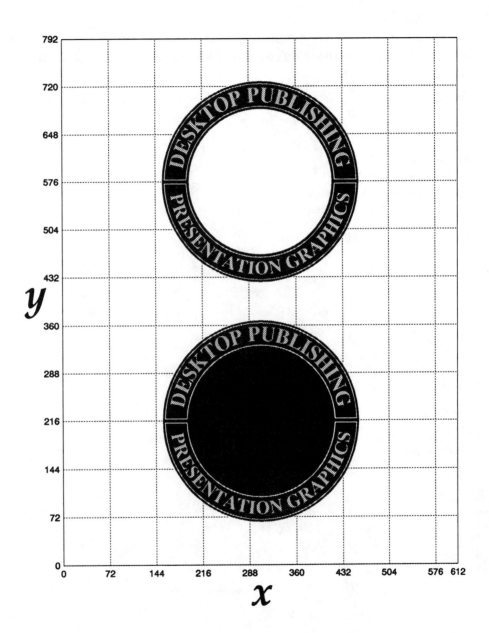

# setrgbcolor

The *setrgbcolor* operator requires three operands that specify the primary colors red, green, and blue used in the RGB color model. The intensity values for the three colors range from 0 (no color) up to 1 (maximum intensity). Color mixtures are shown on page 8-41.

```
/font {findfont exch scalefont setfont } bind def

1.2  3 scale
-42 -234 translate

7 setlinewidth
0 0 1 setrgbcolor % Blue
55 332 moveto 540 332 lineto stroke
55 400 moveto 540 400 lineto stroke
60 340 moveto
72 /Helvetica-BoldOblique font
(POSTSCRIPT) true charpath clip

newpath
gsave
    35 setlinewidth
    50 376 moveto 600 376 lineto stroke
grestore
1 0 0 setrgbcolor % Red
55 355 moveto 510 355 lineto stroke
55 342 moveto 510 342 lineto stroke

showpage
```

We don't show the routine for drawing stars, but one can be found on pages 51–53 of the Blue book.

# sethsbcolor

The HSB color model also uses three operands, but only the first operand designates *hue,* or color; the others describe the *saturation* and *brightness* of the hue. The hue ranges from 0 for red, to .333 for green, .667 for blue, and 1 for red again. Accordingly, *sethsbcolor* is ideal for use in a for loop, to cycle through any range of hues.

The sample below produces a rainbow of 256 vertical bands of color, clipped into the string "COLOR." (Be sure you include the *font, box,* and *center* procedures with the code below.)

```
/rainbow {
    /height exch def
    /width exch def
    /xwidth width 256 div def
    gsave
        currentpoint translate
        0 1 256 div 1 {
            /hue exch def
            hue 1 1 sethsbcolor
            0 0 moveto
            xwidth height box fill
            xwidth 0 translate
        } for
    grestore
} bind def

0 270 translate
108 /NewCenturySchlbk-Bold font
306 90 moveto
(COLOR) center
true charpath clip

newpath
306 80 moveto
(COLOR) center
stringwidth pop
108 rainbow
showpage
```

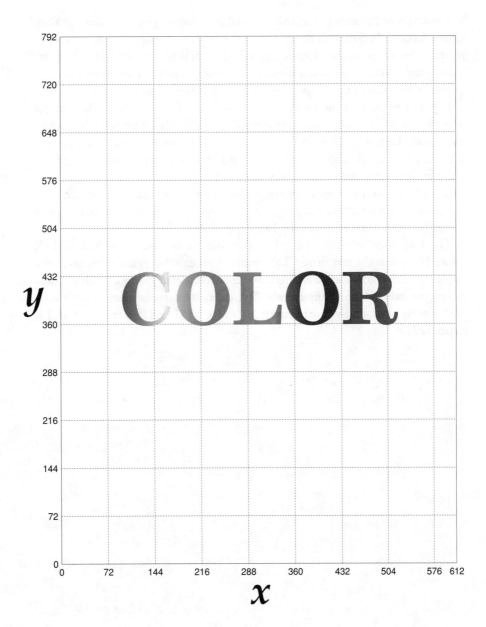

# setcmykcolor

In 1988, Adobe Systems published the *PostScript Language Color Operator Definitions,* in conjunction with the release of the first Adobe-based color PostScript printer. This specification defined support for additional color operations, including the CMYK (for cyan, magenta, yellow, and black) color model.

Unlike RGB and HSB, which are luminance models that use additive colors, CMYK is a reflectance model that uses subtractive colors that are the complements of the RGB colors. Hence, in the RGB model, 1 is a dark color (no light), and 0 is an absence of color (all light); in the CMYK model, 1 is a dark color (all ink), and 0 is an absence of color (no ink). The four operands required for *setcmykcolor* correspond to the colors CMYK.

The accompanying color conversion chart is a rainbow generated in the same way as in the previous sample program. The top two lines show the correspondences between color values in the RGB and HSB models.

The line directly under the color spectrum shows the equivalent CMYK colors. Note how the first three CMY color operands are the complements of the opposing RGB colors—cyan and red, magenta and green, yellow and blue. These complementary relationships are also indicated by the equivalent gray values produced by black-and-white printers: .07 and .03, .41 and .59, and .89 and .11, respectively.

# COLOR CONVERSION

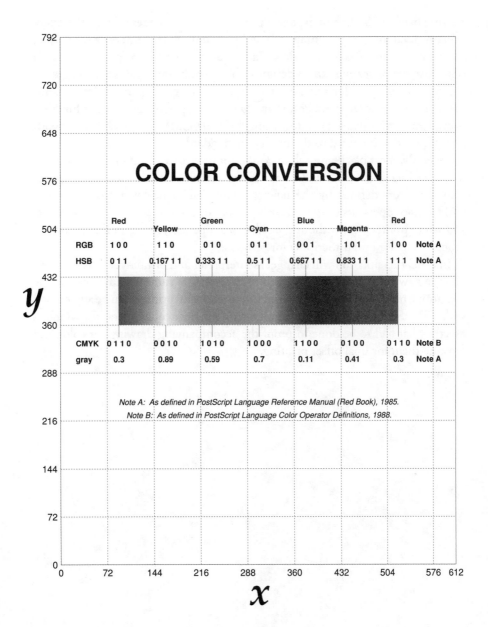

| | Red | Yellow | Green | Cyan | Blue | Magenta | Red | |
|---|---|---|---|---|---|---|---|---|
| RGB | 1 0 0 | 1 1 0 | 0 1 0 | 0 1 1 | 0 0 1 | 1 0 1 | 1 0 0 | Note A |
| HSB | 0 1 1 | 0.167 1 1 | 0.333 1 1 | 0.5 1 1 | 0.667 1 1 | 0.833 1 1 | 1 1 1 | Note A |

| | Red | Yellow | Green | Cyan | Blue | Magenta | Red | |
|---|---|---|---|---|---|---|---|---|
| CMYK | 0 1 1 0 | 0 0 1 0 | 1 0 1 0 | 1 0 0 0 | 1 1 0 0 | 0 1 0 0 | 0 1 1 0 | Note B |
| gray | 0.3 | 0.89 | 0.59 | 0.7 | 0.11 | 0.41 | 0.3 | Note A |

*Note A: As defined in PostScript Language Reference Manual (Red Book), 1985.*
*Note B: As defined in PostScript Language Color Operator Definitions, 1988.*

# colorimage

Because black-and-white interpreters print all colors as shades of gray, the *image* operator used for doing fountain fills on black-and-white printers prints only in shades of gray on a PostScript color printer—even when a color is specified. This is because the *image* operator is designed for use only with gray-scale images.

The new Adobe color standard defines a new imaging operator designed for use with color printers. The PostScript *colorimage* operator performs a function equivalent to the *image* operator, using RGB or CMYK color, but only with interpreters that conform to the new color standard.

Presently, most black-and-white PostScript interpreters and printers conform to the existing PostScript standard as defined in the Red book; they don't support color operators defined by the new standard. Paradoxically, a program using CMYK color operators or the *colorimage* operator can not be run on most black-and-white printers. Yet without the *colorimage* operator, fountain fills cannot be proofed in color on PostScript color printers.

In time, this situation will change, as interpreter and printer vendors incorporate the new color standard into their interpreters, as some already have. In the meantime, black-and-white PostScript interpreters and printers can be augmented with a PostScript program that implements the new color operands, which is exactly what had to be done to proof the accompanying drawings in color and separate them for final offset printing.

792

720

648

576

504

432

$y$

360

288

216

144

72

0

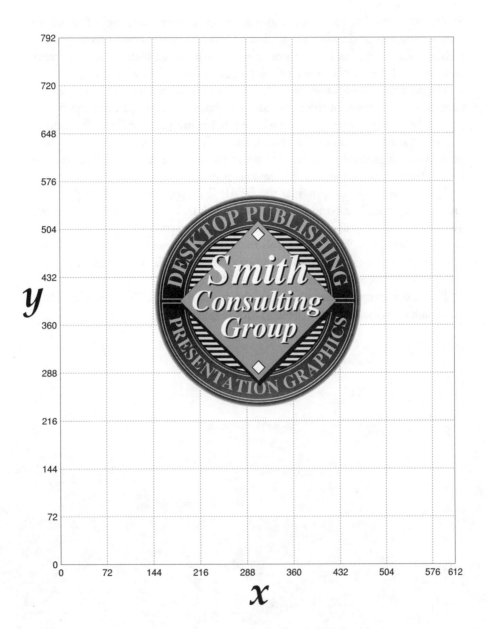

0       72      144     216     288     360     432     504     576  612

$x$

# Color Separations

As the name implies, color separations are pages in which the individual colors constituting a color drawing are printed on separate pages. Each color is printed in black and white, and made into a separate printing plate. Using different colored inks for each plate on a printing press, a full-color image results.

The final color logo was encoded in PostScript using procedures shown in this chapter and elsewhere in the book, and proofed on a 300-dpi color PostScript printer. Separations were tested on a laser printer using a color filtering program that we developed especially for this purpose. Finally, the color separations were printed on a high-resolution imagesetter, to produce the camera-ready film used for printing the color logo on the previous page.

This special filter also provides the facility for testing and printing the color fountain fill on any black-and-white PostScript printer by translating the *colorimage* operator to the *image* operator recognized by interpreters conforming only to the Red book standard. We mention this to acquaint you with the process, but do not show it because it is beyond the scope of the book. (The Orange book has a very good discussion of color, pages 193–225).

The accompanying sample shows the respective CMYK separations (the drawing has no magenta) for the logo on the previous page.

CYAN                    MAGENTA

YELLOW                  BLACK

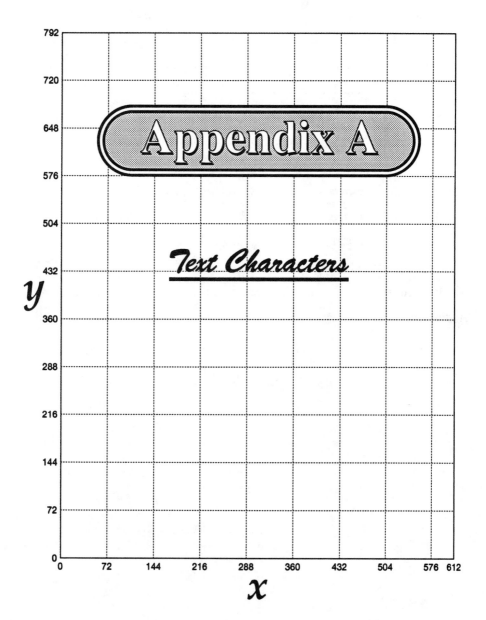

# Appendix A

## Text Characters

# Appendix A

# Text Characters

This section provides additional information about the characters available in PostScript typeface outlines—primarily how to access individual characters and how PostScript places character strings on the page.

# Individual Characters

As we mentioned in chapter 2, the Bézier outline for each character in each typeface defines a character 1000 points (13.89 inches) high along the Y axis, and as wide as necessary to form the character along the X axis.

Vertical placement of each character is determined with respect to a baseline, an imaginary horizontal line drawn along the Y axis. All characters are aligned along this common baseline.

The horizontal position of each character is determined with respect to points of origin along the X axis. Each character has an beginning point of origin, as well as an ending point of origin for alignment of the next character in a string of characters.

The string width of each character is the distance between these two points of origin.

The actual characters are offset from the beginning point of origin a distance determined by the left side bearing. Side bearings can be positive or negative, so the beginning point of origin can fall either inside or outside the "path bounding box" (the smallest rectangle that completely contains the formed character).

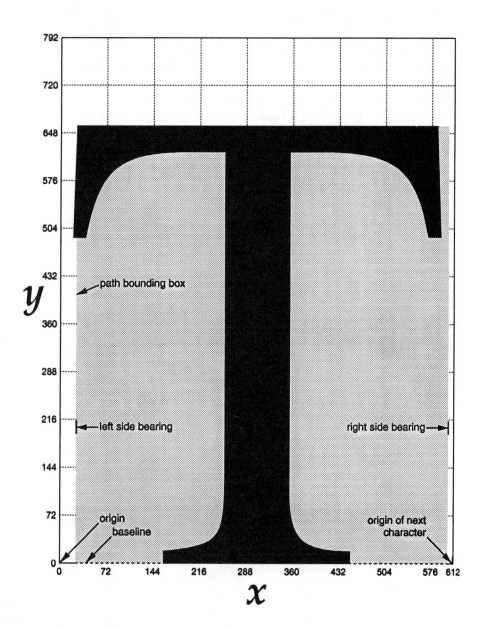

# Font Size

Look again at the accompanying drawing from chapter 2, which describes the basic elements that comprise a string of text for a 144-point (2-inch) font. The shaded gray area defines the horizontal and vertical space taken by the character string. Its vertical height is exactly 2 inches, and its horizontal width (string width) is the distance between the beginning point of origin of the first character and the ending point of origin of the last character in the string.

Notice that there is some space between the highest ascender and the top of the shaded area, and also between the lowest descender and the bottom of the gray area. This white space, which is roughly five percent of the point size in this typeface, is necessary to separate successive lines of text. Therefore text is not usually as tall as its stated point size.

Furthermore, because the point size must include space for descenders, which comprise roughly one-quarter of the point size, the largest point size that can be printed on an 11-inch vertical page is approximately 864 points, or 12 inches, for all normal characters. (Some foreign and special characters in some typefaces may take more space.)

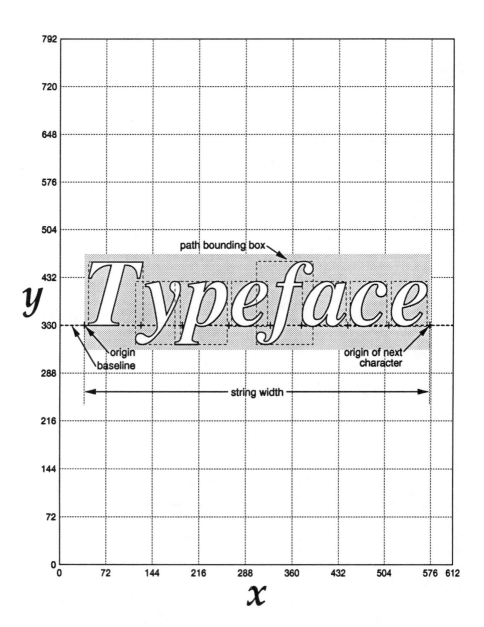

# 12-inch "T"

The accompanying drawing is an 864-point (12-inch) uppercase "T" from the Times-BoldItalic typeface. Notice how we have elevated the baseline 184 points (nearly 2.75 inches, or 1⁄4 of 11 inches), to allow space for descenders for other characters in the typeface.

Notice also that because this character has a negative right side bearing, the ending point of origin is "inside" the path bounding box.

The width of the character is roughly 7 1/4 inches (528 points), measured between the beginning and ending points of origin.

```
/Times-BoldItalic findfont 864 scalefont setfont

0 184 moveto    % Elevate baseline
(T) true charpath stroke

showpage
```

The code that draws the character's bounding box and labels is not shown.

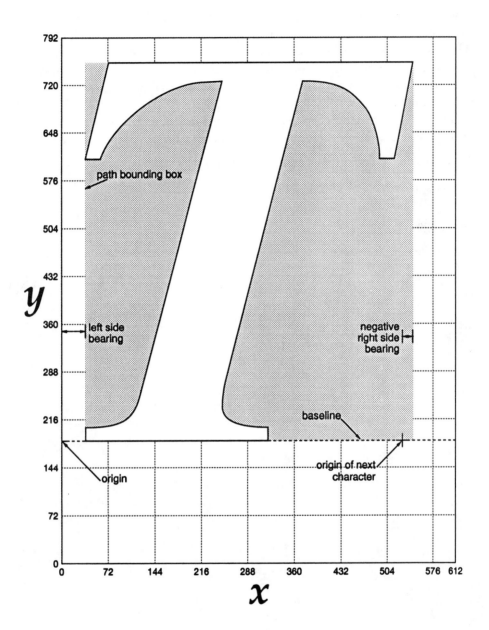

# 12-inch "f"

The lowercase "f" from the same typeface, which has both ascenders and descenders, demonstrates the full height of a 12-inch font on an 11-inch page. There is roughly one-half inch of space above and below the font.

This character has negative side bearings both left and right. Hence, we have shifted the beginning point of origin 144 points (2 inches) right in this sample, to allow the full character to be displayed on the page.

The string width of the character is just under 4 inches, measured between the two points of origin—significantly less than the actual width of the character.

```
/Times-BoldItalic findfont 864 scalefont setfont

144 184 moveto      % Elevate baseline
(f) true charpath stroke

showpage
```

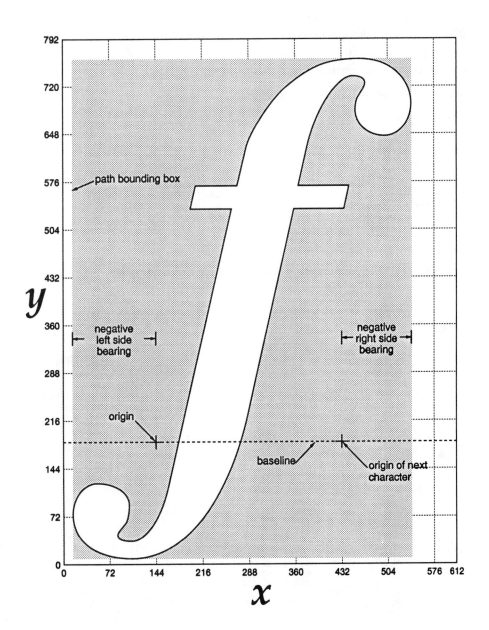

# 15-inch Question Mark

The tallest uppercase character that can be printed on an 11-inch page is usually 1080 points (15 inches), depending on the shape of the character and how close to the edge of the page the imaging device can print. Of course, the character also has to fit on the page vertically, or be scaled to fit.

```
/Times-Bold findfont 1080 scalefont setfont

gsave
    .99 setgray
    54 30 moveto
    (?) show
grestore

54 30 moveto
(?) true charpath stroke

showpage
```

This would make an interesting background for a questionnaire.

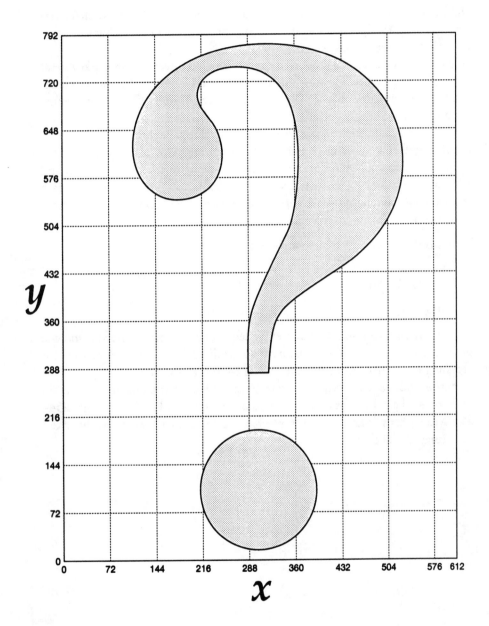

# Character Sets

On the next several pages we show the standard and extended ASCII characters for internal PostScript typeface outlines, together with unencoded characters that are included in the character sets.

Standard characters are those that can be specified directly from the keyboard by simply typing a key. They include the upper- and lowercase letters, numerals, and basic punctuation marks. These characters comprise ASCII decimal values 32 through 126.

Extended characters are those with an ASCII value greater than 126. These are accessed by their octal value (see character sets on the following pages), preceded by the backslash character. For instance, the following instructions place left and right double quote marks (octal values 252 and 272) around the backslash character. Because the backslash is a special character, two backslashes are required to print one backslash (see page 2-26).

/Times-Bold findfont 72 scalefont setfont

36 648 moveto
(\252 \\ \272) show

showpage

In addition to the standard and extended characters, most typefaces include unencoded characters—those that have no specified ASCII value. A method for accessing these characters will be discussed later in this section.

Earlier Adobe PostScript printers have 149 encoded characters and 54 unencoded characters, for a total of 203, as shown in the Red book, pages 254–255. More recent PostScript printers have an additional 25 unencoded characters for a total of 228 characters.

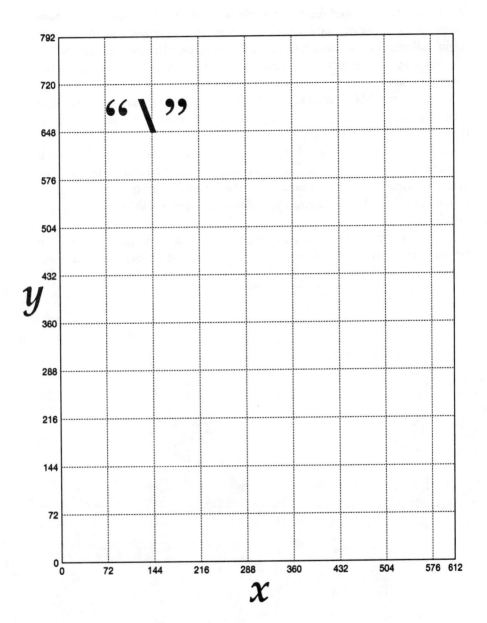

# Times-Roman Characters

In the character sets that follow, each character is shown enclosed in its path bounding box, indicated by a dashed line, with beginning and ending points of origin indicated by solid cross hairs, as noted previously. Baselines are not shown, but they would connect the beginning and ending points of origin along the horizontal axis.

We show two ASCII values below each character—decimal and octal. The octal value is preceded by a backslash, which is how the character is accessed. Below these numbers is the character name.

Of the 35 standard internal typefaces, 33 character sets are identical with respect to character names, ASCII values, and general character shapes. On the next three pages we show the characters in the Times-Roman typeface, which are typical. The Zapf Dingbats and Symbol character sets are shown on the pages that follow.

For each character set, standard characters are on the first page, followed by extended characters on the second page, and unencoded characters on the third.

# Times-Roman

| | | | | | | | |
|---|---|---|---|---|---|---|---|
| 32 \040 space | 33 \041 exclam | 34 \042 quotedbl | 35 \043 numbersign | 36 \044 dollar | 37 \045 percent | 38 \046 ampersand | 39 \047 quoteright |
| 40 \050 parenleft | 41 \051 parenright | 42 \052 asterisk | 43 \053 plus | 44 \054 comma | 45 \055 hyphen | 46 \056 period | 47 \057 slash |
| 48 \060 zero | 49 \061 one | 50 \062 two | 51 \063 three | 52 \064 four | 53 \065 five | 54 \066 six | 55 \067 seven |
| 56 \070 eight | 57 \071 nine | 58 \072 colon | 59 \073 semicolon | 60 \074 less | 61 \075 equal | 62 \076 greater | 63 \077 question |
| 64 \100 at | 65 \101 A | 66 \102 B | 67 \103 C | 68 \104 D | 69 \105 E | 70 \106 F | 71 \107 G |
| 72 \110 H | 73 \111 I | 74 \112 J | 75 \113 K | 76 \114 L | 77 \115 M | 78 \116 N | 79 \117 O |
| 80 \120 P | 81 \121 Q | 82 \122 R | 83 \123 S | 84 \124 T | 85 \125 U | 86 \126 V | 87 \127 W |
| 88 \130 X | 89 \131 Y | 90 \132 Z | 91 \133 bracketleft | 92 \134 backslash | 93 \135 bracketright | 94 \136 asciicircum | 95 \137 underscore |
| 96 \140 quoteleft | 97 \141 a | 98 \142 b | 99 \143 c | 100 \144 d | 101 \145 e | 102 \146 f | 103 \147 g |
| 104 \150 h | 105 \151 i | 106 \152 j | 107 \153 k | 108 \154 l | 109 \155 m | 110 \156 n | 111 \157 o |
| 112 \160 p | 113 \161 q | 114 \162 r | 115 \163 s | 116 \164 t | 117 \165 u | 118 \166 v | 119 \167 w |
| 120 \170 x | 121 \171 y | 122 \172 z | 123 \173 braceleft | 124 \174 bar | 125 \175 braceright | 126 \176 asciitilde | |

# Times-Roman

| | | | | | | | | |
|---|---|---|---|---|---|---|---|---|
| 161 \241 exclamdown | 162 \242 cent | 163 \243 sterling | 164 \244 fraction | 165 \245 yen | 166 \246 florin | 167 \247 section | 168 \250 currency |
| 169 \251 quotesingle | 170 \252 quotedblleft | 171 \253 guillemotleft | 172 \254 guilsinglleft | 173 \255 guilsinglright | 174 \256 fi | 175 \257 fl | 177 \261 endash |
| 178 \262 dagger | 179 \263 daggerdbl | 180 \264 periodcentered | 182 \266 paragraph | 183 \267 bullet | 184 \270 quotesinglbase | 185 \271 quotedblbase | 186 \272 quotedblright |
| 187 \273 guillemotright | 188 \274 ellipsis | 189 \275 perthousand | 191 \277 questiondown | 193 \301 grave | 194 \302 acute | 195 \303 circumflex | 196 \304 tilde |
| 197 \305 macron | 198 \306 breve | 199 \307 dotaccent | 200 \310 dieresis | 202 \312 ring | 203 \313 cedilla | 205 \315 hungarumlaut | 206 \316 ogonek |
| 207 \317 caron | 208 \320 emdash | 225 \341 AE | 227 \343 ordfeminine | 232 \350 Lslash | 233 \351 Oslash | 234 \352 OE | 235 \353 ordmasculine |
| 241 \361 ae | 245 \365 dotlessi | 248 \370 lslash | 249 \371 oslash | 250 \372 oe | 251 \373 germandbls | | |

# Times-Roman

| | | | | | | | |
|---|---|---|---|---|---|---|---|
| Õ | Ÿ | õ | ó | š | ° | ÷ | ¬ |
| Otilde | Ydieresis | otilde | oacute | scaron | degree | divide | logicalnot |
| Ñ | ñ | ú | Ó | ï | ü | ² | Ü |
| Ntilde | ntilde | uacute | Oacute | idieresis | udieresis | twosuperior | Udieresis |
| í | þ | ž | ã | é | ¦ | × | Í |
| iacute | thorn | zcaron | atilde | eacute | brokenbar | multiply | Iacute |
| ¼ | Ç | å | Å | ç | Ä | è | Ã |
| onequarter | Ccedilla | aring | Aring | ccedilla | Adieresis | egrave | Atilde |
| ä | Ï | Ð | Û | µ | Ú | û | ð |
| adieresis | Idieresis | Eth | Ucircumflex | mu | Uacute | ucircumflex | eth |
| Ž | Ö | ô | Š | ± | Ô | ò | ™ |
| Zcaron | Odieresis | ocircumflex | Scaron | plusminus | Ocircumflex | ograve | trademark |
| ù | ³ | − | ö | Ù | Î | î | Ý |
| ugrave | threesuperior | minus | odieresis | Ugrave | Icircumflex | icircumflex | Yacute |
| ½ | ¹ | ý | © | Â | È | Ò | Ê |
| onehalf | onesuperior | yacute | copyright | Acircumflex | Egrave | Ograve | Ecircumflex |
| ê | â | É | Ì | Þ | Á | ¾ | À |
| ecircumflex | acircumflex | Eacute | Igrave | Thorn | Aacute | threequarters | Agrave |
| ì | ÿ | á | Ë | à | ® | ë | |
| igrave | ydieresis | aacute | Edieresis | agrave | registered | edieresis | |

# Zapf Dingbats Characters

The Zapf Dingbats typeface has 188 encoded characters and 14 unencoded characters, for a total of 202 characters.

# ZapfDingbats

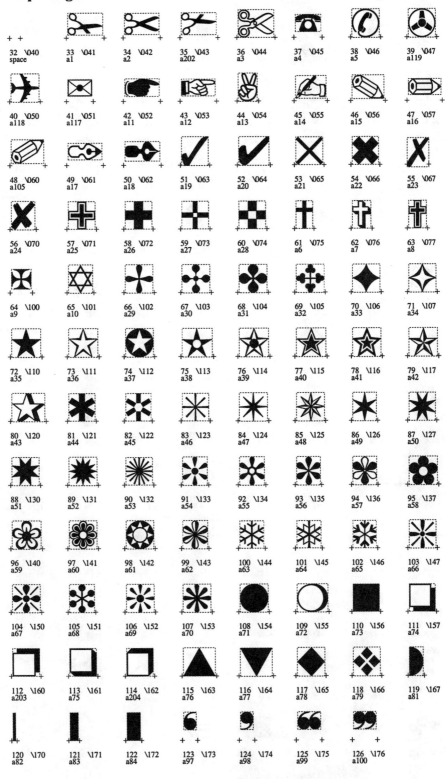

| | | | | | | | |
|---|---|---|---|---|---|---|---|
| ++ | 33 \041 | 34 \042 | 35 \043 | 36 \044 | 37 \045 | 38 \046 | 39 \047 |
| 32 \040 space | a1 | a2 | a202 | a3 | a4 | a5 | a119 |
| 40 \050 a118 | 41 \051 a117 | 42 \052 a11 | 43 \053 a12 | 44 \054 a13 | 45 \055 a14 | 46 \056 a15 | 47 \057 a16 |
| 48 \060 a105 | 49 \061 a17 | 50 \062 a18 | 51 \063 a19 | 52 \064 a20 | 53 \065 a21 | 54 \066 a22 | 55 \067 a23 |
| 56 \070 a24 | 57 \071 a25 | 58 \072 a26 | 59 \073 a27 | 60 \074 a28 | 61 \075 a6 | 62 \076 a7 | 63 \077 a8 |
| 64 \100 a9 | 65 \101 a10 | 66 \102 a29 | 67 \103 a30 | 68 \104 a31 | 69 \105 a32 | 70 \106 a33 | 71 \107 a34 |
| 72 \110 a35 | 73 \111 a36 | 74 \112 a37 | 75 \113 a38 | 76 \114 a39 | 77 \115 a40 | 78 \116 a41 | 79 \117 a42 |
| 80 \120 a43 | 81 \121 a44 | 82 \122 a45 | 83 \123 a46 | 84 \124 a47 | 85 \125 a48 | 86 \126 a49 | 87 \127 a50 |
| 88 \130 a51 | 89 \131 a52 | 90 \132 a53 | 91 \133 a54 | 92 \134 a55 | 93 \135 a56 | 94 \136 a57 | 95 \137 a58 |
| 96 \140 a59 | 97 \141 a60 | 98 \142 a61 | 99 \143 a62 | 100 \144 a63 | 101 \145 a64 | 102 \146 a65 | 103 \147 a66 |
| 104 \150 a67 | 105 \151 a68 | 106 \152 a69 | 107 \153 a70 | 108 \154 a71 | 109 \155 a72 | 110 \156 a73 | 111 \157 a74 |
| 112 \160 a203 | 113 \161 a75 | 114 \162 a204 | 115 \163 a76 | 116 \164 a77 | 117 \165 a78 | 118 \166 a79 | 119 \167 a81 |
| 120 \170 a82 | 121 \171 a83 | 122 \172 a84 | 123 \173 a97 | 124 \174 a98 | 125 \175 a99 | 126 \176 a100 | |

# ZapfDingbats

161 \241 a101  162 \242 a102  163 \243 a103  164 \244 a104  165 \245 a106  166 \246 a107  167 \247 a108  168 \250 a112

169 \251 a111  170 \252 a110  171 \253 a109  172 \254 a120  173 \255 a121  174 \256 a122  175 \257 a123  176 \260 a124

177 \261 a125  178 \262 a126  179 \263 a127  180 \264 a128  181 \265 a129  182 \266 a130  183 \267 a131  184 \270 a132

185 \271 a133  186 \272 a134  187 \273 a135  188 \274 a136  189 \275 a137  190 \276 a138  191 \277 a139  192 \300 a140

193 \301 a141  194 \302 a142  195 \303 a143  196 \304 a144  197 \305 a145  198 \306 a146  199 \307 a147  200 \310 a148

201 \311 a149  202 \312 a150  203 \313 a151  204 \314 a152  205 \315 a153  206 \316 a154  207 \317 a155  208 \320 a156

209 \321 a157  210 \322 a158  211 \323 a159  212 \324 a160  213 \325 a161  214 \326 a163  215 \327 a164  216 \330 a196

217 \331 a165  218 \332 a192  219 \333 a166  220 \334 a167  221 \335 a168  222 \336 a169  223 \337 a170  224 \340 a171

225 \341 a172  226 \342 a173  227 \343 a162  228 \344 a174  229 \345 a175  230 \346 a176  231 \347 a177  232 \350 a178

233 \351 a179  234 \352 a193  235 \353 a180  236 \354 a199  237 \355 a181  238 \356 a200  239 \357 a182  241 \361 a201

242 \362 a183  243 \363 a184  244 \364 a197  245 \365 a185  246 \366 a194  247 \367 a198  248 \370 a186  249 \371 a195

250 \372 a187  251 \373 a188  252 \374 a189  253 \375 a190  254 \376 a191

# ZapfDingbats

a91　　a96　　a85　　a92　　a205　　a95　　a93　　a86

a89　　a87　　a90　　a88　　a206　　a94

# Symbol Characters

There are 188 total encoded characters in this typeface, plus the Apple logo, which is unencoded and undocumented in the Red Book and Adobe printers.

# Symbol

| | | | | | | | |
|---|---|---|---|---|---|---|---|
| 32 \040 space | 33 \041 exclam | 34 \042 universal | 35 \043 numbersign | 36 \044 existential | 37 \045 percent | 38 \046 ampersand | 39 \047 suchthat |
| 40 \050 parenleft | 41 \051 parenright | 42 \052 asteriskmath | 43 \053 plus | 44 \054 comma | 45 \055 minus | 46 \056 period | 47 \057 slash |
| 48 \060 zero | 49 \061 one | 50 \062 two | 51 \063 three | 52 \064 four | 53 \065 five | 54 \066 six | 55 \067 seven |
| 56 \070 eight | 57 \071 nine | 58 \072 colon | 59 \073 semicolon | 60 \074 less | 61 \075 equal | 62 \076 greater | 63 \077 question |
| 64 \100 congruent | 65 \101 Alpha | 66 \102 Beta | 67 \103 Chi | 68 \104 Delta | 69 \105 Epsilon | 70 \106 Phi | 71 \107 Gamma |
| 72 \110 Eta | 73 \111 Iota | 74 \112 theta1 | 75 \113 Kappa | 76 \114 Lambda | 77 \115 Mu | 78 \116 Nu | 79 \117 Omicron |
| 80 \120 Pi | 81 \121 Theta | 82 \122 Rho | 83 \123 Sigma | 84 \124 Tau | 85 \125 Upsilon | 86 \126 sigma1 | 87 \127 Omega |
| 88 \130 Xi | 89 \131 Psi | 90 \132 Zeta | 91 \133 bracketleft | 92 \134 therefore | 93 \135 bracketright | 94 \136 perpendicular | 95 \137 underscore |
| 96 \140 radicalex | 97 \141 alpha | 98 \142 beta | 99 \143 chi | 100 \144 delta | 101 \145 epsilon | 102 \146 phi | 103 \147 gamma |
| 104 \150 eta | 105 \151 iota | 106 \152 phi1 | 107 \153 kappa | 108 \154 lambda | 109 \155 mu | 110 \156 nu | 111 \157 omicron |
| 112 \160 pi | 113 \161 theta | 114 \162 rho | 115 \163 sigma | 116 \164 tau | 117 \165 upsilon | 118 \166 omega1 | 119 \167 omega |
| 120 \170 xi | 121 \171 psi | 122 \172 zeta | 123 \173 braceleft | 124 \174 bar | 125 \175 braceright | 126 \176 similar | |

# Symbol

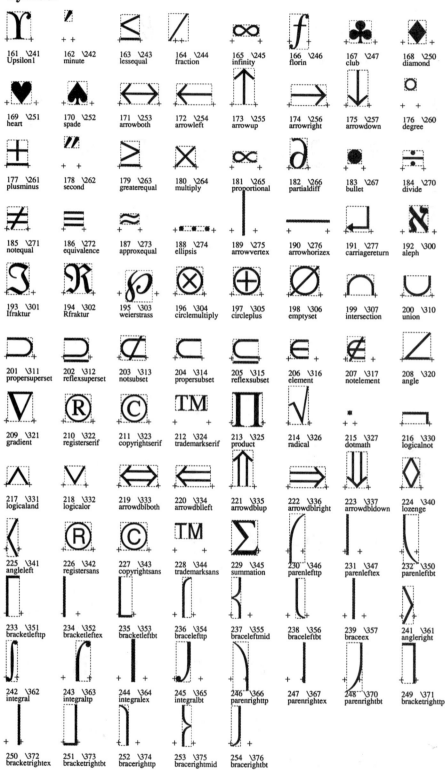

| | | | |
|---|---|---|---|
| 161 \241 Upsilon1 | 162 \242 minute | 163 \243 lessequal | 164 \244 fraction |
| 165 \245 infinity | 166 \246 florin | 167 \247 club | 168 \250 diamond |
| 169 \251 heart | 170 \252 spade | 171 \253 arrowboth | 172 \254 arrowleft |
| 173 \255 arrowup | 174 \256 arrowright | 175 \257 arrowdown | 176 \260 degree |
| 177 \261 plusminus | 178 \262 second | 179 \263 greaterequal | 180 \264 multiply |
| 181 \265 proportional | 182 \266 partialdiff | 183 \267 bullet | 184 \270 divide |
| 185 \271 notequal | 186 \272 equivalence | 187 \273 approxequal | 188 \274 ellipsis |
| 189 \275 arrowvertex | 190 \276 arrowhorizex | 191 \277 carriagereturn | 192 \300 aleph |
| 193 \301 Ifraktur | 194 \302 Rfraktur | 195 \303 weierstrass | 196 \304 circlemultiply |
| 197 \305 circleplus | 198 \306 emptyset | 199 \307 intersection | 200 \310 union |
| 201 \311 propersuperset | 202 \312 reflexsuperset | 203 \313 notsubset | 204 \314 propersubset |
| 205 \315 reflexsubset | 206 \316 element | 207 \317 notelement | 208 \320 angle |
| 209 \321 gradient | 210 \322 registerserif | 211 \323 copyrightserif | 212 \324 trademarkserif |
| 213 \325 product | 214 \326 radical | 215 \327 dotmath | 216 \330 logicalnot |
| 217 \331 logicaland | 218 \332 logicalor | 219 \333 arrowdblboth | 220 \334 arrowdblleft |
| 221 \335 arrowdblup | 222 \336 arrowdblright | 223 \337 arrowdbldown | 224 \340 lozenge |
| 225 \341 angleleft | 226 \342 registersans | 227 \343 copyrightsans | 228 \344 trademarksans |
| 229 \345 summation | 230 \346 parenlefttp | 231 \347 parenleftex | 232 \350 parenleftbt |
| 233 \351 bracketlefttp | 234 \352 bracketleftex | 235 \353 bracketleftbt | 236 \354 bracelefttp |
| 237 \355 braceleftmid | 238 \356 braceleftbt | 239 \357 braceex | 241 \361 angleright |
| 242 \362 integral | 243 \363 integraltp | 244 \364 integralex | 245 \365 integralbt |
| 246 \366 parenrighttp | 247 \367 parenrightex | 248 \370 parenrightbt | 249 \371 bracketrighttp |
| 250 \372 bracketrightex | 251 \373 bracketrightbt | 252 \374 bracerighttp | 253 \375 bracerightmid |
| 254 \376 bracerightbt | | | |

# Reencoding Unencoded Characters

This is an application of *RE* (ReEncode) that appears on page 116 of the Green book. We show how you can use this procedure to access some very useful un-encoded characters, reencoding them into the gap of 16 positions from decimal 209 through 224. However, you can reencode characters into any position.

The sample page description reencodes the Helvetica typeface, but any other internal typeface can be reencoded into the positions shown, except for Zapf Dingbats or Symbol. The same procedure could also be used with downloaded typefaces, but encoding positions would probably need to be changed.

The sample code on the next page produces the encoded characters on the page following. The two pages following show a portion of the Helvetica character set before and after reencoding. Compare characters 209 through 222 decimal.

# RE (ReEncode)

First, copy the *RE* procedure into the beginning of the page description below, where shown. Then add the name of the new reencoded font as "ReEncodedFont" by placing an "underline" character in front of any internal or downloaded typeface, shown as "ExistingFont." Then list up to 16 character names between the lines */stdencoding [209* and *]def* as we have here with 14 characters, each preceded by a slash "/." Finally, enter the same number of octal codes as reencoded characters in the strings at the bottom, beginning with octal 321. Make sure to use the exact names from the character sets on the preceding pages.

```
/RE {
    % ...
    % Include RE procedure from Green book, page 116
    % ...
} bind def

/ReEncodedFont /_Helvetica def  % Make new typeface from old typeface
/ExistingFont /Helvetica def        % Typeface being reencoded
/stdencoding [209
/trademark/copyright/registered/onequarter/onehalf
/threequarters/plusminus/divide/multiply/minus
/onesuperior/twosuperior/threesuperior/degree
] def

stdencoding ReEncodedFont ExistingFont RE

ReEncodedFont findfont 30 scalefont setfont
72 648 moveto
( \321 \322 \323 \324 \325 \326) show
72 504 moveto
( \327 \330 \331 \332 \333 \334 \335 \336) show

showpage
```

You can use this routine as a preamble to a program that requires special characters, or make the changes permanent using the *exitserver* routine discussed in appendix B.

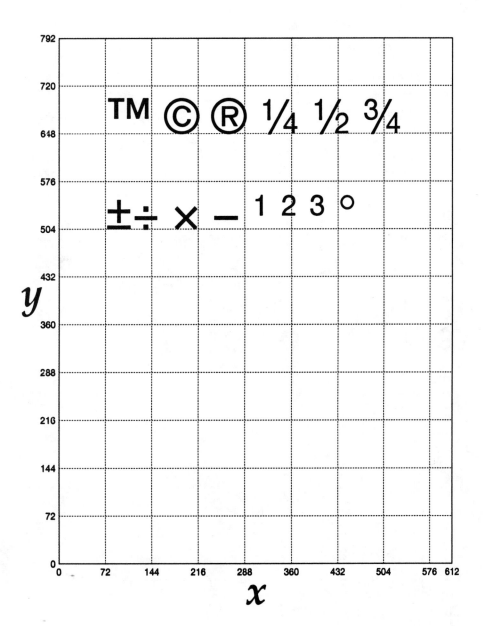

# Helvetica

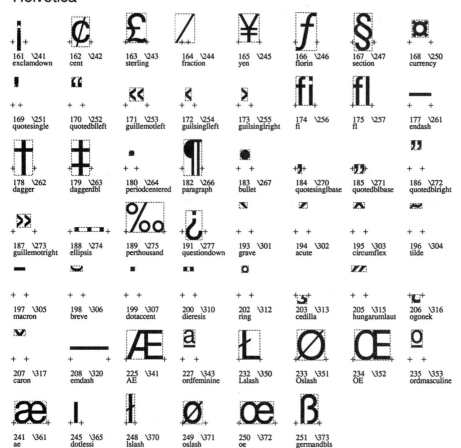

| | | | | | | | |
|---|---|---|---|---|---|---|---|
| 161 \241 exclamdown | 162 \242 cent | 163 \243 sterling | 164 \244 fraction | 165 \245 yen | 166 \246 florin | 167 \247 section | 168 \250 currency |
| 169 \251 quotesingle | 170 \252 quotedblleft | 171 \253 guillemotleft | 172 \254 guilsinglleft | 173 \255 guilsinglright | 174 \256 fi | 175 \257 fl | 177 \261 endash |
| 178 \262 dagger | 179 \263 daggerdbl | 180 \264 periodcentered | 182 \266 paragraph | 183 \267 bullet | 184 \270 quotesinglbase | 185 \271 quotedblbase | 186 \272 quotedblright |
| 187 \273 guillemotright | 188 \274 ellipsis | 189 \275 perthousand | 191 \277 questiondown | 193 \301 grave | 194 \302 acute | 195 \303 circumflex | 196 \304 tilde |
| 197 \305 macron | 198 \306 breve | 199 \307 dotaccent | 200 \310 dieresis | 202 \312 ring | 203 \313 cedilla | 205 \315 hungarumlaut | 206 \316 ogonek |
| 207 \317 caron | 208 \320 emdash | 225 \341 AE | 227 \343 ordfeminine | 232 \350 Lslash | 233 \351 Oslash | 234 \352 OE | 235 \353 ordmasculine |
| 241 \361 ae | 245 \365 dotlessi | 248 \370 lslash | 249 \371 oslash | 250 \372 oe | 251 \373 germandbls | | |

# _Helvetica

| | | | | | | | |
|---|---|---|---|---|---|---|---|
| 161 \241 exclamdown | 162 \242 cent | 163 \243 sterling | 164 \244 fraction | 165 \245 yen | 166 \246 florin | 167 \247 section | 168 \250 currency |
| 169 \251 quotesingle | 170 \252 quotedblleft | 171 \253 guillemotleft | 172 \254 guilsinglleft | 173 \255 guilsinglright | 174 \256 fi | 175 \257 fl | 177 \261 endash |
| 178 \262 dagger | 179 \263 daggerdbl | 180 \264 periodcentered | 182 \266 paragraph | 183 \267 bullet | 184 \270 quotesinglbase | 185 \271 quotedblbase | 186 \272 quotedblright |
| 187 \273 guillemotright | 188 \274 ellipsis | 189 \275 perthousand | 191 \277 questiondown | 193 \301 grave | 194 \302 acute | 195 \303 circumflex | 196 \304 tilde |
| 197 \305 macron | 198 \306 breve | 199 \307 dotaccent | 200 \310 dieresis | 202 \312 ring | 203 \313 cedilla | 205 \315 hungarumlaut | 206 \316 ogonek |
| 207 \317 caron | 208 \320 emdash | 209 \321 trademark | 210 \322 copyright | 211 \323 registered | 212 \324 onequarter | 213 \325 onehalf | 214 \326 threequarters |
| 215 \327 plusminus | 216 \330 divide | 217 \331 multiply | 218 \332 minus | 219 \333 onesuperior | 220 \334 twosuperior | 221 \335 threesuperior | 222 \336 degree |
| 225 \341 AE | 227 \343 ordfeminine | 232 \350 Lslash | 233 \351 Oslash | 234 \352 OE | 235 \353 ordmasculine | 241 \361 ae | 245 \365 dotlessi |
| 248 \370 lslash | 249 \371 oslash | 250 \372 oe | 251 \373 germandbls | | | | |

# Adding Typefaces

Additional PostScript typeface outlines are available from Adobe, Bitstream, and other vendors. Previously, Adobe typefaces could only be used with PostScript interpreters from Adobe Systems, but other interepreters are currently using Adobe typefaces, and most if not all will handle them by the end of 1990. PostScript typeface outlines from other vendors are compatible with most PostScript interpreters, including Adobe-based devices.

The ability to download typefaces depends upon the memory available on the PostScript printer or interpreter you are using. PostScript typeface outlines generally require from 40K to 70K each.

Most PostScript software interpreters and some PostScript controller/interpreters can access additional typefaces directly from disk using the PostScript *run* operator, and therefore do not require downloading. Downloading typefaces and accessing typeface from disk with *run* are discussed in appendix B.

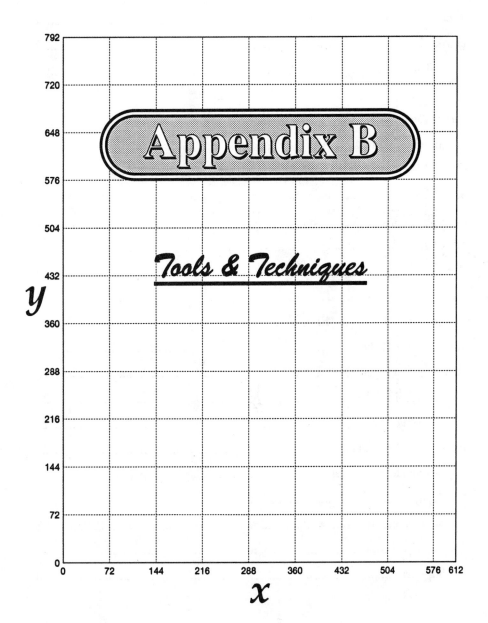

# Appendix B

*Tools & Techniques*

# Appendix B

# Tools and Techniques

We have written a number of useful routines that could best be characterized as tools or utilities. They do everything from downloading fonts to printing envelopes to letting us import our encoded PostScript into page composition programs.

A PostScript printer cannot, for instance, handle the simple task of "typing" a straight ASCII text file without being told what it is receiving, what typeface to use, and where to place it on the page. Here we show you a small PostScript program (PSTYPE.PS) that solves the problem. That's just one example.

Many of these utilities take advantage of MS-DOS "batch" files (text files with the extension .BAT that contain one or more DOS commands for batch execution) combined with PostScript code. We use these batch files to automate everything we send to the interpreter—PostScript files, parameters, instructions, typefaces, and the visual page grids used throughout this book.

Like PostScript operators, our batch files use operands (actually they're called "command line parameters"). The batch files pass the command line parameters to PostScript programs, which define the parameters as variables for use in the program.

The PostScript programs discussed here don't require that you use DOS. You can send them from any computer to any PostScript interpreter, and they'll work. On page B-6, we show you how to modify the programs so they'll work without batch files.

# Harnessing PostScript's Power

In this section, we will show how you can use batch files to send encoded PostScript files and other information to the PostScript interpreter; how to access additional typeface outlines by downloading them or accessing them from a hard disk; how to add your own procedures to a PostScript dictionary; how to "encapsulate" an encoded PostScript file so it can be imported directly into page composition software; and how to convert encapsulated PostScript files back into encoded PostScript files that you can embellish and send directly to your printer.

And finally, we'll introduce you to some environments that allow you to display PostScript output on your monitor. An interactive on-screen environment will assist you in learning the language, writing PostScript programs, or creating PostScript screen presentations.

# DOS Batch Files

In the PC environment, encoded PostScript files are normally sent to the printer attached to any parallel (lpt*n:*) or serial (com*n:*) port using the DOS *copy* command: *copy filename.ps lpt2:*.

This can be partially automated with a simple DOS batch file. Using batch files for transmitting PostScript files saves the trouble of entering the .ps file extension and the printer port each time you send a file to the printer.

SEND.BAT sends to the printer any encoded PostScript file with the extension .ps as specified in the command *send filename* (where *filename* is the name of the file you want to send).

```
echo off
rem SEND.BAT - Send PostScript file to printer
rem SYNTAX: SEND filename
echo Sending %1.ps using %PS% . . .
copy %1.ps %PS%
```

Note that in batch files, you use *rem* to denote remarks in the same way that you use a % sign to denote comments in PostScript code. A % sign in a batch file denotes a "replaceable parameter."

This batch file, for instance, replaces *%1* with whatever you enter on the command line for *filename*. If you type *send mandala* at the command line, the batch file will replace %1 with *mandala*. The result will be *copy mandala.ps %PS%*.

*%PS%* is an environmental variable designating any port with a PostScript printer attached. We define it beforehand with the DOS *set* command (e.g., *set ps=lpt2:*). The advantage of using an environmental variable is that you don't have to change the batch file if the port address of the PostScript printer is changed, or if more than one PostScript printer is on the system. You can also use *set* to send the output to a file, for transporting to another system (e.g. *set ps=filename.ps*).

SCALE.BAT centers and scales to half-size any PostScript file specified on the command line with *scale filename*.

```
echo off
rem SCALE.BAT - Print a 4.25 by 5.5 inch PostScript file
rem SYNTAX: SCALE filename
echo Reducing and printing %1.ps using %PS% . . .
echo 153 198 translate .5 .5 scale > %PS%
copy %1.ps %PS%
```

# echo >

The DOS *echo >* command used in the preceding example sends PostScript *translate* and *scale* instructions directly to the PostScript interpreter prior to sending the file specified on the command line. This causes the ensuing file to be scaled to one-half its normal size and centered on an 8.5-by-11-inch page.

COPIES.BAT prints *n* (number of) copies of any PostScript file specified in the command *copies filename n.*

```
echo off
rem COPIES.BAT - Print n copies of PostScript file
rem SYNTAX: COPIES filename n
echo Printing %2 copies of %1.ps using %PS% . . .
if //==/%2/ goto nocopies
echo /#copies %2 def > %PS%
:nocopies
copy %1.ps %PS%
```

We can also use the *echo >* command to send a PostScript instruction (e.g., */#copies n def*) that includes a variable inserted by the batch file, from information entered as the second parameter on the command line (*%2*). Batch files can also logically determine that if no value for *n* is entered (as the second parameter on the command line), the instruction is not sent. In this case, the PostScript interpreter would default to printing only one copy of the filename specified.

GRID.BAT is similar to SCALE.BAT, above; it also scales and centers a file specified on the command line. But GRID.BAT is used in conjunction with the PostScript program GRID.PS to created the visual page grids used throughout this book.

```
echo off
rem GRID.BAT - Reduce & Grid PostScript file
rem SYNTAX: GRID filename
echo Gridding %1.ps using %PS% . . .
echo (%1.ps) 8.5 11 0 > P:\params.ps
copy P:\params.ps+P:\grid.ps+%1.ps %PS%
```

# Visual Page Grid

In the previous sample, instead of sending PostScript *translate* and *scale* instructions directly to the interpreter, we sent four variables to an interim file, PARAMS.PS, which is then appended to a group of three files sent to the printer as one single file: *params.ps+grid.ps+%1.ps*. Note that *p:\* is any subdirectory on the path, (e.g., c:\ps); or it can be a virtual disk created with the DOS *subst* (for "substitute") command (e.g., *subst p: c:\ps* together with *lastdrive=z* in CONFIG.SYS).

The variables sent to PARAMS.PS are as follows.

1. A string with *filename.ps* (supplied by the batch file) enclosed in parentheses

2. The width of the page

3. The height of the page

4. A center flag that specifies the origin of the coordinate system (0 is normal lower-left corner; 1 is the center of the page)

GRID.PS can create a grid for any size page: 8.5-by-11-inch letter, 8.5-by-14-inch legal, 11-by-17-inch tabloid, etc., where the page width and height are expressed in inches (the first line of GRID.PS can be modified to accept metric dimensions). The grid is drawn in the normal portrait orientation, but can be changed to landscape by simply reversing the order of X and Y in the batch file. For example, the next to last line of LGRIDL.BAT, for producing an 8.5-by-14-inch legal size grid in landscape orientation, would read as follows.

echo (%1.ps) 14 8.5 0 > P:\params.ps

The batch file TGRIDC.BAT would produce an 11-by-17-inch tabloid size grid in portrait orientation, with a center origin.

echo (%1.ps) 11 17 1 > P:\params.ps

# Gridding without Batch Files

The tabloid grid on the next page was created with TGRIDC.BAT, shown on the preceding page. It is the same grid that appears on the cover of this book. It has been scaled an additional 75 percent of its half-scale size to fit in this book, but at normal half scale it fits nicely on an 8.5-by-11-inch page. Being able to grid files intended for output devices with larger page sizes, such as color printers and high-resolution imagesetters, is the only way you can see what they will look like before sending them to such a device.

There is an obvious advantage to using a number of different simple DOS batch files in conjunction with a single PostScript file for creating different formats based in parameters supplied by each batch file. However, the PostScript file that creates the grid, GRID.PS, shown on page 8-10, can be modified to create any grid without using batch files, by simply modifying the four lines that define the variables.

For instance, the fifth line that reads */x exch in cvi def* can be modified to read */x 8.5 in def*, for an 8.5-inch page in portrait mode. Each of the four parameter definitions should be similarly modified, by substituting for the *exch* operator the value of the parameter as shown in the batch file. And don't forget to put parentheses around the program name, and to give a distinctive name to each PostScript program created in this manner.

Variations of GRID.PS thus created can be sent to the printer with SEND.BAT.

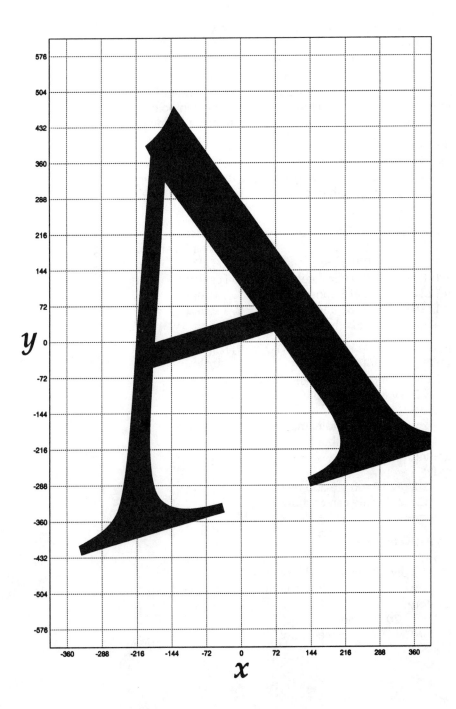

**B-7**

# GRID.PS

```
(Copyright 1990 Smith Consulting Group) /CR exch def
/in {72 mul} def
% The following 4 parameters are passed from the batch file
/c exch def           % Page origin 0=lower-left 1=center
/y exch in cvi def     % Vertical page length in points
/x exch in cvi def     % Horizontal page length in points
/name exch def         % Name of program being gridded

/font {findfont exch scalefont setfont} def
/box {1 index 0 rlineto 0 exch rlineto neg 0 rlineto closepath} def
/center {dup stringwidth pop 2 div neg 0 rmoveto} def
/right {dup stringwidth pop neg 0 rmoveto} def
/s 4 string def

x y gt {612 0 translate 90 rotate} if      % Landscape
x 4 div y 4 div translate                  % Center letter grid on page
y 1008 eq {0 -100 translate} if            % Legal
x 1008 eq {-100 0 translate} if            % Legal
y 1224 eq {-85 -216 translate} if          % Tabloid
x 1224 eq {-216 -85 translate} if          % Tabloid
.5 .5 scale % 1/2 inch scale

gsave                                      % Start with titles
60 /Palatino-BoldItalic font
x 2 div -60 moveto (x) center show
-25 y 2 div 8 sub moveto (y) right show
gsave
    x y 40 add moveto name
    .3 .3 scale right show
grestore
gsave
    x 2 div 10 sub y 6 add moveto
    CR .2 .2 scale center show
grestore

14 /Helvetica font
gsave
    x 2 div 10 sub y 40 add moveto
    2 2 scale (VISUAL PAGE GRID) center show
grestore
x 2 div y 20 add moveto
(1/2 INCH SCALE) center show
```

```
c 0 eq {                              % if center grid:
    /ox 0 def /oy 0 def
}
{                                     % integer div for center origin
    /ox x 2 div 72 idiv 72 mul def
    /oy y 2 div 72 idiv 72 mul def
    x 2 div y 2 div translate
} ifelse

[2] 0 setdash                         % Grid lines
.24 setlinewidth
0 72 y {                              % Grid line loop for y
    /i exch oy sub def
    0 i moveto
    c 0 ne {i oy gt {exit} if
        x 2 div neg 0 rmoveto} if
    gsave x 0 rlineto stroke grestore
    -5 -7 rmoveto
    i s cvs right show
} for

0 72 x {                              % Grid line loop for x
    /i exch ox sub def
    i 0 moveto
    c 0 ne {i ox gt {exit} if
        0 y 2 div neg rmoveto} if
    gsave 0 y rlineto stroke grestore
    0 -17 rmoveto
    i s cvs center show
} for

% show 612 only for normal grid
c 0 eq x 72 mod 0 ne and
    {x -17 moveto
    x s cvs center show} if
grestore                              % grid is done

0 0 moveto x y box clip               % clip the grid
stroke                                % and draw the box around the grid
x y gt {-90 rotate -612 0 translate} if   % landscape

% end
```

# Server Loop

A server loop is the name of the process by which any PostScript interpreter receives and renders encoded PostScript files on a raster imaging device. A *save* is executed automatically at the beginning of each file, and a *restore* is executed at the end. This *save/restore* process returns the interpreter to the state that existed before each job.

Each new job begins as soon as the interpreter begins receiving a file. The end-of-job is not determined by a *showpage* instruction, because a single PostScript file can contain many pages. Instead, it is determined by the occurrence of either the elapse of 30 seconds (a modifiable default timeout parameter) or the receipt of a PostScript end-of-file character—a "Control-D" (ASCII decimal 04). You can send a Control-D end-of-file character at either the beginning or end of each file, or not at all.

We normally send a Control-D at the end of each file, by simply creating a separate file named CTRL_D.PS. The file consists of an ASCII 04 character only, with no carriage return. We place the file in the same subdirectory on the path that contains our batch files, and append it to the file being sent to the printer by any batch file, using the same technique we used for sending multiple files in GRID.BAT. If the Control-D character appears at the end of any print job sent to the printer, it identifies the end-of-file, causing the interpreter to exit from what would otherwise be an infinite loop. The example on the next page shows how this is done.

# PSTYPE

You cannot simply "type" an ASCII file to a PostScript printer as you can other DOS printers, because the PostScript interpreter recognizes only PostScript instructions. But you can get the same results with the program below, which is invaluable for printing the ASCII representation of your encoded PostScript files.

```
% PSTYPE.PS prints text file specified by PSTYPE.BAT
/printloop {
        {    currentfile cvlit              % Read line from file
             =string readline               % Put line in string
             not {exit} if                  % Exit on ending Ctrl-D
             show                           % Or show line

             currentpoint exch pop          % Get y coordinate
             10.5 sub dup 36 le             % Test new y coordinate
                 {pop showpage 72 730 moveto}   % Newpage
                 {72 exch moveto}           % Or newline
             ifelse
        } loop
        showpage
} bind def
/Courier findfont 10 scalefont setfont
72 730 moveto
printloop
```

PSTYPE.PS is used in conjunctions with PSTYPE.BAT, which identifies the file to be typed, and also appends the required CTRL_D.PS file to the end of the sequence.

```
echo off
rem PSTYPE.BAT - Type an ASCII text file on any
rem PostScript device using PSTYPE.PS
rem SYNTAX: PSTYPE filename.ext
echo Typing %1 using %PS% . . .
copy P:\PSTYPE.PS+%1+P:\CTRL_D.PS %PS%
```

Note how we use the complete DOS filename with extension, so we can type any text file, not just those with the extension ".ps."

For a discussion of =string, see the White book, page 7-7.

# exitserver

At the end of chapter 7, we showed how to modify the PostScript *showpage* operator, using the instruction *serverdict begin password exitserver*, where *password* is either "0" or any password established beforehand.

This instruction escapes from the normal server loop *save/restore* context, for making "permanent" changes to the PostScript interpreter that will endure until the interpreter is reinitialized (or the printer is turned off and on).

Here, we show how to permanently download any PostScript typeface, using PSDL.BAT. Please note that PSDL.BAT assumes that the typeface outlines to be downloaded are located in the subdirectory c:\psfonts, and that we send a Control-D both before and after the typefaces, just to be sure that we are not impacting any other print jobs.

```
echo off
rem PSDL.BAT 9/29/89 rrs
rem SYNTAX: PSDL typeface1, typeface2, ... typefacen
copy P:\ctrl_d.ps %PS%
:loop
if //==/%1/ goto exit
echo Downloading %1...
echo serverdict begin 0 exitserver > %PS%
copy c:\psfonts\%1 %PS%
shift
goto loop
:exit
copy P:\ctrl_d.ps %PS%
```

We use another batch file to send a large number of predetermined typefaces to PSDL.BAT. To send the whole Galliard family, for instance, we use a file named GALLIARD.BAT, which contains one instruction line—*psdl cupq.pfa cvpq.pfa cwpq.pfa cxpq.pfa.*

# *run*

It is not necessary to download typefaces for use with PostScript interpreters that can access typefaces directly from a hard disk. This includes all software interpreters, most high-resolution imagesetters, some printers that have a hard disk attached, and at least one controller of which we are aware. (If in doubt, refer to your user manual.)

If you are using such an interpreter, you can access typefaces from a hard disk by using the PostScript *run* operator with each typeface used in your program, and including it at the beginning of the program.

Assuming you will be using four typefaces from the ITC-Galliard family, identified as CU-, CV-, CX-, and CXPQ.PFA, located in the disk subdirectory c:\psfonts, the appropriate instructions for accessing these typeface outlines would be as follows.

```
(c:\\psfonts\\cupq.pfa) run
(c:\\psfonts\\cvpq.pfa) run
(c:\\psfonts\\cwpq.pfa) run
(c:\\psfonts\\cxpq.pfa) run
```

It is not necessary to use lowercase characters to identify the disk, subdirectory, and typeface names, but the DOS backslash must be entered twice for the interpreter to recognize a single backslash, in accordance with the PostScript convention (see pages 2-26 and A-12).

If you will be running the same program on another system, such as a high-resolution imagesetter at a service bureau, you must ascertain whether the desired typefaces are available, and stored in the same subdirectory as indicated in the *run* instruction. You may have to transport the typeface outlines to the other system, but be certain you will not violate any licensing agreements by doing so.

# Preambles

There are three ways to access procedures that will be used many times in your encoded PostScript programs. You can keep them in a separate file (you might call it PREAMBLE.PS), and use one of the following techniques.

1. Begin each new program with that preamble included on the first several lines.

2. Send the preamble file to the printer on a separate line in SEND.BAT.

3. Exit the server loop and permanently download the procedures followed by a Control-D, in the same way that you download fonts.

If you use either of the first two approaches, be certain that *showpage* is not included in the preamble file. If you use the third approach, add the line *serverdict begin 0 exitserver* before your procedures, as we have done before the procedures */font, /box,* and */center* in this example.

```
serverdict begin 0 exitserver
/font {findfont exch scalefont setfont} bind def
/box {1 index 0 rlineto 0 exch rlineto neg 0 rlineto closepath} bind def
/center {dup stringwidth pop 2 div neg 0 rmoveto} bind def
```

Note that if you choose method two or three above, you will have to transport your PREAMBLE.PS file with any PostScript files you will be printing on another system.

# Encapsulated PostScript (EPS) Files

If you want to import your encoded PostScript files into page composition programs, you need to "encapsulate" the PostScript program by adding comments that tell the page composition program how to handle the file.

The Encapsulated PostScript file format (EPS or EPSF) lets page composition software accept a PostScript file, scale it to any size, position it anywhere on the page, and pass it directly to the PostScript interpreter, which executes the drawing.

EPS files are encoded PostScript files that conform to the *Encapsulated PostScript File Format,* EPSF Version 1.2, published by Adobe Systems. Converting an encoded PostScript file to this format can be as simple as adding two brief instruction lines at the beginning of your file. On the next page we show you the minimum requirements for encapsulation.

It is important to distinguish between two types of EPS files—those that are simply encoded PostScript files that have some comments added to allow them to be imported into page composition software, and displayable EPS files that provide a displayable bitmap, added to the PostScript code by another application (usually graphic drawing software).

You cannot send displayable EPS files directly to a PostScript printer, because the PostScript interpreter does not recognize non-PostScript code (the displayable bitmap). You should also be aware that EPS files created from encoded PostScript files (described on the next page) are not in the same format as the EPS files that can be imported directly into graphic drawing software.

# Creating an EPS File

There are only two simple statements that need to be added to any encoded PostScript file to meet the minimum requirements for creating an EPS file that can be imported into page composition software. These two lines must be reproduced exactly as shown below except for the four bounding box coordinates on the second line, which describe the boundaries of a rectangle enclosing the drawing you are encapsulating.

```
%!PS-Adobe-2.0  EPSF-1.2
%%BoundingBox:  0  0  612  792
```

The first line identifies the file as an EPS file, and the second line describes a rectangle that encloses the drawing, according to the PostScript coordinate system. The numbers are replaceable values that represent the lower-left x and y, *llx* and *lly*, and upper-right x and y, *urx* and *ury*, respectively. The bounding box line above describes a full 612-by-792-point (8.5-by-11-inch) image.

The example below describes a bounding box that encloses the logo on the next page, to the nearest one-quarter inch (which makes it easy to describe the frame for importing the drawing). Note that the difference between *urx* and *llx*, and *ury* and *lly*, is the same: 324 points, or 4.5 inches.

```
%!PS-Adobe-2.0  EPSF-1.2

%%BoundingBox:  144  234  468  558
%LOGO.EPS Sample EPS File
```

You will find the visual page grid useful for visually determining the coordinates you use for the bounding box. Be sure to use a portrait grid with an origin in the lower-left corner, as bounding box coordinates are always described with respect to the default page origin, regardless of any subsequent transformations you might perform.

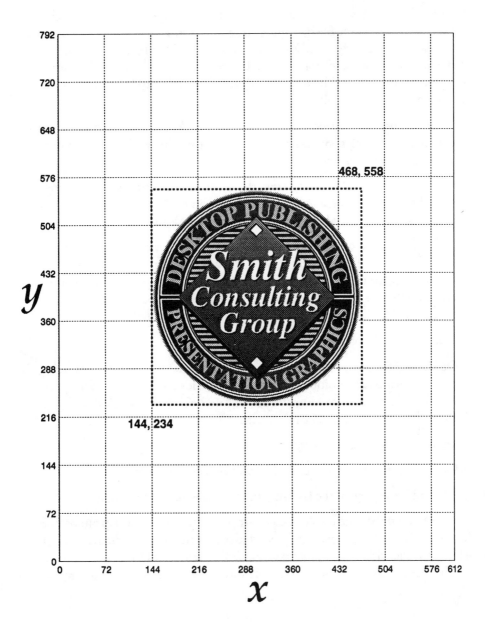

**468, 558**

**144, 234**

# Stripping Displayable EPS Files

You can also edit displayable EPS files created by graphic drawing or other software, and modify the file by adding PostScript instructions as you would any other encoded PostScript file. However, certain displayable information, if it exists, must be eliminated from the file before it can be sent to any PostScript interpreter for printing. The steps for editing displayable EPS files created for IBM-compatibles are as follows.

1. Copy *filename.eps* to *filename.ps* and modify the *filename.ps* file. This protects the original and helps you distinguish between the displayable (.eps) and non-displayable (.ps) versions.

2. Delete the first 30 bytes, if any, from the header on the first line, immediately preceding *%!PS-Adobe-2.0 EPSF-1.2* which should be left intact. (This 30-byte header is generated by the application that adds the bitmap.)

3. Delete the entire displayable bitmap at the end of the file, following the PostScript code. This is fairly easy to recognize by the abundance of "^@" (ASCII 0) characters, and may be preceded by the words *end* or *%Trailer.* If you are in doubt, the Adobe specification explains how to locate the elements of the EPS file from information contained in the 30-byte header.

Then add the following information.

1. On the first line, translate the negative of *llx, lly,* as it appears in the bounding box information, to position the drawing in the lower-left corner of the page. For example, for the *BoundingBox: 55 -614 482 -63* on the sample drawing on the next page, we used *-55 614 translate.*

2. On the next line enter *save mark.*

3. On the first line below the EPS file, enter *cleartomark restore.*

4. Then add *showpage* on the last line, and send the file to the printer.

Note that on the Macintosh, you can strip the displayable bitmap out of EPS files by changing the file "type" to TEXT with a program like ResEdit or DiskTop, editing the file with a word processor, and saving it as Text Only.

The panda illustration in this example was created with Adobe Illustrator.

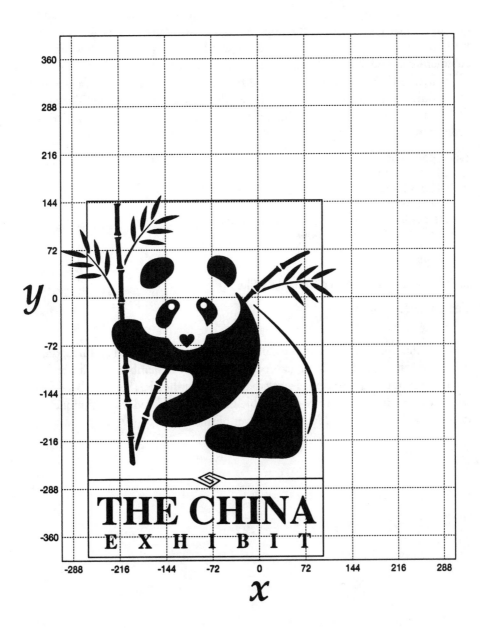

THE CHINA
E X H I B I T

# Modifying EPS Files

If the file prints successfully, you can now reposition or scale the drawing, or add any additional PostScript instructions necessary to modify the page. For the previous sample file, we first computed the width and height of the drawing by subtracting *llx* and *lly* from *urx* and *ury*, respectively. Then we translated half the difference between this and the page width and height, to center the drawing in the middle of the page. Next, we added the title you see in the example. The new file now includes the following additional information, surrounding the PostScript code from the original EPS file.

```
%newpanda.ps
-55 614 translate          % To lower-left corner
97.5 120.5 translate       % To center drawing
36 720 moveto
/Times-BoldItalic findfont 72 scalefont setfont
(Encapsulated PostScript:) show

save mark

% PostScript section from original EPS file

cleartomark restore
showpage
```

When this prints successfully, the file can then be re-encapsulated for importing into page composition software (see page B-16). But remember, it will not be displayable, since you've stripped away that portion of the file. (See page B-24 for an explanation of how to create displayable EPS files.) We used this technique to include the Peachpit Press logo on the cover of this book.

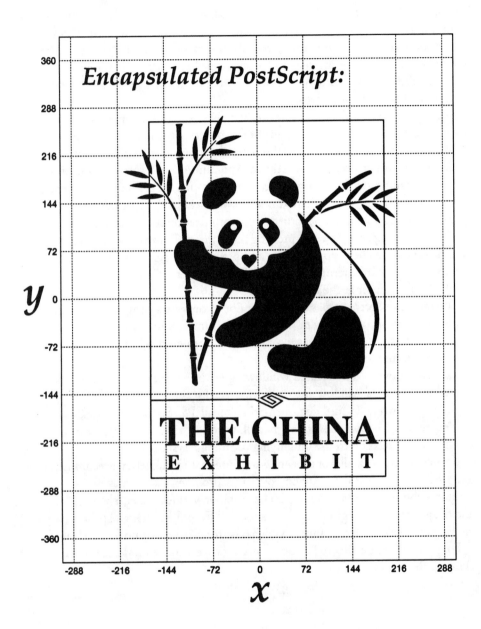

# Interactive PostScript

You can talk directly to a PostScript printer by using the "executive," or interactive, mode of the PostScript interpreter. There are many advantages to learning PostScript interactively, including the ability to interrogate the PostScript interpreter to determine the status of stacks and dictionaries. If you anticipate doing a substantial amount of PostScript programming, using an interactive environment is almost mandatory.

But be warned if you're using a networked printer in interactive mode. When you're working in interactive mode, no one else on the network can use the printer.

You'll need two-way communication with the interpreter to use the executive mode, either through a serial connection and communication software, a software interpreter running on your computer, a program like LaserTalk from Emerald City Software, or any other method that lets you see the interpreter's responses.

If you're using a serial connection and communication software, make sure it's working by typing *showpage* and pressing the Enter or Return key. A blank page should come out. Then type *executive* and press Enter again. You'll see the PS> prompt, and can start entering instructions. The interpreter digests each instruction when you press Enter at the end of a line.

Emerald City Software was the first vendor to provide a complete interactive PostScript learning environment with Lasertalk for the Macintosh and Lasertalk PC. This is an ideal environment for communicating interactively with a PostScript printer connected to a serial interface.

Lasertalk provides a structured windowing environment with a full-function text editor, a status window for displaying stacks and variables, a PostScript dictionary browser, on-line documentation of all PostScript operators, and a preview feature that includes rulers that allow you to view your PostScript page descriptions in relation to the underlying coordinate system.

If you must use a parallel or other one-way interface exclusively, we recommend using ERHANDLR.PS, an Adobe PostScript program that comes with many desktop publishing applications or can be found on various bulletin boards. Send it to the printer at the beginning of a session, and from then on it will print a page showing the first error it encounters, which is better than getting no feedback at all.

For more on connecting to PostScript printers in executive mode, see appendix D of the Red book.

# Interactive Operators

There are two PostScript instructions that are particularly useful in an interactive programming environment—*pstack* and *forall.*

You can use *pstack* at any time to determine the condition of the stack. It displays on the screen every object on the stack, without changing the contents of the stack. This is useful not only for testing and debugging new procedures, but also for learning what specific PostScript operators do. For example, use *pstack* to see what the PostScript interpreter leaves on the stack after a *curveto* operation. Or use it to examine how to use the *roll* operator.

You can also use the PostScript == operator together with *forall* to examine the contents of various PostScript dictionaries, such as *systemdict, userdict, statusdict,* or *FontDirectory* (see the White book, appendices I and II for more information).

*userdict {exch == ==} forall* returns all keys and values

*userdict {== pop } forall* returns values (or procedures) only

*userdict {pop ==} forall* returns keys (names) only

The *forall* operator takes each entry in the specified dictionary and places it on the stack, then == pops it off and displays it on the screen. The first instruction above displays keys (procedure or variable names) and values (or procedures). The other two instructions display one or the other.

An example of the last instruction is shown on page B-26. The same sequence used with *systemdict* would show a list of all the PostScript operators available in the PostScript interpreter you are using.

# Interactive Host Facilities

Most, but not all, computer-resident PostScript controllers and software inter-preters provide an interactive mode that functions like the executive mode of a PostScript printer (consult your user's manual for more information). Communicating directly with a host-resident PostScript interpreter has the advantage of not having to use a serial interface, which makes these interpreters very easy to use. Software interpreters that provide this interactive facility are an inexpensive, hassle-free way to communicate directly with a PostScript interpreter.

The EiconScript controller from Eicon Technology can read from and write to the host computer's hard disk. Eicon offers a separate utility called EiconView, that is used in conjunction with the EiconScript controller, to provide a complete programming/learning environment under Microsoft Windows, similar to that provided by Lasertalk PC. EiconView captures bit-mapped images of PostScript files interpreted by EiconScript for interactive editing. It also includes a facility for creating displayable EPS files from encoded PostScript files, by appending the bitmap to the file.

The illustration on the next page is an EiconView screen showing a bitmap of the logo we designed and encoded in PostScript, captured and displayed by EiconView. Using EiconView, we were able to convert this encoded PostScript file to a displayable EPS file. This facility adds a significant new dimension to the art of PostScript programming, and greatly enhances the functionality of encoded PostScript files.

Another important step in this direction is provided by a utility called Decipher, that is included with the latest version of the Arts & Letters Graphics Editor from Computer Support Corporation. Decipher will read an encoded PostScript file and convert it to a format that can be imported into their graphic drawing software, where the file can be modified interactively, if desired, and exported as a displayable EPS file.

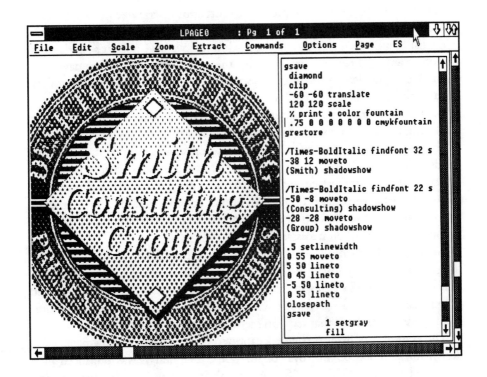

# Displaying PostScript

Because PostScript software interpreters run in system memory, they have the advantage of being able to directly access system resources, such as the hard disk and visual display. We are just now beginning to see interpreters like PreScript from Pan Overseas Corporation and PSView from ImageSoft that are using these capabilities to display PostScript on the system monitor. And Adobe's own Display PostScript has been introduced on IBM, NeXT, and DEC platforms.

LaserGo, the first vendor to provide a PostScript interpreter in software, has just released a version of GoScript that adds support for EGA and VGA monitors to the list of printers it already supports. Although we have not yet seen the final version of any of these new products, for the past several months we have been evaluating a prerelease version of GoScript 3.0, and will discuss some of the features and uses for displaying PostScript on the screen.

Because PostScript software interpreters are relatively inexpensive, and because displaying PostScript files on a monitor eliminates the need for paper and toner or ribbons, this is a very cost-effective interactive learning environment, particularly for displaying PostScript output in color. Because monitors are low-resolution devices, they are very fast compared to most printers. Although monitors lack some of the detail you can get from a laser printer, screen resolutions are improving, and you always have the option of sending the file to any number of different supported printers when necessary.

GoScript 3.0 provides a versatile environment that allows you to display only the graphic representation of the PostScript file, or the text and graphics together. One big advantage of writing to the screen is that each operation can be displayed as soon as it is painted—without having to wait for a *showpage*—so you get immediate visual feedback that lets you see when problems arise.

The example on the next page is a captured GoScript screen showing an early design for a section of the cover of the book. The design was produced by a combined program (GRID-A.PS, not shown). It was run from inside GoScript, together with the results obtained from *userdict {pop ==} forall*, which was also entered interactively. Although you can't tell from looking, the underlying grid was drawn in red, to contrast with the black lettering created by the procedure that draws the letter A.

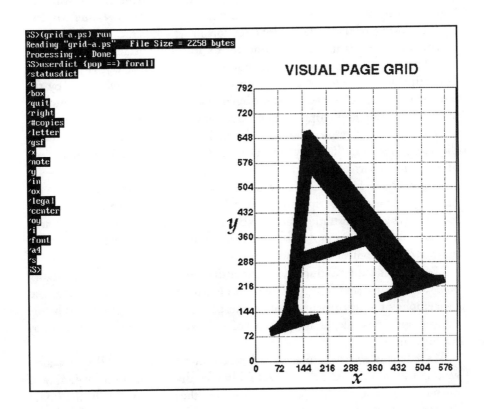

# PostScript Presentations

In the previous example, you will note that the drawing was done on the right side of the screen, while the accompanying text appears on the left. GoScript 3.0 provides the flexibility to use all or any part of the screen for the drawing. For full screen drawing, text can be suppressed by entering the program with the command *gs > nul,* which sends the text to a nul device. Or, the command *gs > log* will send the text to a log file. We used this technique with *systemdict {pop ==} forall* to obtain a printed listing of all the PostScript operators in systemdict.

The split screen is an ideal environment for learning PostScript interactively, because it permits a dialog with the interpreter. The full screen is perfect for PostScript presentations, where a script of PostScript programs is run by the interpreter. These techniques could also be combined in a presentation for teaching any subject, using PostScript to draw the screens. This book, for example, could be adapted to a screen presentation quite easily, and benefit readers by allowing them to interact with the interpreter. The possibilities for PostScript presentations of this kind are virtually unlimited.

To give you an idea of how to create a PostScript presentation, we show on the next page a typical PostScript script, which is a continuous presentation designed to be used as a demonstration that runs the scenario until halted by the operator. The *present* procedure simply places the *run* operator for the individual programs in a *save/restore* context so they won't impact each other.

We designed the procedures *pause* and *wait* especially for screen presentations; *pause* accepts any keystroke from the console (*con*) to continue processing, and *wait* employs the *usertime* operator to wait a specific number of seconds before displaying the next file, or any portions of a file, according to the interval set by the user.

We redefined *showpage* to erase each screen in preparation for the next, after waiting five seconds. And SIGN-ON.PS is a file that is run at the beginning of the presentation to tell the operator how to stop the scenario. Finally, the *loop* at the end runs any number of programs that comprise the scenario until halted.

# A PostScript Script

```
% script01.ps

/present { % Each screen
    /save0 save def
    run
    save0 restore
} def

/pause { (con) (r) file read } def

/wait { % In milliseconds
    usertime add  {
        dup usertime sub 0 le {
            exit
        } if
    } loop
    pop
} def

/showpage {       % Clear screen
    5000 wait    % 5 seconds
    erasepage
} def

(sign-on.ps) present

{ % Continuous script
    (file01.ps) present
    (file02.ps) present
    % ... etc.
    (filenn.ps) present
} loop
```

# Fax Support

Last, but by no means least, there are presently at least three PostScript interpreters—GammaScript (from GammaLink, based on QMS UltraScript), HiJaak PC (from Inset Systems, Inc., based on GoScript), and EiconScript (using EiconView)—that can convert a PostScript file to the compressed TIFF format used for transmissions to group III fax machines from supported fax boards, at 200 dot-per-inch resolution.

Adobe Systems has also announced support for fax transmissions with future versions of their PostScript interpreter. PostScript controllers with this feature should be able to route PostScript files to either the local PostScript printer or to any remote fax machine. PostScript significantly improves the quality of fax transmissions, even at 200-dpi resolution.

Given the recent popularity of fax transmissions, PostScript fax support should prove very important for telepublishing applications.

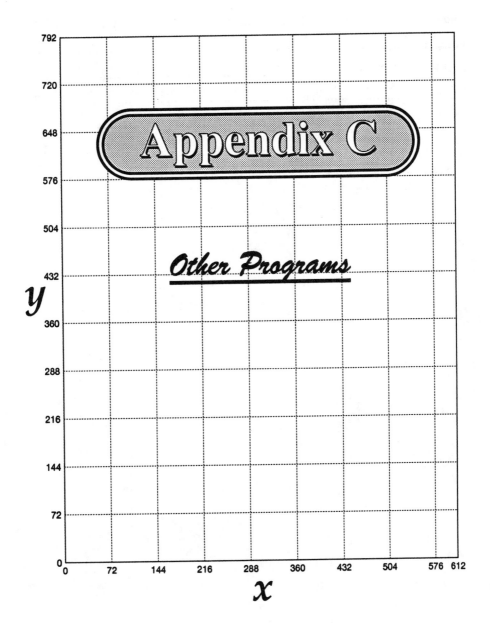

# Appendix C

## Other Programs

# Appendix C

# Other Programs

In this appendix we present three complete programs that not only provide functions you may find useful, but also demonstrate principles you might find useful in other situations.

First, CALENDAR.PS produces an instant calendar for any month of any year in this and the next century, by simply entering the desired month and year from your keyboard. This handy program demonstrates how to send information to a generalized PostScript program, to tell it specifically what to do.

Next, ENVELOPE.PS creates envelopes complete with addresses obtained from separate address files specified on the command line, together with your return address and logo, if you desire. This useful program demonstrates how to use PostScript to access information in other files, and combine this information under the control of one program.

Finally, PSSTAT.PS provides useful information about the PostScript interpreter you are using, complete with samples of all the typefaces available—internal and downloaded. It demonstrates how to interrogate the interpreter to find out what facilities it provides.

Please acquaint yourself with the use of batch files in appendix B before using the programs in this section.

# Calendar

You can use CALENDAR.PS to print a calendar for any month in any year from 1901 to 2099, in a variety of different formats, from information you enter on the command line of CAL.BAT (below). The sample on the next page is a full-page calendar for January, 1990, printed in landscape mode, scaled to fit in this book, and produced with the DOS command *cal 1 1990* using the following batch file.

```
rem CAL.BAT
rem SYNTAX: CAL mm yyyy
rem use with CALENDAR.PS for any month in 1901 to 2099
echo off
echo Print calendar for month #%1 in year %2...
echo %1 %2 %PS%
copy P:\calendar.ps+p:\ctrl_d.ps %PS%
```

The various formats are listed at the end of CALENDAR.PS. Choose any format by removing the preceding percent sign and inserting one in front of the other three formats. To run CALENDAR.PS without the batch file, enter any *mm yyyy* in front of the format you desire and send the file to the interpreter.

# Smith Consulting Group

## JANUARY 1990

| S | M | T | W | T | F | S |
|---|---|---|---|---|---|---|
|   | 1 | 2 | 3 | 4 | 5 | 6 |
| 7 | 8 | 9 | 10 | 11 | 12 | 13 |
| 14 | 15 | 16 | 17 | 18 | 19 | 20 |
| 21 | 22 | 23 | 24 | 25 | 26 | 27 |
| 28 | 29 | 30 | 31 |   |   |   |

DECEMBER 1989

FEBRUARY 1990

# calendar.ps

```
/font {findfont exch scalefont setfont} bind def
/center {dup stringwidth pop 2 div neg 0 rmoveto} bind def

% Syntax: month year calendar
/calendar {
    /year exch def
    /month exch def

    month  1 lt {
        /year year month 12 idiv sub 1 sub def
        /month month 11 add 12 mod 1 add def
    } if
    month 12 gt {
        /year year month 12 idiv add def
        /month month 11 add 12 mod 1 add def
    } if

    % Array of weekday letters
    /Aweekday [(S) (M) (T) (W) (T) (F) (S)] def

    % Array of the names of the months
    /Amonthname [
        (JANUARY) (FEBRUARY) (MARCH) (APRIL) (MAY) (JUNE) (JULY)
        (AUGUST) (SEPTEMBER) (OCTOBER) (NOVEMBER) (DECEMBER)
    ] def

    % Array of the number of days in a month
    /Amonthdays [31 28 31 30 31 30 31 31 30 31 30 31] def

    % Array of starting days for the perpetual scale
    /pcal [6 1 2 3 4 6 7 1 2 4 5 6 7 2 3 4 5 7 1 2 3 5 6 7 1 3 4 5] def
```

```
% get the month name from the array of month names
/monthname Amonthname month 1 sub get def

% get the number of days in the month
/monthdays Amonthdays month 1 sub get def

% get the first day of the year from the pcal array
% 1904 = 1, 1905 = 2, etc.
/year_start pcal year 28 mod get def

% Number of days in the year up to the current month
/yeardays 0 def
0 1 month 2 sub {
    /i exch def
    /yeardays yeardays Amonthdays i get add def
} for

% The first day of the month = the first day of the year + the
% number of day in the year up to the current month
/month_start year_start 1 sub yeardays add 7 mod 1 add def

% This logic will work from 1901 to 2099
year 4 mod 0 eq {        % if year is divisible by 4 then it's a leap year
    month 3 ge {          % if the month >= 3 then
        % month_start = month_start + 1
        /month_start month_start 1 add def
        month_start 8 eq {
            /month_start 1 def
        } if
    } if
    month 2 eq {      % If the month = 2 then
        /monthdays monthdays 1 add def          % add February 29th
    } if
} if
```

```
/yearname year 4 string cvs def        % Print centered title at the top
/title 32 string def
title 0 monthname putinterval
/l monthname length def
title l ( ) putinterval
/l l 1 add def
title l yearname putinterval
/l l 4 add def
/title title 0 l getinterval def
24 /Helvetica-Bold font
314 735 moveto
title center show

16 /Helvetica-Bold font

63 72 567 {                            % Vertical line loop
    396 moveto
    0 333 rlineto
    stroke
} for

396 63 711 {                           % Horizontal line loop
    63 exch moveto
    504 0 rlineto
    stroke
} for

63 711 moveto                          % Draw dark band at the top
504 0 rlineto
0 18 rlineto
-504 0 rlineto
closepath
fill

gsave                                  % Print the days of the week at the top
    1 setgray
    0 1 6 {
        /d exch def
        d 72 mul 93 add 715 moveto
        Aweekday d get show
    } for
grestore
```

```
/str 30 string def              % Get ready to print the days of the month
/x month_start 1 sub 72 mul 66 add def
/y 695 def

month_start 1 eq {
     /y y 63 add def
} if

    1 1 monthdays {             % Print the days of the month
        /n exch def
        n month_start add 2 sub 7 mod 0 eq {     % if n + month_start - 2 = 7
            /y y 63 sub def                        % then start a new week
            /x 66 def
            y 443 lt {                            % if > 5 weeks then print in
                /y 403 def                        % the middle of the cell
            } if
        } if
        x y moveto
        n str cvs show
        /x x 72 add def
    } for
} bind def    % calendar
```

```
/fullpage {
     /Year exch def
     /Month exch def

     612 0 translate
     90 rotate
     gsave
          30 /Palatino-BoldItalic font
          .5 setlinewidth
          385 550 moveto
          (Smith Consulting Group) center
          true charpath
          stroke
     grestore

     -55 -530 translate
     1.4 1.4 scale
     Month Year calendar

     51 652 translate
     .2 .2 scale
     Month 1 sub Year calendar

     2010 0 translate
     Month 1 add Year calendar
} bind def    % fullpage
```

```
/halfpage {
    /Year exch def
    /Month exch def

    Month Year calendar

    35 35 translate
    .45 .45 scale
    65 325 moveto
    gsave
        2 2 scale
        (NOTES:) show
    grestore
    Month 1 sub Year calendar

    612 0 translate
    Month 1 add Year calendar
} bind def    % halfpage

/double {
    /Year exch def
    /Month exch def

    Month Year calendar

    75 translate
    Month 1 add Year calendar
} bind def    % double

% Place "%" before three of the following four lines to select the other

fullpage     % Landscape, full page with small last and next month
%halfpage    % Portrait, with last and next month
%double      % Half-size portrait, this and next month
%calendar    % Landscape, full page only

showpage
```

# Envelope

Instead of using a batch file to feed parameters to the PostScript program, ENV.BAT appends a file with a name and address to ENVELOPE.PS. The interpreter prints that name and address on the envelope. This can be used with any printer—such as those using the Canon SX engine—that feeds any size envelopes in landscape orientation from the middle of the paper tray (or you can modify it for other printers).

```
echo off
rem ENV.bat - Print an address on an envelope

rem Syntax: ENV filename
rem Where filename is any filename.ADR file
echo Printing address for %1.ps using %PS%...
rem the next line is optional
copy P:\env\wavelogo.ps %PS%
copy P:\env\envelope.ps+P:\env\%1.adr+p:\ctrl_d.ps/a %PS%
```

Address files (filename.adr) are separate ASCII files you create with exactly four lines of information (remember to follow the last line with a carriage return). Be sure that these files are kept in the subdirectory specified in the batch file, above. This is PEACHPIT.ADR, the file we used for the sample envelope.

```
Peachpit Press
Attn: Ted Nace
1085 Keith Avenue
Berkeley, CA 94708
```

The DOS command to produce the sample on the facing page is *env peachpit*.

Note that in this example we also sent the file WAVELOGO.PS (not shown), that places a design in the corner of the envelope. If you use this technique, be sure that this file does not include a *showpage*, so that both it and the address will be printed on the envelope. If you don't want to include anything else on the envelope, delete the line from the batch file. You can use this same technique to place the output from any number of PostScript files on the same page.

SMITH CONSULTING GROUP • 834 THIRD ST SUITE B • SANTA ROSA CA 95404

*Peachpit Press*
*Attn: Ted Nace*
*1085 Keith Avenue*
*Berkeley, CA 94708*

# ENVELOPE.PS

```postscript
/font {findfont exch scalefont setfont} bind def

/lines     4 def              % Number of lines per envelope
/addressX      280 def        % Left margin of address
/addressY      315 def        % Top margin of address
/fontsize      36 def         % Point size of address font

% print the envelope
/printenvelope {
        612 0 translate
        90 rotate
        50 0 translate
        fontsize /Palatino-BoldItalic font

        /y addressY def

        0 1 linesread {               % For i from 0 to linesread
            /i exch def
            addressX y moveto
            line i get                % Place line[i] on stack
            show
            /y y fontsize sub def     % y = y - fontsize
        } for

        8 /AvantGarde-BookOblique font
        addressX 100 sub addressY fontsize add 20 add moveto
        gsave
            (SMITH CONSULTING GROUP   \267   ) show
            (834 THIRD ST   SUITE B   \267   SANTA ROSA   CA 95404) show
        grestore
        0 -3 rmoveto
        450 0 rlineto
        -450 -3 rmoveto
        450 0 rlineto
        stroke

        showpage
} def     % printenvelope
```

```
/main {
    /line lines array def              % Create an array line[lines]

    currentfile cvlit                  % Pseudonym for standard input
    40 string readline                 % Read \n after 'main'
    not {stop} if                      % stop if eof found
    pop                                % Discard unneeded string

    /linesread -1 def                  % Set to -1 in case no lines are read
    0 1 lines 1 sub {                  % for i from 0 to lines - 1 step 1
        /i exch def

        line i                         % line[i] = next line read
        currentfile cvlit              % Pseudonym for standard input
        256 string
        readline                       % Read next line of address
        not {pop pop pop exit} if      % exit for loop if eof
        put
        /linesread i def   % linesread = loop variable
    } for
    printenvelope
} def

% Everything following main is treated as addresses, until EOF
main
```

# Psstat

To wrap this up, we include one last program that is very useful for getting information about a PostScript interpreter, and for learning how to get that information. If you must know more about the inner workings of PostScript interpreters and how PostScript dictionaries are organized, we recommend the White book.

You can use SEND.BAT to print PSSTAT.PS, just like any other file. But before you do, we want to give you a small word of warning. Unless you have one of the fast RISC-based PostScript devices, do not make a habit of sending PSSTAT.PS without first changing the first line of the program from 1 to 0, so that the typefaces are all printed in Helvetica. As shown here, PSSTAT.PS prints all the internal fonts in their native typeface, which can involve 35 or more font changes. You can do this once or twice to get a copy of the native fonts for your permanent records, but you should normally print the typefaces in Helvetica. PSSTAT.PS is also ideal for checking to see what typefaces are downloaded.

| | | |
|---|---|---|
| interpreter | UltraScript | Helvetica-Narrow-BoldOblique |
| product | Laserport PS600 | Helvetica-Narrow-Oblique |
| version | 12.0 | Helvetica-Oblique |
| revision | 1 | Lucida |
| | | Lucida-Bold |
| Device resolution: | 600 dpi | Lucida-BoldItalic |
| | | Lucida-Italic |
| left margin | 14.4, 0.2 in. | LucidaSans |
| bottom margin | 13.92, 0.193333 in. | LucidaSans-Bold |
| imageable height | 764.28, 10.615 in. | LucidaSans-BoldItalic |
| imageable width | 583.2, 8.1 in. | LucidaSans-Italic |
| Device type: | Color | LucidaSans-Typewriter |
| Red screen frequency: | 60.0 | LucidaSans-Typewriter-Bold |
| Green screen frequency: | 60.0 | LucidaSans-Typewriter-BoldOblique |
| Blue screen frequency: | 60.0 | LucidaSans-Typewriter-Oblique |
| Black screen frequency: | 60.0 | NewCenturySchlbk-Bold |
| Red screen angle: | 45.0 | NewCenturySchlbk-BoldItalic |
| Green screen angle: | 45.0 | NewCenturySchlbk-Italic |
| Blue screen angle: | 45.0 | NewCenturySchlbk-Roman |
| Black screen angle: | 45.0 | Palatino-Bold |
| Number of shades of red: | 99 | Palatino-BoldItalic |
| Number of shades of green: | 99 | Palatino-Italic |
| Number of shades of blue: | 99 | Palatino-Roman |
| Number of shades of gray: | 99 | Symbol |
| Number of possible shades: | 970299 | Times-Bold |
| | | Times-BoldItalic |

321986 of 520208 bytes remaining

Times-Italic
Times-Roman
ZapfChancery-MediumItalic
ZapfDingbats

47 fonts available:
AvantGarde-Book
AvantGarde-BookOblique
AvantGarde-Demi
AvantGarde-DemiOblique
Bookman-Demi
Bookman-DemiItalic
Bookman-Light
Bookman-LightItalic
Courier
Courier-Bold
Courier-BoldOblique
Courier-Oblique
Helvetica
Helvetica-Bold
Helvetica-BoldOblique
Helvetica-Narrow
Helvetica-Narrow-Bold

*Downloaded typeface

# PSSTAT.PS

```
1 /native exch def    % 1 = print fonts in their native typeface
% Change above to 0, for faster printing of fonts in single typeface

/font {findfont exch scalefont setfont} bind def
/box {1 index 0 rlineto 0 exch rlineto neg 0 rlineto closepath} bind def

/tab {
    currentpoint exch pop
    leftmargin 120 add exch
    moveto
} def

/nl {
    currentpoint leftmargin exch ptsize sub moveto
    currentpoint exch pop bottommargin le {
        /leftmargin leftmargin columnwidth add def
        leftmargin topmargin moveto
    } if
} def

/sshow {s cvs show} def
/tshow {tab sshow nl} def

/printerinfo {
    statusdict begin
        /printername where
        {pop (printer name) show 64 string printername tshow} if
        /product where {pop (product) show product tshow} if
        /version where {pop (version) show version tshow} if
        /revision where {pop (revision) show revision tshow} if
        nl
    end % statusdict
} def
```

```
/otherinfo {
    72 72 matrix defaultmatrix      % Calculate the number of device
    dtransform                      % Pixels for one inch in the x dimension
    /hres exch round abs cvi def % Stack: abs(y') x'
    /vres exch round abs cvi def  % Stack: abs(x') abs(y')
    /eres vres hres mul sqrt cvi def
    vres hres eq {
        (Device resolution:) show tab hres sshow ( dpi) show nl
        }{
        (horizontal resolution:) show tab hres sshow ( dpi) show nl
        (vertical resolution:) show tab vres sshow ( dpi) show nl
        (effective resolution:) show tab eres sshow ( dpi) show nl
    } ifelse
    nl

    /height y2 y1 sub def      % height = top margin - bottom margin
    /width x2 x1 sub def % width = right margin - left margin
    (left margin) show tab x1 sshow (, ) show
    x1 72 div sshow ( in.) show nl
    (bottom margin) show tab y1 sshow (, ) show
    y1 72 div sshow ( in.) show   nl
    (imageable height) show tab height sshow (, ) show
    height 72 div sshow ( in.) show nl
    (imageable width) show tab width sshow (, ) show
    width 72 div sshow ( in.) show nl
} def % otherinfo

/colorinfo {
    /color systemdict /currentcolorscreen known def
    (Device type: ) show tab
    color {(Color)} {(Black & White)} ifelse
    show nl
    color {
        /rlevels 1 def
        /glevels 1 def
        /blevels 1 def
        /klevels 1 def
        gsave
            currentcolorscreen
            pop /kangle exch def /kfreq exch def
            pop /bangle exch def /bfreq exch def
            pop /gangle exch def /gfreq exch def
            pop /rangle exch def /rfreq exch def
```

```
            rfreq rangle {pop pop /rlevels dup load 1 add def 1 }
            gfreq gangle {pop pop /glevels dup load 1 add def 1 }
            bfreq bangle {pop pop /blevels dup load 1 add def 1 }
            kfreq kangle {pop pop /klevels dup load 1 add def 1 }
            setcolorscreen
        grestore

        (Red screen frequency:   ) show rfreq tshow
        (Green screen frequency: ) show gfreq tshow
        (Blue screen frequency:  ) show bfreq tshow
        (Black screen frequency: ) show kfreq tshow
        (Red screen angle:   ) show rangle tshow
        (Green screen angle: ) show gangle tshow
        (Blue screen angle:  ) show bangle tshow
        (Black screen angle: ) show kangle tshow
        (Number of shades of red:  ) show rlevels tshow
        (Number of shades of green:) show glevels tshow
        (Number of shades of blue: ) show blevels tshow
        (Number of shades of gray: ) show klevels tshow
        (Number of possible shades:) show
        rlevels glevels mul blevels mul tshow

    }
    {   /klevels 1 def
        gsave
            currentscreen pop /kangle exch def /kfreq exch def
            kfreq kangle {pop pop /klevels dup load 1 add def 1 } setscreen
        grestore
        (Black screen frequency: ) show kfreq tshow
        (Black screen angle: ) show kangle tshow
        (Number of shades of gray:) show klevels tshow
    } ifelse % color
    nl
} def % colorinfo

/memoryinfo {
    vmstatus            % savelevels used max
    dup                 % savelevels used max max
    3 -1 roll           % savelevels max max used
    sub sshow ( of ) show
    sshow ( bytes remaining) show nl nl
    pop
} def
```

```
/bubblesort {
    /v exch def
    /n v length 1 sub def

    n -1 1 {
        /i exch def
        0 1 i 1 sub {
            /j exch def
            /t1 v j get def
            /t2 v j 1 add get def
            t1 t2 gt
            {
                v j t2 put
                v j 1 add t1 put
            } if
        } for
    } for
} def % bubblesort

/fontinfo {
    /FontArray [ FontDirectory {pop 128 string cvs} forall] def
    FontArray bubblesort
    FontArray length sshow ( fonts available:) show nl
    FontArray {
        /fontname exch def
        gsave
            % Comment out next line to disable native mode
            native 0 ne {
                ptsize fontname cvn font
            } if
            fontname show
            FontDirectory fontname cvn get
            /FontType get 3 eq { (*) show } if
        grestore
        nl
    } forall
    nl
    (*Downloaded typeface) show nl
    nl
} def % fontinfo
```

```
gsave
    initgraphics      % Reinstate default clipping path
    clippath          % Set current path to clipping path
    pathbbox          % Place path bounding box on the stack
    /y2 exch def
    /x2 exch def
    /y1 exch def
    /x1 exch def
grestore

/ptsize 10 def
/s 128 string def
/columnwidth 220 def
/topmargin y2 ptsize sub 5 sub def
/leftmargin x1 5 add def
/bottommargin y1 10 add def

ptsize /Times-Roman font

newpath      % draw a box around the defined clipping region
x1 y1 moveto
x2 y2 box
stroke

leftmargin topmargin moveto
printerinfo
otherinfo
colorinfo
memoryinfo
fontinfo
showpage
```

# INDEX

# Smith Consulting Group

Smith Consulting Group specializes in PostScript-based systems for desktop publishing or related applications. We evaluate and review dozens of new PostScript hardware and software products annually, and use the most promising on a continuing basis.

We provide national consulting and support services for all phases of PostScript operations, including requirements evaluation, system specifications, acquisition, installation, documentation, training, and ongoing technical support. We also undertake custom PostScript programming projects, and prepare product literature and training material.

A visual learning seminar based on the principles in this book is available on a regional or corporate basis. For more information on any Smith Consulting Group services, please feel free to contact us.

*Smith Consulting Group*
*834 Third St, Suite B*
*Santa Rosa, CA 95404*

# Registration Card

If you are interested in being added to a database of PostScript users who are interested in receiving periodic information about new PostScript products and developments, we encourage you to complete and return the registration card on the following page. You can either copy and cut the registration card, or use the PostScript program on the back of the page to create your own. (Note the use of special Zapf Dingbats characters to aid in completing the card.)

We are particularly interested in hearing any comments you may have about the book. Please include them with your registration, in the space provided.

# Program Diskette

For the convenience of our readers we provide a diskette of all sample programs and batch files shown in this book, including one that produces individual character sets for any typeface shown in appendix A. The price is $20 ($21.25 for California residents; $25 outside North America). Please include a check, money order, or cash with your registration card. IBM-PC 5.25-inch media will be provided unless otherwise indicated. Quantity prices are available for corporate or user groups.

FULL NAME

COMPANY NAME (IF COMPANY ADDRESS USED)

STREET ADDRESS

CITY, STATE, AND ZIP CODE

POSTSCRIPT PRINTER OR INTERPRETER NAME & MODEL OR VERSION

COMPUTER MAKE, MODEL & DISKETTE FORMAT

CHECK
3.5 INCH

PHONE ( ) _____ FAX ( ) _____

FOLD HERE

YOUR COMMENTS:

SEND REGISTRATION TO: Smith Consulting Group, 834 Third St, Suite B, Santa Rosa, CA 95404

```
% register.ps
/Times-Roman findfont 8 scalefont setfont
125 600 moveto 330 0 rlineto stroke
130 592 moveto (FULL NAME) show
125 565 moveto 330 0 rlineto stroke
130 557 moveto (COMPANY NAME (IF COMPANY ADDRESS USED)) show
125 530 moveto 330 0 rlineto stroke
130 522 moveto (STREET ADDRESS) show
125 495 moveto 330 0 rlineto stroke
130 487 moveto (CITY, STATE, AND ZIP CODE) show
125 460 moveto 330 0 rlineto stroke
130 452 moveto (POSTSCRIPT PRINTER OR \
INTERPRETER NAME & MODEL OR VERSION) show
125 425 moveto 330 0 rlineto stroke
130 417 moveto (COMPUTER MAKE, MODEL & DISKETTE FORMAT) show

130 390 moveto (PHONE ) show
gsave
       0 5 rmoveto
       1 1.5 scale
       ((             ) ) show % 18 spaces
grestore
0 0 rmoveto 138 0 rlineto
gsave
       stroke
grestore
0 0 rmoveto ( FAX )
gsave
       0 5 rmoveto
       1 1.5 scale
       ((             ) ) show % 18 spaces
grestore
0 0 rmoveto 138 0 rlineto stroke
130 350 moveto (YOUR COMMENTS:) show
270 370 moveto (FOLD HERE) show
128 136 moveto
(SEND REGISTRATION TO: Smith Consulting Group, \
834 Third St, Suite B, Santa Rosa, CA 95404) show
432 417 moveto (CHECK) show
430 410 moveto (3.5 INCH) show

[3] 0 setdash 2 setlinewidth
100 130 moveto 0 500 rlineto 382 0 rlineto
       0 -500 rlineto closepath stroke
1 setlinewidth
100 380 moveto 382 0 rlineto stroke
/ZapfDingbats findfont 30 scalefont setfont
105 605 moveto (\355) show          % Arrow
435 430 moveto (\157) show          % Box
497 113 moveto 90 rotate (\043) show    % Scissors

showpage
```